IN BED

WITH THE

ANCIENT
EGYPTIANS

IN BED

WITH THE

ANCIENT EGYPTIANS

CHARLOTTE BOOTH

AMBERLEY

To my mum, Margaret Dorothy Hanna (1939–2014).
When I told her I was writing this book, she said with a twinkle,
'But that's rude!'
I hope she is reading it and blushing.

First published 2015

Amberley Publishing
The Hill, Stroud
Gloucestershire, GL5 4EP

www.amberley-books.com

Copyright © Charlotte Booth, 2015

The right of Charlotte Booth to be identified
as the Author of this work has been asserted
in accordance with the Copyrights, Designs
and Patents Act 1988.

ISBN 978 1 4456 4343 4 (hardback)
ISBN 978 1 4456 4351 9 (ebook)

British Library Cataloguing in Publication Data.
A catalogue record for this book is available
from the British Library.

Typesetting and Origination by Amberley Publishing
Printed in the UK.

CONTENTS

TIMELINE

Predynastic Period
Before 3150 BCE

Early Dynastic Period
Dynasty 0: 3150–3050 BCE
Dynasty 1: 3050–2890 BCE
Dynasty 2: 2890–2686 BCE

Old Kingdom
Dynasty 3: 2686–2613 BCE
Dynasty 4: 2613–2500 BCE
Dynasty 5: 2498–2345 BCE
Dynasty 6: 2345–2181 BCE

First Intermediate Period
Dynasty 7 and 8: 2180–2160 BCE
Dynasty 9 and 10: 2160–2040 BCE

Middle Kingdom
Dynasty 11: 2134–1991 BCE
Dynasty 12: 1991–1782 BCE

Second Intermediate Period
Dynasty 13: 1782–1650 BCE

Dynasty 14: exact dates unknown
Dynasty 15: 1663–1555 BCE
Dynasty 16: 1663–1555 BCE
Dynasty 17: 1663–1570 BCE

New Kingdom
Dynasty 18: 1570–1293 BCE
Dynasty 19: 1293–1185 BCE
Dynasty 20: 1185–1070 BCE

Third Intermediate period
High Priests (Thebes): 1080–945 BCE
Dynasty 21 (Tanis): 1069–945 BCE
Dynasty 22 (Tanis): 945–715 BCE
Dynasty 23 (Leontopolis): 818–715 BCE
Dynasty 24 (Sais): 727–715 BCE
Dynasty 25 (Nubians): 747–656 BCE
Dynasty 26 (Sais): 664–525 BCE

Late Period
Dynasty 27 (Persian): 525–404 BCE
Dynasty 28: 404–399 BCE
Dynasty 29: 399–380 BCE
Dynasty 30: 380–343 BCE
Dynasty 31: 343–332 BCE

Graeco-Roman Period
Macedonian Kings: 332–305 BCE
Ptolemaic Period: 305–30 BCE

ILLUSTRATIONS

All illustrations and photographs are by the author unless otherwise stated.

1-a. Lower Egypt. Courtesy of the Thomas Cook Archives.
1-b. Upper Egypt. Courtesy of the Thomas Cook Archives.
2. Amun-Min, Karnak. Photograph courtesy of BKB Photography.
3. Cosmetic items beneath the chair of the wife of Remini, El Kab.
4. Sety I with Ramses II, wearing the side-lock of youth, Abydos. Photograph courtesy of BKB Photography.
5. Hathor stela showing the Hathor wig, Serabit el Kadim. Photograph courtesy of Roland Unger Wikimedia Commons.
6. Noblemen wearing unguent cones, tomb of Khaemhat TT57, Luxor. Photograph courtesy of BKB Photography.
7. Khnum creating the king on a potter's wheel, Denderah. Photograph courtesy of BKB Photography.
8. Faience Bowl, Leiden Museum.
9. Hathor nursing the king, Edfu.
10. Graffiti of Hatshepsut and Senenmut, Deir el Bahri (after Tyldesley 1996, fig 7.3).
11. Throne room in the palace at Medinet Habu. Photograph courtesy of BKB Photography.
12. Harem at Medinet Habu. Photograph courtesy of BKB Photography.

13. Bes, Denderah.
14. Heket, the frog goddess of childbirth, Abydos. Photograph courtesy of BKB Photography.
15. Seven Hathors, Medinet Habu.
16. Weighing of the Heart with Meskhenet above the scales, Deir el Medina. Photograph courtesy of Olaf Tausch, Wikimedia Commons.
17. Hatshepsut's mother, Ahmosis, pregnant, Deir el Bahri. Photograph courtesy of BKB Photography.
18. Hieroglyph showing childbirth, Edfu. Photograph courtesy of BKB Photography.
19. Making offerings to Amun-Min, Karnak. Photograph courtesy of BKB Photography.
20. Niankhkhnum and Khnumnakht embracing. Photograph courtesy of the Egypt Archive and Jon Bodsworth.
21. Hathor holding a sistrum, Edfu.
22. Middle Kingdom birth-brick, Abydos. (Drawing after Szapakowska 2008, fig 2.1).
23. Tutankhamun embracing Osiris with his ka behind him. Reconstructed tomb of Tutankhamun, Luxor.
24. Dancers from the Red Chapel, Karnak.
25. The sacred lake at Karnak. Photograph courtesy of BKB Photography.
26. Benben stone which represents the petrified semen of Atum, Cairo Museum.
27. Shu, the god of the air, Kom Ombo.
28. Nut giving birth to the sun-god, Denderah.
29. Amun, Luxor Temple. Photograph courtesy of BKB Photography.
30. Amaunet, Luxor Temple. Photograph courtesy of BKB Photography.

31. Sety I making offerings of incense, Abydos. Photograph courtesy of BKB Photography.

32. Bringing incense trees from Punt, Deir el Bahri. Photograph courtesy of BKB Photography.

33. Amenirdis, God's Wife of Amun, Karnak. Courtesy of user Neithsabes, Wikimedia Commons.

34. Resurrection of Osiris with Isis as a kite above him and Heket at the foot of the bed, Denderah. Photograph courtesy of BKB Photography.

35. Driving of the calves, Luxor Temple. Photograph courtesy of BKB Photography.

36. Sekhmet offers the menat to Sety I, Abydos. Photograph courtesy of BKB Photography.

37. Anukis, consort of Khnum the creator nursing Ramses II, Beit el Wali.

38. Scene from the Turin Erotic Papyrus showing the application of lipstick and use of external stimuli.

39. Ka statue of Djoser, Saqqara.

40. Cutting penises from the enemies during battle, Medinet Habu. Photograph courtesy of BKB Photography.

41. Hieroglyph of a couple making love, Beni Hasan, Middle Kingdom (after Manniche 1997, fig 21).

42. Hathor as a cow licking the hand of Hatshepsut, Deir el Bahri. Photograph courtesy of BKB Photography.

43. The Osireion, Abydos. Photograph courtesy of BKB Photography.

44. Banquet scene of Paheri, El Kab. Photograph courtesy of BKB Photography.

Introduction

THE ANCIENT EGYPTIAN
ATTITUDE TO SEX

'Spending a pleasant hour together'

Writing a book of this kind was a daunting task, as it needed to
be fun, factual but not gratuitous. For many people, the idea of a
book on sex is considered a little taboo, a little 'naughty', but in
ancient Egypt (as today), sex was an important part of everyday
life. It is important, however, to identify what is intended with a
book of this nature. This is not a book simply about the sexual
exploits of the ancient Egyptians, as the evidence is lacking and
it would make for a short volume. Instead, it concerns itself with
all aspects of sex, from the ideals of beauty, fertility, sexuality and
childbirth, the ultimate result of the act of intercourse. We will, in
short, be delving into the most intimate moments of the ancient
Egyptians' lives, using their own words, artwork and sculptures
to guide us.

Before starting on this journey, it is important to ascertain what
their approach to sex as a subject was. The concept of gratuitous
sex or sex as a taboo subject is very much a modern one, introduced
by medieval puritans and embraced by the Victorians to ludicrous

ends. Such embarrassment at sex is not something that would be fully understood by an ancient Egyptian, as sex was an integral part of life and not something considered shameful.

The Egyptian language had at least a dozen words for sexual intercourse[1], which were suitable for daily use. One of the most common words for the act of penetrative sex was *nk*,[2] which was used generally to describe the male agent of the sexual act rather than the female.[3] However, there were numerous phrases for intercourse that were used in poetry and literary texts, which were less graphic, such as 'spending a pleasant hour together', 'entering a house', 'to know', 'to sleep with', 'to enjoy oneself with' or 'to unite oneself with'.

The act of ejaculation was also referred to in the texts and was spelt using the sign for an ejaculating penis. However, this sign was additionally used for numerous words connected with sex, fertility and virility. The female climax was not so readily referred to, and when it was, it was shrouded in mystery. One record states that after the age of sixty 'you lust after a woman, her moment does not come'.[4] Whether this is referring to the female climax is uncertain, but seems likely. In the text describing the divine conception of Hatshepsut at Deir el Bahri (*see* chapter 3), Hatshepsut's mother, the queen, is thought to cry out at the moment of climax during her intercourse with the god Amun.

Sexual language was used in a remarkably similar way to modern societies. For example, it was not uncommon to use a sexual word when swearing or insulting another person. To hurry along a work colleague in a jovial manner, an Egyptian may have yelled: 'Come on you fornicator,' as attested by the boatmen in the Old Kingdom tomb of Ti at Saqqara.[5] To an unpopular individual, an ancient Egyptian may have exclaimed: 'May a donkey copulate with your wife and children',[6] 'May a donkey violate him! May a donkey violate his wife'[7] or 'Your mouth does not fornicate'.[8] This latter insult is rather interesting, as it makes reference to fellatio. Generally, this sexual act is only mentioned in reference to the earth god Geb, who is sometimes depicted performing this act upon himself. However, how common the act was with a female (or indeed a male) partner is not mentioned or depicted.

The act of masturbation is also only referred to in religious texts where the creator god Atum masturbates in order to create the next generation of gods (*see* chapter 8). It was also referenced in the religious title 'hand of the god', which was given to the God's Wives of Amun at Karnak (*see* chapter 8). How common such acts were among the general populace, or how they were perceived, unfortunately goes unrecorded. For the most part, written evidence and artwork concerning sexual life in ancient Egypt were produced by men and, therefore, provide a biased view of attitudes.[9]

The Egyptian language was a rich one, and there were various hieroglyphic renderings for male and female genitalia. A penis was known as an Hnn and could be written with a penis determinative or an ejaculating penis determinative. Female genitalia, on the other hand, had many more words, including *Xnmt* (uterus), *iwf* (flesh), *kns* (pubic area) and *k3t* (vulva). All of these were rather anatomical in nature, whereas *keniw* or 'embrace' was a more poetic way of describing it. For example, a poem might state: 'she showed me the colour of her embrace'. Colour was considered an erotic characteristic and appears in numerous poems and may have been a euphemism for skin: 'seeing the colour of all her limbs' or 'her colour was smooth'.[10] Some poetic euphemisms were not quite so subtle. One young man longed to 'charge towards her grotto'.[11] The simile does not really need explaining.

Despite the numerous sexual words that existed in ancient Egypt, there is only one example of a hieroglyphic sign of a couple making love. It was discovered in a Middle Kingdom tomb at Beni Hasan, but unfortunately due to hundreds of tour guides and visitors touching it over the years, this unique image has long since been erased.[12]

Artistic scenes at best only hint at intercourse and often depict servants near the couple, presumably in case they need something, demonstrating that sex was not a particularly private event in ancient Egypt.[13] Indeed, the examination of the archaeological remains of Egyptian homes at sites like Amarna, Deir el Medina and El Lahun shows that they were cramped and overcrowded. Most middle- and lower-class homes comprised four rooms and a flat roof, which accommodated a couple and their children, which may have numbered as many as ten in addition to grandparents, siblings and unmarried female relatives. With so many people in such a confined area, it is surprising young couples had any time or privacy to have sex. It is therefore likely that ancient attitudes were different to modern ones, and sex was not seen as something performed in seclusion but through stolen moments and opportunity.

It is interesting to note that fertility figurines, depicting a naked woman lying on a bed, are often accompanied by a child, normally a boy (*see* chapter 1).[14] The eroticism of the object is not hampered by the presence of this child, if anything a male child enhances the fertility aspects making it more desirable. Moreover, it is very possible that in addition to servants who may have been in the vicinity while couples were having sex, children may not have been very far away.

This question of privacy leads to the popular discussion regarding the role of box-beds which were bed-shaped structures found in the first room of most houses. They were made of mud brick and built into one of the walls creating an enclosed space reached by a couple of small steps. A number of female clay figurines have been discovered in these beds, and some are decorated with images of the pregnant hippopotamus deity, Taweret, and the dwarf god, Bes (*see* chapter 4). This has led some scholars to suggest they were associated with fertility and acted as a marital bed where a young couple could go and be shielded from the rest of the room. Some scholars go so far as to suggest that these structures were used as birthing beds, providing a secluded place that helped keep mother and baby safe during a particularly vulnerable time.

However, these mud-brick structures were relatively small at 1.7 m long, 80 cm wide and 75 cm high. Once enclosed inside, it would have felt hot and claustrophobic and may not have provided ample room for lovemaking. Considering the common depictions of couples having intercourse, (albeit in the form of graffiti) indicating that it was common for the man to be behind the woman, in a space this size such a common position would not be possible.

Furthermore, images of women in childbirth show they squatted on two birthing bricks in what appears to be a temporary arbour (*see* chapter 4). This squatting position would also be impossible while confined in this structure.[15] While it is possible to argue that the ancient Egyptians may have felt less embarrassment about sexual intercourse, it does seem unlikely that such intimate acts as intercourse and indeed childbirth would be carried out in the first room of the house. This room traditionally opened directly onto the street. The latter naturally would be carried out somewhere more secluded in order to safeguard the health of the mother and child.

It is more likely that the box-bed structures were in fact shrines dedicated to the household deities Taweret and Bes. This provides an adequate explanation for the images decorating them and the clay figurines found within them, which may have been given as votive offerings. The first room of the house in general was considered a feminine room, and this shrine may have been dedicated to aspects of fertility and childbirth protection rather than the practicalities of giving birth or even conception.

One of the more frustrating aspects of Egyptology is that many common Egyptian activities, like childbirth and mummification, were not considered interesting or important enough to be recorded. This means such events, which occurred often, remain a mystery to modern Egyptologists. Sex is included in this group of common daily activities. Sex was on a par with eating, sleeping and defecating[16] and was linked to all aspects of life: domestic, religious (*see* chapter 8), practical (childbirth and fertility) and the afterlife (*see* chapter 9).[17]

A lover records on an ostracon (O. Berlin P12635): 'I long for my sister more than for meat', clearly connecting the two in his mind. It was intended as an insult to the food he had just eaten but clearly places sexual desire and food together[18] as a staple of daily life. It was generally only the abnormal practices like adultery (*see* chapter 2) and homosexuality (*see* chapter 5) that were recorded in any way.[19]

Whenever the Egyptians were kind enough to record something about sex, the prudishness of Victorian excavators did not help matters regarding retention of such artefacts. Many erotic drawings discovered were not passed onto museums, as they would not have been displayed and, therefore, ended up in private collections. Now they are lost and mostly unpublished.[20] Those that were passed onto museums had penises removed or covered up, as with the famous example from the Petrie Museum, London. A Middle Kingdom inscription depicts Senusret I running the sed festival in front of Amun-Min, an ithyphallic deity. The god's erect phallus was covered with a sign declaring the museum number in order to save the blushes of visitors to the museum.

There were two types of erotic images from ancient Egypt: religious and non-religious. We have already mentioned religious images showing Geb performing fellatio upon himself, or shown partaking in stylised intercourse with Nut, the sky goddess.

Ithyphallic deities such as Amun-Min, Osiris and Geb are also generally depictured with enormous phalli. The non-religious form of art is generally satirical, humorous or graffiti. They often depict mortal men with oversized penises in various positions. It is possible that these items held some religious significance but the meaning has since been lost to the modern audience.

Such misinterpretation is a major problem with deciphering the intimate lives of ancient Egyptians. It can be difficult for modern scholars to decide if something was intended to be erotic or if there was some deeper underlying meaning. For example, the numerous sexual words with penises as determinatives, or sketches of male and female genitalia, may represent fertility rather than something erotic[21] and could therefore be grossly misinterpreted. There is also the additional possibility that an Egyptian artist drawing genitalia or a couple having intercourse could be doing so due to personal pleasure of drawing rather than trying to relay some deeper meaning. A modern alternative would be an artist attending a life-drawing class. Although the models are naked, it is about anatomy and artistic representation, not sex or eroticism.

We can assume however, that it was considered inappropriate to show images of couples having intercourse on temple or tomb walls, as they do not appear there. However, it seems strange that there are no images of couples kissing until the Amarna Period, when art styles in general became more fluid and less regimented.

Prior to this period, the most intimate positions depicted showed couples nose to nose, as in the tomb of Niankhkhnum and Khnumnakht (*see* chapter 5). This is likely due to strict artistic conventions, where it was important to view the key parts of the body and face in a recognisable form in order for the deceased to be able to use it in the afterlife. This is why there are unusual perspectives in Egyptian art, with the face in profile, for example, and the eye from a frontal viewpoint. Therefore, people kissing may have necessitated obscuring parts of the face, which may affect how the person could interact in the afterlife.

However, in the Amarna Period, artists became a little more adventurous while trying to maintain these strict artistic conventions. In one scene, Nefertiti has her head tilted back and her lips are about to touch Akhenaten's in a kiss. In another scene, Nefertiti is kissing the lips of one of her daughters.[22] No other members of the Egyptian royal family from the Pharaonic Period are shown in such intimate poses.

Written evidence is a little more informative about ancient Egyptian attitudes to sex. In the Middle Kingdom texts, women are described as wives, mothers and pleasure providers, making their sexual and fertility roles clear.[23] Yet, later, Herodotus (fifth century BCE) records that the Egyptians made it:

> an offence against piety to have intercourse with women in temples, or to enter temples after intercourse without having previously washed.[24]

Ptolemaic records also indicate that a priest should not enter a temple after having intercourse with a woman without first purifying himself. Furthermore, throughout Egyptian history, all priests, whether they had intercourse of not, were required to purify themselves before entering a temple by plunging into the sacred lake:

> The priests shave their bodies all over every other day to guard against the presence of lice, or anything else equally unpleasant, while they are about their religious duties ... They bath in cold water twice a day and twice every night.[25]

Although in the Ptolemaic Period sex with a woman rendered the man unclean and unable to enter a temple, in the earlier periods, it was viewed as a more common aspect of daily life, so much so that sex features prominently in the dream interpretation texts. For the Egyptians, sleep was a potentially dangerous time when the gods (or demons) could interact and potentially harm the sleeper. In some cases, dreams were taken as advice from the god in order to solve a problem or answer a prayer (*see* chapter 8), but others could be a portent or sign of a future to come. One Demotic dream interpretation text states:

> If a man sees himself in a dream his phallus becoming large: GOOD. It means that his possessions will multiply.
>
> Having intercourse with his mother: GOOD. His companions will stick to him.
>
> Having intercourse with his sister: GOOD. It means that he will inherit something.
>
> Having intercourse with a woman: BAD. It means mourning.
>
> Seeing his phallus erect: BAD. It means that he will be robbed.
>
> Having sex with his wife in the sun: BAD. The god will see his miseries.[26]

Some of these interpretations are somewhat surprising, as incestuous relationships were a good omen in a dream but not acceptable in life (*see* chapter 2), and yet dreaming of having sex with one's wife was considered a bad thing. The interpretations for dreams about sex were different for a woman as we learn from the Demotic papyrus Carlsberg XIIb:

> If a woman dreams she is married to her husband, she will be destroyed. If she embraces him she will experience grief.

If a horse has intercourse with her, she will use force against her husband.

If a donkey has intercourse with her, she will be punished for a great sin.

If a he-goat has intercourse with her, she will die soon.

If a Syrian has intercourse with her, she will weep for she will let her slaves have intercourse with her.[27]

A woman dreaming about sex was considered a negative thing, and all aspects of sexual dreams were bad, although it is interesting to consider how these dreams were recorded. Did women approach a scribe and ask him what her dream was about? Or did a scribe write what he thought women dreamed about? The dreams are a little odd, to say the least, to the modern mind. However, it needs to be considered that many of the animals featuring in these dream interpretations were avatars of specific gods. For example, the donkey was associated with the god Seth, the horse was associated with Horus (at least in the Graeco-Roman Period) and the goat was associated with the cult of Mendes (*see* chapter 8). Perhaps these dreams were believed to be spiritual in some way rather than admissions of bestiality.

Furthermore, while dreaming about sex was definitely taboo for women, the prescribed cure for many gynaecological problems was in fact penetrative sex,[28] obviously with her husband. It was not encouraged for women to be promiscuous, but rather it was expected that all women should be married and, therefore, have marital intercourse regularly. Sex within marriage, however, was not for pleasure in its own right, but rather for procreation. Relationships which did not produce children were considered unproductive, and this was grounds for a divorce (*see* chapter 2), or considered a waste, as in the case of homosexuality (*see* chapter 5).

It was considered the norm for everyone to want to get married, and from a young age searching for a husband or wife was important. Chapter 1 outlines what ancient Egyptians considered attractive and provides some insight into what was expected from an ideal woman. Once a mate had been chosen, love and then marriage followed, and this is expanded on in chapter 2 as well as looking at the legal aspects of marriage and divorce. Chapter 3 investigates the sex lives and relationships of the royal family and how these differed from that of the ordinary people. The one thing that truly sets them apart is the divine conception and birth scenes, which demonstrate the king's divinity and this can be compared with the childbirth experience of most Egyptian women in chapter 4. For such a dangerous time in a woman's life, it is not surprising that women required the doctor through all stages of her pregnancy, and some of the remedies prescribed are discussed in chapter 7, along with other medicaments for various aspects of beauty, fertility and feminine ailments.

Inevitably, there were people who were not married and had chosen alternative lifestyles such as homosexuality, which is discussed in chapter 5, or prostitution (chapter six). While evidence is lacking for both homosexuality and prostitution, it is possible to present a picture of these activities and discuss how they were accepted by the wider population.

Sex was also a major concern of ancient Egyptian religion-forming aspects of the creation myths, and myths of kingship, as well as being a focus of daily religious practices carried out in the home. In chapter 8, gods associated with sex, fertility and virility will be introduced, as well as sexual activities carried out in the temples themselves.

Sex even featured in the afterlife, as the main aspect of death was the concept of rebirth, a repeat of childbirth, and therefore all the same associations were in play. These will be discussed in chapter 9. Additionally this chapter will outline how the deceased was able to maintain an active sex life once he was reborn.

Sex truly does feature in all aspects of the lives of the ancient Egyptians from a young age when they were contemplating marriage and choosing a suitable partner through to death and rebirth when the whole cycle started again.

I

IDEALISED BEAUTY

'The mouth of my beloved is like a lotus bud'[1]

In any kind of relationship, whether sexual or otherwise, attraction is key. What is considered attractive however is not static and changes from decade to decade. Using the modern West as an example, the ideal body shape for women has changed drastically over the decades, with a cinched waist being ideal in the 1910s, a straight up-and-down figure in the 1920s, to the curvy hourglass of the 1950s and the waif of the 1960s. This changing image of idealised beauty is no different to changing fashions in ancient Egypt.

However, as we are reliant on formal artwork in temples and tombs to be our fashion guide, a decade-by-decade approach is not practical; but it is possible to see a changing fashion over the centuries. Starting with the short, slender figures of the Old Kingdom, men and women had chunky ankles and large block-like hands and feet. Men were always presented as youthful with broad shoulders, a low waist, well-developed muscles and a full face with large eyes and a long nose.[2] By the Middle Kingdom, it was fashionable to be taller with wide shoulders and extremely narrow waists. Women were always shown with a high small of the back and no muscle definition.[3]

In the New Kingdom, especially during the reign of Amenhotep III, the eyes became more cat-like while the figures remained tall and slender. His son Akhenaten, however, overhauled the ideal body shape, which now included short legs, large hips, pendulous breasts and a pot belly hanging over the top of the kilt; for both men and women. After the reign of Akhenaten, the rounded stomach remained, albeit it rather reduced, but the legs lengthened, representing the idealised figure as tall, slender and well proportioned.

However, images depicted in tomb and temple artwork present a formal, idealised image which was sometimes archaised in order to lend authority to the scene. Therefore, in the same way fashion magazines do not reflect the reality of a modern population, temple and tomb scenes may not accurately present the ideals of beauty and fashion of the Egyptian populace.

Our other source of evidence for ideals of beauty is written texts, primarily love poetry and literary tales. When consulting them, it must be considered that even the love poetry was written by professional scribes and was not necessarily written to express genuine emotions of the author. However, these resources, combined with the archaeological record, enable us to create an image of idealised feminine beauty and to understand what men found attractive. As most of the records were produced by men, we know how a beautiful woman was expected to look but not how the beauty of men was perceived by women.[4]

To start this discussion, we will look at images of people having sex, which can be found in graffiti or on ostraca and are probably more likely produced by ordinary individuals than professional draftsman. The first thing one notices is that it can be difficult to ascertain the genders depicted, as they are often androgynous in appearance. A wig is sometimes added to identify the female agent, and a penis clearly identifies the male. It has been suggested that in some such images the act of sex is far more important than the actors[5], and therefore they are drawn almost as cartoons. This raises interesting questions about gender representation and how different genders were perceived by the population. As both male and female figures are presented in similar ways, it has been suggested that the Egyptians did not necessarily see much of a difference between the two genders.

A study on skeletons from Gebelein demonstrated that the physical difference between male and female stature and build was slight, indicating that in life the difference between the sexes was not actually so marked, giving rise to a one-sex logic. This manifests itself in such depictions where the masculine body is identified by a penis and the female by the lack of one.

In modern sexually explicit illustrations in the West, there is often a concentration on breasts and penises, normally the bigger the better. Such focus sometimes results in farcical images, often in the realm of caricature, but does give some idea of which body parts are deemed important and, therefore, attractive to the intended audience. The ancient Egyptian view of beauty and sexuality was very different to that of the modern West.

In ancient Egyptian art it is rare, if not unheard of, to depict a woman with enormous breasts as they were not considered an erotic aspect of the female body. Breasts were associated with milk, sustenance and therefore motherhood, rather than sexuality. A poem describing a lovers' tiff demonstrates this well:

Are you leaving because of hunger or thirst?
Take my breast! It overflows for you. It is all yours!
Sweet is the day of your embrace.[6]

Where breasts are emphasised on figurines and artwork, it is normally to emphasise the fertility of a woman. So what was considered sexually attractive in ancient Egypt? Beauty, as they say, is in the eye of the beholder, and therefore we have to look at the texts and artistic representation to see how the Egyptians perceived beauty. Additionally, we need to identify sexuality and eroticism from the same resources and try to understand the cultural and social perceptions of these.

The ideals of beauty and sexuality are described succinctly in the New Kingdom love poetry. Although probably written by professional scribes, in order to be considered believable by the audience they needed to reflect genuine feelings and emotions. The Chester Beatty I Papyrus describes the ideal body shape of a woman:

> With a long neck and white breast,
> Her hair of genuine lapis lazuli
> Her arm more brilliant than gold
> Her fingers like lotus flowers,
> With heavy buttocks and girt waist
> Her thighs offer her beauty
> With a brisk step she treads on the ground.[7]

The body shape described comprises small breasts and waist with large thighs. Her breasts are described as white, indicating that pale skin was attractive and could be an indicator that she was wealthy with no need to work outside. A dark-skinned girl was obviously one that worked in the fields or down by the river.

Her fingers are compared to lotus flowers, which not only describe the shape but also are steeped with erotic symbolism. Lotus flowers often appear in love poems or banqueting scenes, as they were the equivalent of red roses in the modern world and immediately conjure up images of romance, love and eroticism.

Furthermore, the flower itself was associated with creation and, therefore, birth, fertility and even rebirth.

In one of the creation myths, the lotus (more commonly known as the blue water lily) was believed to be the first plant to grow on the mound of creation. From it rose the first dawn in the form of the sun god as a child. The most famous representation of this mythology of the lotus is from the tomb of Tutankhamun, where the head of the king is seen emerging from the lotus flower showing his affiliation with the sun god. With this in mind:

> ... all those individuals depicted holding a lotus [blue water lily] before their noses in tomb scenes may very well have been staring into the first moment of creation, aligning themselves with that sacred energy ... or perhaps focusing on Re himself, in anticipation of riding throughout eternity on his solar barque.[8]

Like the sun, the blue lotus opens only in the daylight and at noon closes its petals, meaning each day is a mini rebirth of the flower. The white lotus, on the other hand, has different habits and flowers at night, representing the nocturnal journal of the sun god. Therefore, it is common for lotus flowers to be depicted on coffins and draped around the deceased in order for them to accompany Ra on his journey. On the coffin of Iset, currently in the Cairo Museum, the lid is painted to resemble the deceased tomb owner and, in addition to having blue water lilies entwined in her headband, her breasts are accentuated by two further flowers, fully open and viewed from above.[9]

In the tomb of Rekhmire (TT100), the tomb owner's son offers lotus flowers to his parents stating:

> Receive the lotus that comes from your garden,
> There is nothing lacking here!

It offers you all the refreshments it bears,

Be pleased with its foods,

Rejoice in its produce, delight in its flowers!

You are cooled by the shade of its trees.

May you do as you wish in it for all eternity.[10]

Lotus flowers were offered to the revered dead and the gods, as they were thought to have a narcotic effect on them. As they sniffed the flower's scent, they immediately relaxed. It is suggested that the natural smells of flowers may have been more powerful in the ancient past, as the ancient Egyptians' sense of smell had not yet been desensitised by artificial fragrances, chemicals and fumes.[11] There is little doubt that the lotus was therefore a powerful flower to hand to a loved one, and describing a woman's hands as lotuses is almost the same as claiming she is divine.

Often mentioned or depicted alongside the lotus was the mandrake fruit. Although it was sometimes used as a medicament to induce sleep, it is also thought to have been an aphrodisiac. In the banquet scenes, the revellers are depicted sniffing the fruit rather than eating it, and the scent alone would be enough for the reveller to lose inhibitions. The scent is described as 'slightly unpleasant according to today's taste', 'musky and not unpleasant', 'sweet smelling' and 'fragrant'.[12] The love poetry uses the shape of the mandrake to describe a beautiful woman: 'The mouth of my beloved is like a lotus bud her breasts are like mandrake fruits'.[13]

The poetry therefore provides us with a mental image of an idealised woman with a small waist, heavy hips, small breasts curved like mandrake fruits, hands like an open lotus and a mouth like a closed lotus. The skin should be pale and the hair blue-black like lapis lazuli. Eye colour is rarely if ever mentioned, and it can be assumed that the majority of people had brown eyes and therefore the colour was deemed an unnecessary addition to these descriptions. This description of an ideal woman is close in appearance to the Middle Kingdom fertility figurines, which display large hips and a small waist, somewhat different to the tall, slim images in New Kingdom tombs.

The love poetry additionally describes the effects love can have, which in some cases is similar to grief. During mourning, it was normal for people to stop adorning themselves with perfume, for men to stop shaving and for women to appear generally dishevelled. This gives the impression that normally people cared for their appearance, were heavily adorned with perfume, smelled pleasant and men were on the whole clean-shaven.

Love, according to the poetry, has a similar affect: 'It lets me not put on a dress, nor wrap my scarf around me'.[14] It is clear this love-starved lyricist is unable to dress, as he or she is so distraught at their love of another. This indicates that being fully clothed was the norm and to be unclothed was not. Moreover, artwork shows that while nudity was fine for dancers and musicians, the majority of women wore fine linen at all times; the more transparent the better. In the eighteenth dynasty tomb of Menna (TT69), his wife Henuttawi is depicted standing with him before Osiris in a dress that is virtually transparent.[15] Although a funerary context, such semi-nudity was clearly considered acceptable and perhaps draws into question whether a transparent dress was considered erotic or simply a sign of wealth. The more transparent the linen, the finer and more expensive it was.

However, while transparent clothes were considered acceptable for noble women, nakedness was not. Servants, on the other hand, were sometimes shown carrying out their daily tasks naked, demonstrating their lack of status.[16] Such naked depictions were not, however, believed to be erotic, although their sexuality is indicated in some cases through their erect nipples. Rather oddly, erect male nipples were not considered erotic.[17] The only elite woman to be regularly shown naked was the sky goddess Nut in her role as a divine mother.[18] Her hips and breasts were therefore emphasised in recognition of her role in giving birth daily to the sun god Ra.

This idea of a woman fully clothed in expensive linen was erotic in the sense that the body could be glimpsed beneath. These clothes could be made even more erotic with the presence of water. As in modern Western and Bollywood movies, wet transparent clothes were considered extremely sensual and one New Kingdom poem (Cairo 25218) describes the scene:

O my god, my lotus flower! It is lovely to go out and ...
I love to go and bathe before you.
I allow you to see my beauty in a dress of the finest linen, drenched with fragrant unguent.
I go down into the water to be with you, and come up to you again with a red fish, looking splendid on my fingers. I place it before you ...
Come! Look at me![19]

Picture the scene, a young woman swimming in front of her lover, in wet linen soaked with beautifully scented perfumes carrying a red fish. To the modern mind, the fish is a little unusual, but fish had phallic associations, especially certain breeds associated with the myth of Osiris and Isis (*see* chapter 8).[20] It is probably unwise to suggest that the red fish was a phallic symbol, but it certainly presented an erotic image to the ancient Egyptian audience.

The wet tunic here was drenched with perfume, indicating that scent was an important part of eroticism. In the Chester Beatty poem, the pining lover declares: 'I put no paint upon my eyes, I am not even anointed'.[21]

Not being able to anoint oneself with perfume was clearly considered a tragic state of affairs, as it was something everyone clearly did on a daily basis; as was the application of cosmetics. Men and women from all levels of society wore eye make-up in addition to other cosmetics, and it was considered an essential part of the daily routine. A New Kingdom letter explains the importance of cosmetics, even to the king:

> Let twice excellent galena suitable for pharaoh's eye-paint be brought to the place where the pharaoh is, and have 15 deben [1 *deben* = 90g] galena brought through [*this official*]. As it was given to the physicians from the office of pharaoh's palace physicians in order to prepare it, it was found that the galena was useless, as there was nothing in it that was worthy of eye-paint for pharaoh's use. One single deben galena was it which one found in it [*that was suitable?*].[22]

Cosmetics were clearly used by all members of society and have been discovered in funerary contexts from the Badarian Period (4000 BCE) throughout the entire Dynastic Period, from both rich and poor graves.[23] Initially, eye make-up was worn as a repellent for flies which carried diseases, as well as for protecting the eyes from the sun and preventing them from drying out. Naturally, it was not long before someone noticed that it enhanced the appearance of the eyes. However, the medicinal purpose was always paramount, and New Kingdom kohl pots were labelled: 'to cause tears', 'good for the sight', 'to staunch bleeding' or 'for cleaning the eyes'.[24]

The colour range for eye make-up was limited to green malachite and dark-grey galena, a lead-based mineral, both imported from the Sinai. Green was generally applied to the brows and the corner of the eyes and the grey galena to the rims and lashes. Then a darker line was drawn from the corner of the eye to the hair-line, and the eyebrow was extended likewise. This style of application is attested from the artwork.

The Old Kingdom statue of Nesa, however, from the Louvre Museum, Paris, shows a thick green line was also applied beneath the eye, in a manner not depicted elsewhere. Although green eye-paint is generally not depicted in the artwork, it has been discovered in a number of tombs and may have been beneficial for eye infections. Malachite, in addition to producing a vibrant green colour, also contained antibacterial properties.[25] Black was used in the later periods and was easily produced from sunflower soot, charred almond shells and frankincense.

Regardless of the colour, the method of producing and applying cosmetics was the same. First it was essential to grind the mineral into powder, which could be stored until needed. When required, a small amount was mixed with water and resin. This was then dropped into the eye and the tears spread it across the lash line in the eye.[26] As mentioned above, both men and women wore eye-paint, and the tomb of Ipuy (TT217) from Deir el Medina has the only image depicting a man applying eye-paint to another man. This scene shows a number of accidents happening in the workplace, and the man applying the cosmetics is probably a doctor and wishes to prevent dust from entering the eyes of the workman.

The Egyptians were also keen wearers of rouge and lipstick, and the tomb of Nefertari in the Valley of the Queens shows her lips as dark red, hinting at lipstick, and the round, red marks on her cheeks suggest the application of rouge. The Turin Erotic Papyrus actually depicts one of the girls applying lipstick with a lip brush, and a Middle Kingdom relief in the British Museum (1658) depicts a woman applying rouge or perhaps powder to her cheeks with a small pad. Rouge and lipstick were made of hematite and red ochre combined with oil or animal fat, and remnants of this substance have been discovered in funerary contexts, showing it was important enough to take to the afterlife.

Naturally, caring enough to apply cosmetics to enhance the appearance meant that washing it off at the end of the day was essential. Soap comprised natron, soda, ashes or niter (a type of potassium). Oil and lime were also added to the water, but they probably irritated the skin necessitating one of many oils, combined with honey, milk, fragrant resins and flowers, to be applied to the skin.[27]

Soap has been found in reed containers in tombs alongside hair gel that comprised a fatty material used to keep the hair in place. A study was carried out in 2011 on the hair of a number of mummies to see if there was any evidence of such a fatty substance coating it. A large number of the sample did have this substance in the hair, which was different from other materials used in the embalming process, and it is believed to have been styling gel.[28]

Hair was, in fact, a particularly significant aspect of personal beauty, status and eroticism. When the ancient Egyptians were young, they wore a side-lock of hair on an otherwise shaved head, which comprised a curl, or a series of braids. With the onset of puberty, this side-lock was shaved off, showing a transition from childhood to adulthood. This side-lock was common for all strata of society including royalty. The artwork from Amarna shows all the princesses wearing side-locks, with the oldest having the longest and thickest one. At Deir el Medina, the mummies of two princes were discovered with the side-lock still in place. One was the son of Amenhotep II and aged about eleven years, and the other was a son of Ramses III aged about five years. On statues, the king is often depicted as a child being suckled by Isis while wearing the lock of youth and with his forefinger in his mouth showing that he is the son of the goddess and therefore divine. When the child reached puberty, this side-lock was shaved off and they were now no longer children but were considered adults within the community. It is clear that these side-locks were sometimes kept, and four examples from the sixth dynasty have been found in the archaeological record, including a plaited example in the British Museum which was discovered in a child's tomb.[29]

Hairstyles were used not only to display status differentiating the child from the adult but also to display the status of both men and women. For example, New Kingdom elite men wore a shoulder-length wig with beautifully arranged curls and braids. In tomb scenes, the tomb owner is often shown in this wig, whereas those making offerings to him wore a short wig or a shaved head showing their inferior status to the tomb owner.[30] For women, there was an intermediary hairstyle between a child and adult, which was a tripartite style with the section at the back in a ponytail exposing the back of the head. This may have been to show they were sexually mature but not yet married.

Women often wore elaborate wigs over the top of their natural hair, which peeped out on the forehead, which in itself was considered a sign of their sexuality. It was common for both men and women to shave their heads against lice and the hot climate, and wear either wigs, or simple linen head-cloths which were cooler in the heat. However, women who did not shave their heads were seen as closer to nature, and therefore natural hair was considered a sign of sexuality and fertility.[31]

An erotic scene in the tale of The Herdsman and the Goddess (1900–1800 BCE) describes the herdsman's first encounter with the goddess:

Lo and behold when I went down to the swamp which borders on this low ground, I saw a woman there, and she looked not like an ordinary mortal. My hair stood on end when I saw her tresses, because her colour was so smooth ... The goddess met him at the pool and she had stripped off her clothes and disarrayed her hair.[32]

The fact that she was naked, and wore her natural hair rather than a wig, which she shakes out for him, emphasises the sensuality of the scene. The words 'colour' and 'skin' were the same in Egyptian, so this could refer to freshly shaved skin 'ready for lovemaking'.[33]

Another literary tale describes a lock of hair which had lodged at the area of the Nile where the king's laundry was carried out. It was so fragrant that the laundry smelt of perfume even after being washed. The head laundryman was blamed:

'... the smell of unguent is in pharaoh's garments!' he exclaimed. And pharaoh harangued them day after day, and they did not know what to do. Pharaoh's chief laundryman was extremely annoyed because of these daily rebukes and he betook himself to the riverbank. He stopped on the sand bank near the spot [where the clothes had been laundered] and he saw the lock of hair in the water. He sent someone to go down into the river and bring it up to him. The hair gave off an exceedingly sweet smell, and he took it back to pharaoh.[34]

A hunt began for the woman to whom the lock of hair belonged to, and when she was discovered, the king wanted to marry her at once, although she was already married. A rather strange story, but one where the eroticism of natural hair and perfume combine, making a woman so desirable that the king goes to extreme lengths to marry her.

Another New Kingdom love poem shows why women still wore wigs even when they had natural hair:

My heart is once again filled by your love when only part of my hair is braided ... So I'll trouble myself no longer over my hairdressing and put on a wig and be ready at once.[35]

Although it appears that natural hair was considered erotic and sensual, wigs were also a feature of the sexuality of women as well as being convenient for moments like this when she does not have time to finish braiding her natural hair. Hair was considered so erotic that to walk in on someone in the process of doing their hair or putting on a wig was perhaps the equivalent of seeing someone in the process of getting dressed. In the *Tale of the Two Brothers*, the younger brother Bata walks in on his sister-in-law as she is braiding her hair. Later she elaborates on this while she is talking to her husband and claims he said to her: 'Come, let us spend an hour lying together: loosen your braids'.[36]

Normally wigs were dark brown, as they were made of a variety of materials including plant fibres, sheep's wool, horse hair or human hair, depending on the wealth of the individual. The cheapest and least attractive wigs were made of palm fibre, which were red in colour and had an unrealistic texture and appearance.[37] Coloured wigs, however, were not unheard of, and the fourth dynasty queen Hetepheres II (2566–2558 BCE) wore a yellow wig, and there is an image of queen Merysankh III (2558–2532 BCE) wearing a short red and yellow wig. Kings were also sometimes depicted wearing blue or green wigs as a sign of their fertility. Whether these were wigs of human hair, or plant fibres dyed these colours, or simply an artistic representation is unknown.

As with any fashion accessory, the wig styles changed over the centuries. In the Old Kingdom, the fashion was to wear short wigs with horizontal rows of curls over the forehead, whereas in the New Kingdom, the bigger the wig the better. One particularly popular wig in the eighteenth dynasty royal court was known as the Hathor wig. The hair was parted in the middle with a plait down each side of the face. The end of each plait was wrapped around a round disc, giving the same shape as the very distinctive wig worn by the goddess and was believed to resemble cow horns. Hathor is sometimes referred to as 'she of the beautiful hair' as well as being a goddess of sexual love.[38] Hair was also an element of erotic dances, some of which were dedicated to Hathor. Dancers plaited weights into the bottom of their hair so when they danced they were able to flip their hair in perfect arcs, which formed part of the dance routine.

Wigs were therefore a common addition to a woman's personal grooming box, regardless of wealth. Wigs have been discovered in the funerary context, but due to their fragility, they are rarely put on display. There are currently examples displayed in the Turin Museum and the Egyptian Museum in Cairo.

The wig currently held in the British Museum (although no longer on display) was examined by a professional wig-maker who determined it an expensive example, as it was made of brown, curled human hair and was covered in a mixture of beeswax and resin. It dates to the eighteenth dynasty and probably comes from Deir el Medina. There were three hundred locks of hair, each comprised of approximately four hundred strands making up the wig. Each of the hair locks was attached to a foundation mesh, also made of human hair, which was relatively elastic, allowing movement. Each strand of hair was wound through the mesh and then itself and sealed with beeswax. As the melting point of the wax was between 62 degrees Celsius and 65 degrees Celsius, they were unlikely to melt through daily wear, as shaded temperatures rarely exceed 60 degrees Celsius in Egypt.

The wig itself does not clearly resemble those depicted on tomb and temple walls, and comprised short blonde-brown curls over the crown, and from the neck of the wig hang hundreds of three-strand plaits in dark brown.[39] The wig discovered in the tomb of Kha and Meryt, currently in the Turin Museum, is, on the other hand, more recognisable as a wig depicted in the tomb scenes with heavy braids falling from a central parting, which framed the face in the manner common in eighteenth dynasty tomb images.

An amazing archaeological find was the wig workshop near the temple of Deir el Bahri, which provided a great deal of information regarding the care and manufacture of wigs. In addition to wigs in various stages of completion, hair wefts, a thread net-foundation and even a model head marked up to show how the wig would attach were discovered. Remnants of a waxy soap made of natron and soda were also found in the workshop, and were likely used for washing the wigs. A dark brown substance of bicarbonate of manganese and quartz grains was used to give the hair body and shine, and if mixed with a waxy substance could have been used as hair dye[40] to ensure that the wig had an even colour tone.

Sometimes a full wig was not required, and men and women simply added hairpieces to their natural hair to add volume or to disguise bald spots, and these have also been found in tombs as well as still attached to the head of mummies. For example, the mummies of Queen Tetisheri and her granddaughter Ahmose-Nefertari had hair pieces woven into their thinning white hair to disguise bald patches.[41]

In a country, where the majority of the population had dark-brown or black hair, it is not surprising that people used dye in order to look different as well as to cover up those tell-tale grey roots. Henna was commonly used, and the hair of an eighteenth dynasty mummy, Honttimihou, was a brilliant red, as were the finger nails of an eleventh dynasty mummy. However, some scholars believe some nail discolouration to be the result of a chemical reaction of the mummification process rather than a widespread use of henna.[42]

So far in this chapter we have discussed the means by which men and women enhanced and improved their appearance making themselves more attractive to the opposite sex, by use of cosmetics, wigs and perfume. However, some women in ancient Egypt went one step further and enhanced their bodies permanently with tattoos and scarification. It is interesting that tattoos were often attributed by archaeologists as being an indicator of an erotic occupation: dancer, musician or prostitute. One wonders if the interpretation would be different today at a time when tattoos are commonplace. In the West, they are considered fashion essentials, and in modern Egypt they are a common indicator of religion, with Copts tattooing a small cross on their wrist. The association of tattoos with rebellion against society is a very nineteenth-century interpretation and one that perhaps needs to be readdressed.

Tattoos in ancient Egypt were not that common, but the surviving evidence shows they were normally worn by women rather than men, and only appear on mummies and faience figurines after the Middle Kingdom. It is thought that the practice may have come to Egypt from Nubia.

The most common representation of female tattoos are in the form of small faience or clay figurines of naked women, with enhanced hips, prominent pubic areas and small breasts. Some of these were placed in tombs, leading to the idea they were concubine figures providing a sexual partner for the deceased in the afterlife. Obviously, this theory did not account for the examples found in the tombs of women or in domestic structures. The possible theories are explained in more detail in chapter 8. These figures, while naked, are often decorated with tattoos, mostly in the form of girdles that cross over the torso, back and the hips. There is obviously a ritualistic element to these figures, as many of them do not have feet, which is often interpreted as a precaution to prevent them from leaving the tomb and taking their sympathetic magic with them. An inscription on the thigh of one of these figures states: 'May a birth be granted to your daughter Seh', indicating that this particular figurine was placed in a man's tomb by his daughter who hoped he could help her to conceive.[43]

Most of the tattooed designs on these figures are simple, comprising a series of small triangles made up of a number of small dots placed closely together. It is suggested that the number of dots may have held some significance; two symbolised duality, and three was plurality, and deities were often worshipped in the form of triads. Five was the sum of duality and plurality together, and seven was the sum of plurality and totality (four) and was considered one of the most sacred numbers along with nine which was three pluralities.[44] Most of the geometric dot tattoos were in multiples of these numbers. A mummy discovered in Nubia dating to 2000 BCE had tattooing around the abdominal region and was buried with a concubine figure whose decoration matched the tattoos. However, the number of tattoos on the fertility figurines always outnumbered those discovered on individual mummies.

Through examination of the potential instruments used to produce tattoos, it is clear that dots and geometric shapes would have been easier to produce than complex images. The Petrie Museum, UCL, has seven small bronze instruments, between 3.4 and 4.8 cm in length, with a sharp point that may have been tattooing instruments. To form the points, the corners were folded in and beaten flat before the item was ready for use.[45] These instruments were discovered at Gurob among cosmetic items and fine pottery, and Petrie initially described them as points for removing thorns, although for a problem that was rather common, it is unlikely there was a special instrument for removing them. In the modern world, there is no specialised instrument solely for removing splinters, as you use whatever is to hand. Other possible tattooing instruments are from Kafr Hassan Dawood in the form of five metal rods measuring 75 mm long and 2 mm thick. They were found in a woman's grave in association with razor blades and could have been used either for tattoos or as a leather working set.[46]

To produce a tattoo, these instruments were dipped into a mixture of soot and oil, producing a blue-black ink, which was then repeatedly stabbed into the skin, leaving a deposit of ink beneath the surface. A similar technique was used in Egypt in the 1920s, where they used seven needles tied to a stick, which was then stuck into the skin. With seven at a time, this process may have been much quicker, although those receiving tattoos often suffered from fever and inflammation after the tattoo had been completed, possibly resulting in blood poisoning.

There are only a few images of women rather than figurines with tattoos, which includes a New Kingdom ostracon from Deir el Medina, which shows a dancer doing a backflip. On her thighs, she has similar tattoos to those on the fertility figures, and therefore it is clear why such tattoos were associated with fertility and sex. She also has a semicircle on her cheek, which could be another tattoo or evidence of scarification. Facial tattoos appear to be unusual, with tattoos mostly presented on the thighs. However, facial tattoos were found on Nubian mummies and may have been introduced to the Egyptians in the twenty-fifth dynasty.[47] Additionally, Gaston Maspero discovered Graeco-Roman mummies at Akhmim which bore tattoos to the side of the nose and the chin,[48] which, according to Herodotus, at this time, meant they were runaway slaves.

He records that a slave caught fleeing could be punished by a hundred lashes and a tattoo on the forehead. However, this idea of tattooing as punishment seems different from the pharaonic examples on dancers and priestesses, indicating the ideologies surrounding tattoos changed over the centuries, as indeed they have in the modern West over the last fifty years.

Herodotus also records that runaway slaves seeking sanctuary in the temple of Heracles in the Delta were exempt from the traditional punishments if they agreed to have the cultic symbols associated with the god tattooed upon their person. Not only did this show the slave's dedication to the god but also that he was under the divine protection of the god. This idea of cultic tattoos was not an unusual one, and in a New Kingdom chapel at Deir el Medina there are images of priestesses who all have a series of little cross tattoos across their breast showing their affiliation to the god.

In total, forty-two mummies bearing tattoos have been discovered from Nubia and Middle Kingdom Egypt. Only one of them was male.[49] Three Middle Kingdom mummies discovered in the royal precinct of Nebhetep-Ra at Deir el Bahri show evidence of tattoos; one, belonging to Amunet, which is currently in the Egyptian Museum of Antiquities in Cairo, and two belonging to dancers of Hathor, which are in the Metropolitan Museum of Art, New York.

Amunet's burial equipment included a painted wooden coffin, and the burial location in the royal temple complex of Deir el Bahri indicates she was a wealthy, if not, influential individual, indicating tattoos were clearly not a sign of low status.[50] The mummy, Amunet, held the title 'priestess of Hathor', and king's favourite ornament, further indicating that her tattoos were religiously significant rather than a sign of promiscuity and sexuality. Amunet's tattoos were on the left shoulder, a number of dotted lines above the naval, on the thigh and on both arms, all in the form of geometric shapes. She also had evidence of scarification on her abdomen, which were described as three horizontal blue and white lines.[51] Keimer also discusses two mummies of dancing girls which have similar tattoos to Amunet as well as scarification on the abdomen. It seems, therefore, that it was possible that body decoration in the form of tattooing and scarification went together.

However, the main difference between Amunet and the dancing girls were the lozenge-shaped tattoos over the abdomen, which would have swelled when she was pregnant, creating a web or netting design which may have offered divine protection to the pregnant woman.[52]

In the New Kingdom, Bremner-Rhind Papyrus, girls playing the role of Isis and her sister Nepththys in the re-enactment of the myth of Osiris and Isis are identified, as 'their name is inscribed into their arms as Isis and Nephthys' and could be evidence of tattooing rather than simply painting the names onto the girls' arms.[53] This indicates that religious tattooing may have been common, further emphasising that not all tattooed women worked in the entertainment industry.

Although the majority of the evidence for tattoos shows geometric designs, there is evidence for more complex designs, even drawings. The Middle Kingdom paddle dolls, for example, sometimes have images of crocodiles near the genitalia, presumably offering some form of protection. A faience bowl, currently in the Rijksmuseum van Oudheden, Leiden, shows a musician playing a lyre. She is naked other than a girdle and a tattoo of Bes on her thigh. This is likely to have an apotropaic function, as Bes is the god of music and childbirth. Perhaps she had the tattoo in order to have his protection over her music or as a symbol of her own fertility and fecundity. Moreover, the rest of the scene is steeped in sexual symbolism. The head of her instrument is in the form of a duck, which is turned to look at her, and a monkey is seated behind her on her cushion playing with her girdle. Monkeys were considered erotic, and sometimes in sexual graffiti the women often look like monkeys. Monkeys are also shown playing musical instruments, and one of Akhenaten's wives (*Kiya*) had a very similar name to the Egyptian word (*ky*) for monkey,[54] which may have been a sexualised nickname.

The musician also seems to be seated in an arbour, with convolvulus leaves forming the canopy. She is wearing a large elaborate wig, which as discussed above was very important when creating an erotic image, on top of which was a scented fat cone. These scented cones are believed to have been made from animal fat steeped with perfume, with the idea that as they heated up they melted and emitted a scent of perfume.

However, some scholars believe these perfume cones were actually just an artistic representation of perfume-wearing, showing a two-dimensional representation of scent.[55] Further indications of wearing of perfume can be seen in the banqueting scenes from the tombs where the white linen dresses of the female revellers are stained a yellowy-brown colour. It is thought this represents dousing the dress in perfume rather than the body, although it is darker where it is in close contact with the body itself.[56] As these images generally only appear in funerary scenes and therefore may have a deeper significance (*see* chapter 9). All of these characteristics combined made the Leiden bowl image incredibly risqué to an ancient Egyptian observer.

A similar image can be found in the Pushkin State Museum of Fine Arts, Moscow, on an ebony and ivory spoon, and in the Philadelphia Museum of Art on two wooden statues of women which also show an image of Bes on the thigh. A musician depicted in house SE8 at Deir el Medina is surrounded by convolvulus leaves (as with the Leiden Bowl) playing a double flute. She has tattoos on her thighs, although the design is no longer clear. There is only one mummy, dated to the fourth century BCE from Aksha in Nubia, which actually shows a tattoo of Bes on the thigh.

There is clearly a connection between music and sex, and quite often where musicians are depicted there are other characteristics in the scene to associate it with sexuality. An eighteenth dynasty leather wall hanging from Deir el Bahri, which is currently in the Metropolitan Museum of Art, depicts a woman playing a harp while a naked man with an enormous phallus dances in front of her. At the beginning of the twentieth century, the phallus was erased, and only a photograph exists of this item now.[57] This scene is possibly connected with the cult of Hathor,[58] although it has been interpreted in many ways: a fertility and harvest ritual, a circumcision ritual, puberty rites or an apotropaic ritual to banish Hathor's dangerous side.[59] Regardless of the meaning, the basic characteristics show a well-endowed man dancing in front of a woman playing a harp, connecting sex, music and dancing.

The association between fertility and tattoos, or at least between women and tattoos, could explain why not many males are represented with them. However, considering some tattoos were cultic rather than sexual, it seems unusual that priests did not have tattoos to show devotion. Changing attitudes to tattoos from associations with religion, sexuality and fertility to connections with submissiveness and slavery meant that, generally speaking, the only men shown with tattoos were foreigners; both Nubians and Syrians are often identified artistically by their elaborate clothing, hairstyles and tattoos.

All the adornments discussed in this chapter (clothes, cosmetics, perfumes, henna, hair and tattoos) ensured that both men and women looked their best, and were able to attract someone of the opposite sex. Each of their adornments provided some information about their status, wealth, sexuality and fertility, and no doubt helped in finding a future wife or husband.

2

LOVE AND MARRIAGE

'I wish I were your mirror, so that you always looked at me'[1]

Once a partner had been chosen, the Egyptians started the complicated courting process before finally getting married. Regarding relationships and emotions, the ancient Egyptians felt exactly the same way as we do today about people. It is only culture that dictates how people act on those feelings. Unfortunately, it is very difficult to ascertain true emotion from the surviving religious or literary texts. For example, in an Old Kingdom tomb chapel a husband laments the virtues of his deceased wife stating: 'she did not utter statement that repelled my heart, she did not transgress whilst she was young in life'. This suggests he had fond memories of her, as did another husband who similarly compliments his wife as 'one who speaks pleasantly and sweetens love in the presence of her husband'.[2] However, as both husbands remark on similar aspects of their wife's character, it could be suggested they were standardised phrases used in funerary texts rather than displays of real affection.

Although women did not leave as many monuments as men, there are some examples of a wife's affection towards her husband. The inscription of Taimhotep, sistrum player and priestess of Ptah at Memphis, currently in the British Museum, is a perfect example. She died during the reign of Cleopatra VII, before her husband, the high priest of Ptah, Psherenptah. From beyond the grave she encouraged him to carry on enjoying life:

> O, My brother, my husband, my friend, high priest,
> Weary not of drink and food, of drinking deep and loving!
> Celebrate the holiday, honour your heart day and night,
> Value the years spent on earth.[3]

A very touching sentiment, but it is not known if Taimhotep commissioned the stela to be carved before her death or whether it was commissioned after her death by her grieving husband. The signature at the end of the stela is that of Imhotep, son of Kha-Hapi, who may have been Taimhotep's brother[4] and, therefore, does not shed much light on authorship. Moreover, the sentiment is also a standardised funerary formula and is also expressed by Nesmut, the wife of Nakhtefmut, from the reign of Osorkon II (874–850 BCE):

> We here wish to dwell together, god not separating us!
> As you love for me, I leave you not!
> Let your heart not grieve! Rather sit at ease each day,
> There is no evil coming![5]

It is difficult to find the true affection behind such formulaic texts, but that is not to say funerary texts cannot reflect loving relationships. A small glimpse of affection can be seen in the survival of nicknames. A number of canopic jars belonging to royal women display such nicknames including: 'The cat like one', 'The much sought after one' and 'She (who is) hot-tempered like a leopard'.[6] Perhaps not as catchy to a modern ear, but to the Egyptians these were probably considered cute and are a small reflection on the feelings of the husband towards his wife.

The most revealing texts about love and romance are the New Kingdom love poetry, although, as mentioned in chapter 1, they were written by professional scribes and therefore represent an idealised scenario rather than reality. But, they do, even now after 3500 years, still present feelings and thoughts that are familiar to us. That is not to say, as literary texts, that some of them do not sound like they were written by teenagers in the first throws of love, like this young man who likens love to an illness:

Seven days it is from yesterday since I saw my sister,
And I am feeling ill.
My limbs are heavy, I forget my body.
If the doctors come, no remedies will cure me,
Even the lector priests know not the cure.
There is no diagnosis for my disease,
What I have said is what revives me.
Her name can get me on my feet.[7]

Many love poems, and indeed letters between husband and wife, are addressed to sister or brother, which concern and confuse modern readers. It must be remembered that these were terms of endearment used to address lovers and spouses without any reference to actual sibling relationships. Such terms have led to the oft-quoted myth about ancient Egypt that they commonly had sibling marriages or other incestuous unions.[8] In reality, sibling marriages were not accepted except for the royal family, which is discussed in chapter 3.

A study of 490 marriages from the First Intermediate Period to the eighteenth dynasty was carried out by Jaroslav Černy, who only identified two apparent sibling marriages. On the other hand, marriages between half-siblings or cousins[9] seemed more common, possibly in order to ensure that family wealth was not divided.

The family of Sennedjem, a workman at Deir el Medina, presented three cousin marriages, and there were five other cousin marriages at Deir el Medina during the Ramesside Period.[10] Therefore, the evidence suggests that incestuous marriages were the exception rather than the norm in pharaonic Egypt. Unfortunately, these examples do not provide enough information to ascertain how widespread this practice actually was. Some of the identifications may also be tenuous, as such research is based solely on names, which can be problematic. It seems rather more common however that, upon the death of the first wife, the widower married her sister, his sister-in-law. Unfortunately, it is difficult to trace such relationships, as parents of wives are not often represented or named in tombs,[11] so Egyptologists have to trace relationships using nomenclature, which is only simple if people have unusual names.

The aim of most of the New Kingdom poetry is love and marriage rather than purely sex, indicating the Egyptians were a romantic bunch. The following from the poems entitled '*The beginning of the songs of pleasant entertainment for your beloved the chosen of your heart when she comes from the field*' gives us some idea of desires and romantic ideals.

O beauteous youth, may my desire be fulfilled to become the mistress of your house.
With your hands resting upon my breasts, you have spread your love over me.

I speak to my innermost heart, with the prayer that my lord may be
with me this night.

I am like one who is in her tomb, for are you not alone my health
and life?

Your touch brings the joy of my well-being, the joy of my heart
seeking after you.[12]

This poem, written from a female perspective, expresses the desire
to become the 'mistress of your house' or wife. Even poetry from
a male perspective refers to marriage and commitment rather than
simply a sexual dalliance. This poem from the sixth century BCE
was recorded in many places, indicating it was a popular and
well-known piece:

I wish I were her doorkeeper, so that at least she would nag me.

Then I might hear her voice, though angry, like a child fearing her.

I wish I were her Nubian slave, who guards her steps.

Then I would be able to see the colour of all her limbs!

I wish I were her laundryman, just for a single month.

Then I would flourish by donning [her garment] and be close to
her body.

I would wash away the unguent from her clothes and wipe my
body in her dress ...

I wish I were the signet ring, which guards her finger, then I would
see her desire every day.

I wish I were your mirror, so that you always looked at me.

I wish I were your garment so that you would always wear me.

I wish I were the water that washes your body.

I wish I were the unguent, O woman, that I could anoint you.

And the band around your breasts, and the beads around your
neck. I wish I were your sandal that you would step on me.[13]

The author or narrator of the poem is clearly besotted with the young lady and wishes to be with her all the time. It does not sound as if there is a relationship at the time of writing, more that he is watching her from afar.

Naturally, while some men wanted such commitment, others were interested in the physical aspect of relationships, as one man comments: 'you shall reach its grotto before your hand is kissed four times'. Perhaps this does not seem very risqué, but in ancient Egyptian 'its' and 'hers' were written the same way, and 'grotto' is a double entendre for vagina and 'the pleasures awaiting the young man' therein.[14] The poem continues 'you are pursuing the love of your sister'. The term 'love' could be used to mean love, beloved, or the sexual act. In the Turin Erotic papyrus (*see* chapter 6), one of the girls encourages the man: 'Come behind me with your love. Your penis is with me', making it clear that love here refers to the sex act.[15] A poem on the Chester Beatty I Papyrus also uses the grotto euphemism:

When you go to the house of the sister
And charge towards her grotto,
The gate is made high
Its mistress cleans it and furnishes it with the palate's delight.[16]

It is perfectly clear what the young man is hoping to happen once he arrives at the home of his intended liaison for the evening.

Another man describes his feeling after a dalliance, although he seems happy with simply kissing and embracing the young woman:

When I embrace her and her arms are open, I feel like a man in incense land

Who is immersed in scent.

When I kiss her and her lips are open

I rejoice without even having drunk beer.[17]

As one would expect, not all men were as articulate as the love poetry suggests, or were not confident enough to instigate such dalliances without a little help. A Graeco-Roman guide offers advice to men on how to flatter and seduce women. It is clear that none of the advice is new and would not look out of place in a modern guide to 'picking up girls':

> *Concerning Seductions.* Accordingly the seducer should be unadorned and uncombed, so that he does not seem to the woman to be too concerned about the matter in hand.[18]

Most will be familiar with the phrase, 'Treat 'em mean to keep 'em keen', and it seems the ancient Egyptians followed this advice too. The idea of being dishevelled is discussed in chapter 1, as personal grooming was important to the Egyptians and was only abandoned in times of mourning. This was to be followed by flattery, as the man is advised to declare:

> ... that the plain woman is the equal of a goddess, the ugly woman is charming, the elderly one is like a young girl.[19]

Unfortunately the text breaks off at the intriguing title of '*Concerning kisses*', which presumably gave advice on what to do once the seduction was successful.

Once courting, a couple no doubt snatched moments alone together, as suggested in the Turin Love Song which is told from the view point of a sycamore tree, which was sacred to Hathor, the goddess of love:

> The little sycamore ... opens her [mouth] to speak ...
> Come, spend time where the young people are:
> The meadow celebrates its day.
> Under me are festival booth and a hut ...
> Come spend the day in pleasure,
> [one] morning, then another – two days,
> Sitting in my shade.[20]

Another similar poem adds alcohol and perfume to make the scene even more erotically charged:

> The sister spends the day with the brother beneath my branches,
> Drunk with grape and pomegranate wine,
> Besprinkled with the fragrance of resin.[21]

The poetry gives the impression that the Egyptians were quite romantic and that love was an important aspect of their lives. Perhaps it was. The institution of marriage, on the other hand, was not always based on mutual love but rather the will of the girl's parents as attested from numerous poems: 'He knows not my wish to embrace him, or he would write to my mother'.[22] The sixth stanza of Papyrus Chesty Beatty I records something similar: 'If only my mother had known my heart, she would have gone in'.[23]

These lines suggest that the young man approached the mother in order to arrange a marriage with the object of his affection rather than asking the girl directly. However, other evidence suggests that it was the father who made the decision. Ankhsheshonq (Ptolemaic Period) advises his son that he 'should choose a prudent husband, not necessarily a rich one, for your daughter'.[24] It seems clear that the daughter probably had little input into the decision regarding her marriage.

Further evidence suggests it could be either parent who ultimately made the decision regarding the marriage:

> Come to me that I may see your beauty.
> My father and mother will be glad,
> Everybody will rejoice at you unanimously.[25]

It seems clear, therefore, that a boy wishing to marry a girl approached her parents (mother or father, perhaps varying from family to family) in order to gain permission. The parents would then assess his suitability as husband material. However, the criteria for a suitable husband are not clear. It was not essential to marry into the same class or financial background, indicating they were judged on other characteristics. This is made clear in a text dating to the reign of Thutmosis III. The royal barber, Sabest, discusses the impending nuptials of his niece:

> … my slave, my property, his name is Imenjui. I fetched him with my own strength when I accompanied the sovereign. I have given to him the daughter of my sister Nebta as a wife. Her name is Takamenet.[26]

The first question raised by this text is why Takamenet's uncle rather than father was making marital decisions for her. Either it was due to the death of her father, or it could be that as her uncle had found a suitable match he was negotiating on behalf of the groom. It is also clear from this that class boundaries were not important, as a slave was considered suitable for his niece. Things had clearly changed by the time Herodotus was writing, as he comments about swineherds: 'Nobody wants to give them a daughter in marriage nor take a wife from them, indicating inter-class marriages were taboo'.[27]

Even in the royal family there is evidence of large class differences with non-royal women marrying the king. One of the most famous was Amenhotep III and his great royal wife, Tiye, a girl from a non-royal family.

While marriage across the classes was acceptable, sexual relationships between different social statuses appear to have been frowned upon, and records from Deir el Medina suggest that sexual acts should take place between equals unless they ended in marriage.[28] For example, a record was made regarding the Deir el Medina workman, Merysekhmet, who impregnated his servant. We do not know if he married her, but as this situation was recorded it was possibly seen as inappropriate, even though it was a mutually desirable relationship.[29] In an eighteenth dynasty text, Amenemhat is adamant that he has not had intercourse with his father's servants, although it is difficult to ascertain whether it was considered inappropriate for him to have had a relationship at all with the servants or if he was overstepping the mark and this was only the prerogative of his father.[30]

Whereas it is clear girls may have had little say in their marriage arrangements, it may have been similar for boys too. In the wisdom text of Ankhsheshonq, he advises: 'Don't let your son marry a bride from another town, in case he is taken away from you'.[31] This idea was embellished on in the Instruction of Hardjedef, who claims a good wife is a 'hearty woman'.[32] Ani adds she should not be a 'stranger, one not known in her town'.[33] Apparently a nice, local girl was the better option to ensure that the son remained close to home, especially when his parents became elderly and needed taking care of. Should the boy wish to marry a girl from another town, it is quite possible that his parents would refuse to allow the marriage to take place.

While families often arranged marriages or at least offered advice as to the ideal husband or wife, that is not to say that there were no protests from the bride or groom about these choices. One poem on Papyrus Harris II makes it clear that the girl will not be parted from her lover:

> I shall not leave him, even if they beat me ...
> And if I have to spend my day in the swamp,
> Or if they chase me to Syria with clubs,
> Or to Nubia with palm ribs,
> Or to the desert with sticks,
> Or to the coast with reeds,
> I will not listen to their plans of giving up the man I love.[34]

It would be interesting to know what happened in such a case. Would the young girl get her way, or would she have to give up the man and marry someone chosen by her parents?

This parental involvement, especially in regard to the girls, is likely due to the age of girls when they were considered old enough for marriage. Lives were short in ancient Egypt, with the lifespan for women being approximately thirty years and men on average dying at thirty-five years. This is supported by an early nineteenth-century study carried out on 709 skulls from the Dynastic Period, which showed the average age at death was thirty-six years.[35] A further study on skeletons from Gebelein and Asyut currently in Turin shows that by thirty years the population was halved and by forty-three years the population was reduced to a quarter.[36]

Therefore, children were expected to grow up quickly, and girls in particular were married at a young age enabling plenty of time to have a large family. However, it was not the same for men, and it was not unusual for a young girl to be married to a man many years her senior. In the Graeco-Roman Period, there is evidence of girls marrying as young as eight years old, and there is a demotic mummy label produced for an eleven-year-old wife.[37] It may not have been much different in the Pharaonic Period.

When a child reached puberty, they were considered to be of marriageable age. For a girl, she was considered an adult when her menstruation cycle began. Some estimate that this started at approximately fourteen years, although it could start earlier or later depending on the individual girl. It is believed that with better health and diet the onset of menarche earlier today than is in the ancient past.[38] For example, the population at Amarna was particularly unhealthy, and therefore the onset of menarche was later than expected, maybe fourteen to seventeen years.[39] It is suggested that menstruation may have happened less frequently than in the modern world due to malnutrition, trauma and stress. It is known that they used linen as sanitary towels, which were sent to the washermen to launder. Although in the Satire of the Trades this task was condemned as something unsavoury, it was not considered unclean or taboo.[40]

There is no evidence that menarche was celebrated in any way, although reference is made to women at Deir el Medina during their monthly cycle. An intriguing New Kingdom ostracon, for example, claims that something unusual happened on: 'the day when these eight women came out [to/from the] place of women while they were menstruating'.[41] Although a short text, it leaves a lot of questions unanswered. We do not know what happened to them on their way to/from the Place of Women, we do not know what this Place of Women was, and who qualified to go there while they were menstruating. It is also interesting that there were eight women who travelled together, almost as if menstruation was a social event.

Additionally, the absentee records from Deir el Medina from year 40 of Ramses II are interesting in regard to menstruation, as nine men were absent from work due to a female member of his family being on her period. Whether it was due to her being incapacitated or absent is unknown, but it has been possible to calculate how many women in Deir el Medina had synchronised cycles. The wife of Simut and Nakhtmin, and the daughters of Rahotep and Wadjmose all fell within days of each other and were in sync throughout the year as were the daughters of Neferobe and Siwadjy and the wife of Inherkhau.[42] Perhaps, if enough women had synchronised cycles, they all travelled together in order to be purified or to sit in isolation. Although the ritual aspects are unknown, it is likely that such an excursion was a fun social event for the women involved, and one that excluded men and children. Imagine the gossip the walls of the Place of Women heard!

A boy's coming of age was a social rather than a biological event. At approximately twelve years, boys went through a public circumcision ritual with other boys from the village. However, with only three representations of circumcision and two textual references, it is uncertain how widespread it actually was. Two of the circumcision images are from the divine birth scenes of Hatshepsut at Deir el Bahri and Amenhotep III at the temple of Mut at Karnak, and therefore of a ritual rather than an actual event. The king and his *ka* (spirit) are depicted being circumcised together as part of the purification rituals required prior to coronation. In the case of Hatshepsut's circumcision scene, she is depicted with a penis and is undergoing a male circumcision, which in her case was biologically impossible.

One textual record, a stela from Denderah states: 'I buried its old people, I circumcised its young people',[43] indicating in the Ptolemaic Period circumcision was a common event for the ordinary populace too. The third pictorial representation comes from the sixth dynasty tomb of Ankhmahor, and is believed to be a record of an actual event. In the scene, a servant holds the boy from behind as a priest kneeling before him numbs his penis and comments: 'Hold him firmly. Don't let him swoon'. In the next scene, the kneeling priest holds a flint knife to the boy's penis and there has been some discussion as to whether this was to remove the foreskin or to shave the pubic hair as part of a purification ritual. The text above the boy's head states: 'I will make it comfortable (well/pleasant/sweet)'.[44]

The final textual reference gives some indication of the extent of the circumcision ritual. It dates to the First Intermediate Period and comes from Naga ed-Dier. A man comments: 'when I was circumcised together with 120 men'. While not offering much detail, this simple phrase tells us circumcisions were public events with numerous boys at a time. If this ritual was indeed as widespread as this text suggests, human remains should offer some supporting evidence, but unfortunately it is difficult to identify this practice in mummies. It seems that Amenhotep II, Thutmosis IV, Ramses IV and Ramses V were circumcised, but this is no indication of how widespread the ritual really was.

The circumcision ceremony was a ritualistic marker of adulthood for the boys, but a clearer marker of manhood was when he received his first paid position. This could follow an apprenticeship or the death of his father, upon which he took over the family profession. Therefore, this age varied from boy to boy and did not have the same impact on them as coming of age did on girls. For both boys and girls at this important stage in their life, their side-lock of youth was shaved off, providing an external sign of their new adult status to the rest of the community.

Whereas a girl was ready to marry upon the onset of menarche, often boys worked at their career for a few years until they were financially in a position to consider marriage and start a family. Both required wealth, stability and dedication, and this is emphasised by the Middle Kingdom teachings of Ptahhotep:

Love your wife with proper ardour ... Fill her belly and clothe her back! Ointment is a good remedy for her limbs. Make her happy as long as you live. She is a good field to her master.[45]

Marriage could not happen prior to menstruation, and in a document from the twenty-seventh dynasty, Horwedja asks a priest of Amun-Ra, Pediaset, if he could marry his daughter. Pediaset replies: 'Her time has not yet come; become a priest of Amunrasonter and I shall give her to you'.[46] This shows that not only did he want to wait until his daughter was older but also until Horwedja had secured a paid position and could care for her properly.

It was not, therefore, unusual for a very young girl to marry a man many years her senior. As an older husband, it was his responsibility 'to make her a wife and teach her to be human'. This phrase is one that is used in relation to both marriage and in child-rearing. To 'make her human' is not a comment about an inferior woman's position but regarding the need to teach your wife how to live within society as one would with a child: as indeed she may still have been.

A perfect example of a large age gap is recorded on the stela of Taimhotep, who we met earlier. She married Psherenptah when she was fourteen years old and he was over thirty years her senior. She claims in this marriage she had 'obeyed her father'. Both Psherenptah and Taimhotep's fathers were high priests of Ptah at the temple of Memphis, and it was clearly an arranged marriage to maintain the family's position in society.

It is thought that, as the girl was young at marriage, she was expected to be a virgin in order to limit questions of illegitimacy with the first child, but there does not seem to be a ceremony to prove her virginity. In modern Egypt, the groom or a female relative will insert a finger covered in gauze into the new bride's vagina to break the hymen proving her purity[47] in what is no doubt a traumatic and humiliating experience for the young bride. As there is no record of this in ancient Egypt, the importance of virginity is questionable. Furthermore, there was no word for virginity in the Egyptian language suggesting perhaps it was not considered essential.

In family-arranged marriages, dowries were often paid between the families and were recorded in marriage contracts or prenuptial agreements. Such agreements often outlined what would happen in the case of a divorce:

> Make Nakhtemut take an oath of the lord, life, prosperity, and health that he swore 'As Amen endures, as the ruler endures, if I go back on my word and abandon the daughter of Tenermonthu in the future, I will receive one hundred blows and be deprived of all the property that I will acquire with her'.[48]

The dowry often comprised goods a bride required in her new life, and legally belonged to her even after a divorce. Some families may have believed that the wealthier the gifts, the better the arrangements that could be made for their daughters. The groom's family may also provide gifts or services to the bride's family in the form of a bride price,[49] which could be a quantity of corn[50] or other prearranged product. Although this process of giftgiving was no doubt common, there is little evidence from the texts regarding the finer details of how they made the arrangements, although there was very much a standardised formula to the contracts that were drawn up. This included the date of the ruling monarch, names of the contracted partners (husband and wife) and their parents, the husband's profession, the name of the scribe who drew up the contract and the names of the witnesses and finally the details of the settlement.

It is suggested that this payment to the wife of goods or corn was not a bride price as such, but a means of obtaining 'rights' to the woman as a wife, perhaps purely sexual rights[51], a sort of compensation for marrying the woman.[52] This did not make the woman her husband's property, but was an assurance that she would act as a good wife and remain faithful.[53] This gift enabled the woman to cut the ties with her father as a new relationship was formed with her husband[54] as well as compensating her father for losing her input in the home.

Although these gifts were sometimes recorded on papyrus and constituted official documents, they were not a requirement for a marriage to be legal, as there are examples of such 'gift' documents being drawn up months or even years after the marriage and birth of children. Needless to say, not all marriages ended up with such a document regarding financial arrangements, and a marriage was legal without it. These documents were signed by a number of witnesses, which legalised them, but there is limited evidence as to whether it was necessary to present the contract before the knbt (court) as part of the procedure. A papyrus in Turin dated to the twentieth dynasty records the procedure of presenting the contract before the vizier. The contract concerned a priest, Amenkhau, whose first wife, Tathari, died, and he remarried a woman called Anoksunozem. He had children with his first wife, but not the second, and the contract essentially concerned the property he was giving to his second wife. His children were to bear witness that this was not the property of their late mother, but that of their father. Whether this was the normal procedure in second marriages is uncertain, and the contract itself has not survived.[55] Instead of involving the vizier to solve a current dispute, this action seemed to be in order to prevent any disputes further down the line.

It was unusual for people to remain unmarried in ancient Egypt. The sole purpose of marriage was the reproduction of the next generation of Egyptians. Therefore, the most important relationship was that between a husband and wife.[56] According to the wisdom texts, getting married young was advisable:

> Take a wife while you are young that you may beget a son and she can bear him whilst you are still young. Happy is the man who has offspring and a large family. He is respected because of his children.[57]

An army captain from the eleventh dynasty took this to heart and boasts that he fathered 'seventy children, the issue of one wife,' in order to show his (and his wife's) great virility.[58] The actuality of his boast must obviously be questioned. At the other end of the fertility scale, a man who was unable to impregnate his wife could be publically ridiculed, as was the case with Nekhemmut who received an anonymous letter stating:

> You are not a man since you are unable to make your wife pregnant like your fellow men. A further matter; you abound in being exceedingly stingy. You give no one anything.[59]

However, a residential inventory of Deir el Medina shows that families were not as large as we are generally led to believe. Of thirty houses that are recorded, one couple had four children, five couples had three, two fathers each had three children with different mothers, six couples had two children, seven families were with one child, four households were with no children and six were unmarried men.[60] It must be noted that Deir el Medina is not necessarily a model for the whole of Egyptian society, as it was an unusual, purpose-built village, with small houses with no possibility of expansion.

As a social norm, anything that deviated from a traditional marriage producing children was seen as a deviation from *Maat* (cosmic balance) and could invoke a hostile response from society. However, there were some men who chose not to marry, albeit a very small number. Of a study of ninety-three New Kingdom funerary contexts, only three burials appear to be of unmarried men,[61] where they are not depicted with a wife or children.[62] Unfortunately, as women were either buried in the tomb of their husband or their father, it is not so easy to ascertain how many women decided not to marry and how they were treated by society.

Should a marriage not produce a child, it was expected that the childless couple would adopt a son. Then in due course this son took over the father's position as well as acted as a 'staff of old age' for the elderly couple, providing them with care when they needed it most. Nekhemmut was also criticised for not taking this logical step in providing his wife with a family:

> As for him who has no children, he adopts an orphan instead to bring him up. It is his responsibility to pour water onto your hands as one's eldest son.[63]

Adoption was not always in the traditional sense where a child was raised as a member of the family. It was acceptable to adopt an adult, whose own parents were still living and have them train alongside the adoptive father so the business could be passed onto him following retirement.

For financial reasons, a childless man could adopt his own wife in order that she should inherit all of his possessions after his death. Traditionally, a wife inherited a third of her husband's possessions, so this ensured she received all of them. By adopting his own (first) wife, the man could remarry in order to bear children while not affecting the first wife's inheritance. This type of situation is recorded in the rather unusual Adoption Papyrus from the reign of Ramses XI (1098–1070 BCE). It discusses a man, Nebnefer, who adopted his wife Naunefer before fathering three children with a household slave. His wife then adopted these three children as her own. Her brother married the oldest of the three children, and Naunefer adopted him as well.[64] Although rather complicated, it was a legal means of manipulating the inheritance in the manner that Nebnefer wanted.

With such complicated marriage and adoption arrangements, the question of legitimacy must be addressed. The question of legitimacy is rarely represented in the texts, and there is only one clear example where an illegitimate boy is mocked for this status. This is in the literary tale, *Truth and Falsehood*:

> Then his companions said to him; 'Whose son are you? You don't have a father!' and they reviled and mocked him: 'Hey you don't have a father!'[65]

A record from Deir el Medina tells of a married woman (*Hmt*) who had an affair and became pregnant. In many modern societies, this in itself would be considered a terrible thing. However, the text is rather more concerned with the behaviour of the man with whom she had the affair, to provide any information about what happened to the woman or her child, indicating it was not considered a priority.

A further issue raised by such complicated family situations is that of polygamy. There was no word for 'ex-' in ancient Egyptian, so it is difficult to ascertain whether wives were concurrent with each other or consecutive. In the case of Amenemhat (TT82), both the issue of incest (discussed above) and polygamy are raised. He is recorded as having had two wives: one represented in his tomb and the other identified from a statue in Berlin (2316). It is thought the statue possibly represents his first wife who died. His second wife, Baket, is clearly identified as the daughter of his sister, in other words his niece, and it is this wife who is represented throughout his tomb with him.[66] This is the only case of an uncle/niece marriage from the eighteenth dynasty, although there is another case of uncle/niece and one of an aunt/nephew marriage from the twentieth dynasty.

However, some so-called cases of polygamy may in fact be cases of a man depicting his deceased wives alongside his current wife. The ninth dynasty tomb of Mery-aa from el-Hagarseh is a case in point, as he depicts six wives, five of whom were mothers to his children. The sixth wife, Isi, who had no children, was however more prominent in the tomb, and it is suggested she was his first wife. Trying to identify the position of the other wives is difficult. Wives were omitted from tomb depiction should they die before the tomb was constructed, infertility, general incompatibility, adultery and divorce. Therefore, we can assume none of Mery-aa's six wives were ex-wives. However, perhaps Mery-aa was unlucky enough to have lost five wives, although this seems unlikely. It is more probable that this is evidence of polygamy, where he had a number of wives living contemporaneously with each other.

Another example can be found in the tomb of Sobekhotep at El Kab, who is depicted with four wives, although in his brother's tomb he is only shown with one. All four women are referred to as *Hmt* (wife) rather than *Hbswt* (concubine), indicating they were all of a similar status, except the one singled out to be depicted elsewhere. Perhaps she was the main wife and the other three were minor wives in an attempt for Sobekhotep to father sons. Even with four wives, he fathered ten daughters but no sons.[67]

In the Theban tomb of Horemheb (TT78), he stands with his mother while two women make offerings to him. However, they are not adequately labelled and they either represent his wife and sister or two wives. Both are presented as equal in status, although only one, Itwy, was represented elsewhere as his wife.[68] Some evidence of multiple wives is much less ambiguous. The Tomb Robbery Papyrus lists two women as being wives of a guard of the King's Treasury:

> The citizeness Herer, the wife of the watchman Paaemtawemet of the treasury of Pharaoh. The citizeness Tanefery, his other wife, making two.[69]

It is interesting that this guard was able to maintain two wives, considering his job was not a particularly elite one.

Perhaps polygamy was easy, if one could afford it, as it required very little legal intervention. Although the majority of people in ancient Egypt got married and had children, there appears to have been no formal wedding ceremony, religious or legal. Moreover, in the Egyptian language there was no word for wedding and instead they used phrases like 'sitting together', 'to eat with', 'to be together with', 'entering a house' or 'bringing the bundle', which is likely to have meant moving into the marital home or the tradition of producing a dowry.[70] Another common phrase was 'to make as a wife', which could describe the male role in organising the wedding,[71] or 'to take a wife'. The phrase to 'take a husband' was not used until the second half of the sixth century BCE, which could simply be due to a lack of documents written by women prior to this. When the woman claims 'you made me a wife', it could refer to the consummation of the marriage. Some fathers comment that they have 'given in marriage'[72] their daughters, and possibly make reference to a marriage arranged by the woman's father and the groom. It certainly suggests the woman had a passive role in the arrangements.

Even the literary texts provide little information about the marriage ceremony, with a love poem on Papyrus Harris 500 stating:

> My heart [desires] your property as the mistress of your house,
> while your arm rests on my arm, for my love surrounds you.[73]

This, as mentioned above, shows the desire of the woman to be the mistress of the house, or the wife of her lover, but gives no further information on how this would come about. The only text that discusses marriage celebration is the Ptolemaic Story of Setne Khamwas (I) and the tale of Ahwere and her brother Naneferkaptah, the children of king Merenebptah. Although brother and sister, they loved each other and wanted to wed. Initially the king forbade it, as he wanted to arrange suitable partners from outside of the royal family. Eventually, he relented and the siblings were married. He demanded:

> Steward, let Ahwere be taken to the house of Naneferkaptah tonight and let all sorts of beautiful things be taken with her.

Then Ahwere discusses the process of her wedding day:

> I was taken as a wife to the house of Naneferkaptah [that night and Pharaoh] sent me a present of silver and gold, and

all Pharaoh's household sent me presents. Naneferkaptah made holiday with me and he entertained all Pharaoh's household. He slept with me that night and found me [pleasing. He slept with] me again and again, and we loved each other.[74]

No ceremonial aspects are described, although the event is marked by a celebratory party with the giving of extravagant gifts. This gives the impression that weddings therefore were entirely social rather than religious or legal events. For a marriage to occur, the woman simply left her father's house and moved into her husband's house or her husband's parental home. It is likely there was a procession through the streets with singing and dancing, although there are no records of such an event. Such a relaxed approach to such an important institution is bound to have caused some confusion or problems. On rare occasions, it would seem, the man moved into the woman's family home in order to get married, and such an attempt is recorded on Ostracon Nash 6 from Deir el Medina. This text tells us of a man who tried to marry a woman, twice, unsuccessfully. On two occasions he packed his belongings, including food, furniture, and clothing and took them to his intended's home. Twice he was told to leave. Apparently she would not even 'provide clothing for his backside'.[75] One has to admire his resolve, as after the first attempt he wanted another try: 'I went again with all my property in order to live with them. Look she acted exactly the same way again'.[76]

Whether such disastrous attempts could be considered as being married is certainly open for debate. It would be fascinating to hear the girl's side of the story. Did she change her mind? Or was he delusional and she had no intention of marrying him at all? As her family had thrown him out, had he succeeded with moving in, even on a temporary basis?

Life would be difficult for a new bride, as she was required at a young age to leave her family home and move in with an entirely new family. Her husband's home would no doubt include himself, his parents, siblings and unmarried aunts or other female relatives. One lady, Takhentyshepse, wrote a heartfelt letter to her sister, Iye, describing some of the problems she was encountering in her new home:

> I shall send you barley, and you shall have it ground for me and add emmer to it. And you shall make bread with it, for I have been quarrelling with Merymaat (my husband) 'I will divorce you', he keeps saying when he quarrels with me on account of my mother questioning the amount of barley required for bread. 'Now your mother does nothing for you' he keeps telling me and says, 'although you have brothers and sisters, they don't take care of you' he keeps telling me in arguing with me daily.[77]

Even though Takhentyshepse was living with her new husband and his family, a marriage was not considered stable and long-term until seven years had passed, and during this time the wife's father may still have provided the couple with food and other goods.[78] The Autobiography of Wedjahorresne states that 'I fed all their children and I established all their homes'.[79]

As with many aspects of daily life, marriage and family situations can be complicated to unravel, as we no longer understand the nuances of the language and titles meaning sometimes clumsy translations are applied, which may not represent the ancient Egyptian reality. The common word for wife is *Hmt*, and this is the widely accepted translation. However, Egyptologists have long debated the exact meaning of another term *Hbswt/Hbsyt*, which from the Middle Kingdom onwards is often applied to a woman and is thought to mean concubine[80], and rather confusingly is sometimes used alongside *Hmt*.

However, not all scholars agree that a *Hbswt* was a concubine, as it seems a *Hbswt* lived within the man's home with his family, and perhaps should be viewed as a living companion, the equivalent of a modern common-law-wife: 'a state of man and woman cohabiting as married persons without the full sanction of legal marriage', indicating a monogamous and long-term relationship.[81] The most common belief, however, is that the term refers to a second wife in a polygamous relationship.[82] In the letters of Hekanakhte, he refers to a problem between his family and his *Hbswt*, indicating that she was not accepted by the family. Hekanakhte was a funerary priest and a prolific landowner, and the surviving records were written by him from his position in the north of Egypt to his estate in the south. He refers to his new bride living with the family, as he had heard news that the other members of the household had been insulting her. He demands the instant dismissal of a maid-servant who appears to have started the name-calling and gives the ultimatum that if they do not accept her to the 'one table' he will cut off his financial aid: 'Now as you don't want her with you – so let 'Iutenheb be brought to me!'[83]

The confusions regarding such terminology is perpetuated by the ancient Egyptians themselves, as they use the terms *Hbswt* and *Hmt* to address the same person. In the New Kingdom Tomb Robbery Papyrus, the gold worker Ramesses is recorded as having four wives. One of them, Mutemheb, was described by the scribe as *Hbswt* (so-called concubine) but she refers to herself as *Hmt*.[84] She explains that of the four wives, two are dead and one was still living.[85] Perhaps this is an indication that the translation 'concubine' is inappropriate, and perhaps there was a difference in status and the scribe was applying the lower status to her on purpose, or perhaps Mutemheb applied the higher status to herself intentionally. The title *Hbswt* was used in secular documents, whereas the title *Hmt* appears in tombs, stelae and statues, indicating there was perhaps a status difference, or one was formal and the other informal.

It is apparent that a *Hbswt* lived with her male partner and had access to servants and wealth but lacked any authority over them or other members of the household. It is possible that this lack of authority was connected with age, indicating the *Hbswt* was perhaps younger than the wife (*Hmt*). Legally, however, the *Hbswt* had the same legal (if not necessarily social) rights as the *Hmt* (wife). A man could take a *Hbswt* even if his main wife (*Hmt*) was alive and bore him children, so they were not always introduced into the family unit because of a barren wife and therefore could be considered as secondary wives rather than concubines. Although polygamous relationships were considered a sign of wealth, those men with a *Hbswt* were from all walks of life including field workers, washermen or priests.[86] A Middle Kingdom governor of a province near Beni Hasan took as his *Hbswt* the treasurer in his household and they had two sons and a daughter together.[87] However, the difference between the two titles seems to be totally lost to us now,[88] if indeed they were not interchangeable words.[89]

There were other terms that were even more nuanced than *Hmt* and *Hbswt*, which include *Hmt t3y*, which was originally thought to mean 'woman and man' but after much discussion is now more commonly believed to mean 'married woman' or more graphically 'a woman who has sexual relations with a man'. Sometimes it is used as a synonym for wife, but whereas *Hmt* often has a possessive connecting the woman to a particular man,

Hmt t3y does not.[90] Perhaps it is a similar difference to 'his wife' and 'she is married'. Then there is the simple phrase of describing a woman as 'with' a man, indicating that while co-habiting they were perhaps of a different status than the wife. However, in the Adoption Papyrus, Taiemniut is described as being both a *Hmt* of, and as being with, Padiu, indicating that this nuance is also lost to us.

Other forms of marriage also existed in ancient Egypt as attested by a particularly strange text that talks about a temporary marriage, not one of divorce, but rather one that was planned to 'expire':

> You will be in my house while you are with me as a wife from today the first day of the third month of the winter-season of the sixteenth year, until the first day of the fourth month of the inundation season of the seventeenth year.[91]

Such an arrangement seems unusual, but obviously as marriage was simply the act of the woman moving into the husband's house, then this was just as valid a marriage as any other. It was considered a 'year of eating' or a trial, enabling the couple to ascertain if the relationship was sound and whether there would be children in the first year.

Marriage could be a happy affair, producing a large family and surviving for the duration of the couple's lifetime, or it could be an unhappy situation that ultimately ended in divorce. Therefore, such trial marriages could be viewed as a rather forward-thinking arrangement on behalf of the Egyptians. Divorce in ancient Egypt was not uncommon, and it was considered acceptable for a man to divorce his wife if she no longer 'fits in' with his rising career and status. In a letter to the dead, a man writes to his wife, Ankhiry, stating he married her:

... when I was a young man. I was with you when I was carrying out all sorts of offices. I was with you and I did not divorce you. I did not cause your heart to grieve. I did it when I was a youth and when I was carrying out all sorts of important offices for Pharaoh ... without divorcing you saying 'She has always been with me' so said I.[92]

His deceased wife is expected to be grateful that he had remained with her regardless of his change in status.

One of the most common factors leading to divorce was adultery on both the husband's and wife's part. In a marriage contract in the Louvre (E7846) dated to 546 BCE, the man Iturekh, son of Petiese, outlines the property settlement his wife will receive if they divorce, except in the case of 'the large crime that is (usually) found in a woman'.[93] It was clearly believed by the Egyptians, or this chap in particular, that adultery was a particularly female predilection. It was something that was considered worse for women than for men, and one Deir el Medina text states: 'a wife (*Hmt*) is a wife. She should not make love. She should not have sexual intercourse'.[94] Naturally, this means she is not expected to have intercourse with anyone other than her husband.

Herodotus records an intriguing story of a king, which may have more social commentary than truth about it. The king had gone blind and the oracle claimed he would regain his sight if he bathed his eyes in the urine of a woman who had only had intercourse with her husband. The king tried his wife, then a number of other women, all to no avail. Finally he regained his sight but:

then he collected within the walls of a town, now called Red Clod, all the women except the one whose urine had proved efficacious, set the place on fire, and burnt them to death, town and all; afterwards he married the woman who had been the means of curing him.[95]

Presumably he encouraged this faithful wife to divorce her husband in order to marry him, but felt it was worth it to get a faithful wife of his own. The Instruction of Ani (twenty-first or twenty-second dynasty) advised that men should also try to remain faithful:

Every man who founds a household, should hold back the hasty heart. Do not go after a woman; do not let her steal your heart.[96]

However, the evidence is rather telling for both men and women in society. Identifying the legal status of adultery is a tricky one, as there is little doubt that adultery was considered unacceptable in society as it broke up homes and brought legitimacy into question in regard to children. Chapter 125 of the Book of the Dead, the so-called negative confession, included adultery, as well as more specifically: 'I have not committed adultery in the sacred places of my city god',[97] indicating it was something the deceased did not want to be accused of in the afterlife in case it affected their rebirth. However, chapter 125 can be a little misleading when trying to ascertain social *faux pas* from crimes, as trivial and major crimes are listed side by side almost as if in the afterlife there was no difference between murder and adultery. Turning to the written evidence, it seems as if in real life whether adultery was classified as a criminal act or a social misdemeanour very much depended on the situation. In the Turin Indictment Papyrus, the wab priest, Penanuqet, from the temple of Khnum at Elephantine, was accused of numerous crimes including theft, fraud, bribery and 'copulation ... with Tabes, daughter of Shuy, she being wife of Ahauty'.[98] It is likely that this accusation was due to a personal vendetta against him and adultery seems to be a popular means of blackening a character.[99] Userhet, who lived during the reign of Ramses III, was accused of adultery with three married women[100] and Paneb, among other things, was also accused of adultery.

The punishment for adultery was not standardised, as it was dependent on the husband and the punishment he wanted administered to his unfaithful wife. Ankhsheshonq advised the relaxed approach: 'If you find your wife with her lover, get yourself a bride to suit you'.[101]

Diodorus Siculus records that an adulterous Egyptian wife would have her nose cut off, while the man would be beaten[102], but this was not the norm. In the Westcar Papyrus, the unfaithful woman was executed and her body set on fire, whereas her lover, a servant, was thrown in a lake to be devoured by a magical crocodile. Adultery could therefore, it would seem, end in execution[103] should the wronged husband so desire it, rendering it a criminal act. However, the most common punishment was divorce, indicating on the whole that, infidelity was a social misdemeanour rather than a crime.

In the *Tale of the Two Brothers* from the New Kingdom, the theme of adultery and feminine scheming is a popular one. The older brother, Anubis, is married to an unnamed woman who tried to seduce his younger brother Bata when he entered the house in order to fetch seed for sowing. He was carrying the seed-sacks over his shoulder, catching the eye of his sister-in-law:

She said 'There is great strength in you. I see your vigour daily' and she desired to know him as a man. She got up, took hold of him, and said to him, 'Come let us spend an hour lying together. It will be good for you and I will make fine clothes for you'.

Then the youth became like a leopard in anger over the wicked speech she had made to him; and she became very frightened. He rebuked her saying, 'Look, you are like a mother to me; and your husband is like a father to me. He who is older than I, has raised me. What is this great wrong you said to me? Do not say it to me again! But I will not tell it to anyone. I will not let it come from my mouth to any man'.[104]

The wife, angry at his refusal and concerned he would tell her husband about her behaviour, scuffed her clothes and dirtied her face, and when her husband found her he believed she had been attacked. She blamed Bata for the attack saying he had propositioned her, to which she rebuked him saying; 'Am I not your mother? Is your elder brother not like a father to you?' She then claimed Bata became angry and beat her. She demanded from her husband: 'Now if you let him live, I shall die! Look when he returns, do not let him live. For I am ill from his evil design which he was about to carry out in the morning'.

Anubis waited in order to attack his younger brother with a spear, but Bata had been warned of his presence by his cows enabling him to flee. After Bata lived in exile for a number of years, Anubis realised his wife was the guilty party, which resulted in her death.

Another literary tale, the Story of Petese, son of Peletum, tells of an unfaithful wife and mother. A young man is sent home by his father to get something from his mother but when he arrives he sees that she is having intercourse with a soldier, 'committing an act of adultery'. Despite hiding, his mother spotted him:

It happened thereafter that his mother came. She stood from him and said: 'Woe and misery! My son has seen me sleeping with the kalasins [soldier]. He will tell it to his father. He will place a curse ... together with everyone who belongs to me'.[105]

Unfortunately, as with many literary tales, the ending is missing so we do not know what happened or if the mother was punished for her behaviour. However, it is likely that the real world was not as dramatic as some of the literary tales would have us believe. If the woman in an adulterous relationship was unmarried, technically there was no harm done. The victim was considered to be the husband, as infidelity with his wife was an affront to him. A woman would have little redress if her husband was unfaithful to her, however. For both men and women, adultery more often than not simply resulted in anger and hurt feelings.

A letter and its reply emphasise the normality of adultery and how ordinary people dealt with it. The letter is from a woman to a man, possibly her friend or a relative warning him about his wife's behaviour:

> I did not take you (aside) to say you should look to what you will do [about] your wife! (and) to say, you are blind about her! You have kept me from deafening you. The crime is the abomination of Monthu! Look, I will make you see this continuous fornication which your [wife] committed against you.

It would be interesting to know exactly what the relationship was between the woman and the man, as she seems angry at the wife's behaviour and the husband's apparent obliviousness to it. She references the situation to the god Monthu, which is intriguing, as perhaps in the mythology Monthu's wife was unfaithful to him and therefore the situation was particularly offensive to him. The husband's reply, however, is a little ambiguous:

> But she is not my wife! Is she my wife? She finished making her speech and she went outside leaving the door open.[106]

Was he denying the behaviour was attached to his wife, had he already divorced her for having an affair, or had she left him?

There is little doubt, however, that the man is a little irritated at the letter received from the woman; perhaps he considers her a meddling relative or a nosy neighbour.

A rather sad tale from Deir el Medina tells the story of a servant of the workman, Amenemenat, who recounts his marriage to the daughter of Payom:

> I brought the bundle to the house of Payom, and I made his daughter my wife. Now when I had spent the night in the house of my father, I set out to go to his house, and I found the workman Merysekhmet, son of Menna sleeping with my wife in the fourth month of summer, day 5. I went out and told the officials; but the officials gave me 100 blows of a stick, saying; 'Really what are you saying?' Then the chief workman Inherkhau said 'Really, what means this giving the 100 blows [to] the one who carried the bundle while another fornicates? What the officials have done is a great crime'.
>
> Then the Scribe of the Necropolis Amennakhte made him [Merysekhmet] swear an oath of the lord, l.p.h saying 'As Amun endures, as the Ruler endures, If I speak with her, the wife, my nose and my nostrils and my ears will be cut off, and I will be exiled to the land of Kush'.
>
> But he went again, and made her pregnant. Then the workman Menna, his father, placed him before the officials, and the scribe Amennakhte made him swear an oath of the Lord, l.p.h. again saying, 'If I go to the place where the daughter of Payom is, I will be set to breaking stone in the quarry of Elephantine' ... the good thing that the officials instituted.[107]

The unnamed servant seems to have got a raw deal here, as he married his wife and found her in bed with another man. Merysekhmet simply had to make an oath stating he would not approach Payom's daughter again, and even when he broke the oath, he was not punished for impregnating her. The only one who seems to have been punished was the husband who received a beating for reporting Merysekhmet. Unfortunately, there is no record of what happened to Payom's daughter who was pregnant by a man who was not her husband, or how this was received in the community. In the Demotic tale of Petese, a similar situation was handled in a most unusual way. The wife of the Prophet of Atum approached the king and told him that her husband was having an affair with the wife of the prophet Nebethetepet and had impregnated her. She implored the king: 'This son whom she shall bear, make him my son for his father is my husband'.[108]

The king obliged, and the son born to the mistress of the priest of Atum was raised by his wife as her own. Whether this was the traditional response to this sort of situation is uncertain, but it does address the lack of importance attached to legitimacy. Moreover, some consideration should be given to the Adoption Papyrus, where Naunefer adopts the children of their household servant fathered by her husband.

Other evidence of kind husbands being treated badly can be found from Deir el Medina about the workman Hesysunebef. His wife Hunro had an affair with notorious village bad-boy Paneb, and he divorced her. However, to ensure she was still cared for, each month for three years someone paid her a small grain ration, although whether it was her ex-husband is not recorded. During their divorce proceedings, he attempted to sell a scarf she had woven at the east bank market, but as it was considered low quality no one bought it. Out of his own pocket he paid her six times the value for it. Without having all the information, it is uncertain whether he owed her a debt and was simply paying it back or whether Hesysunebef was trying to help his ex-wife in her new life. Other evidence we have for possible alimony following a divorce is on a marriage contract recorded on Papyrus Louvre (E7846) dated to 546 BCE. Iturekh, son of Petiese, outlines what arrangements would be made for his wife, Tsendjehuty, should he leave her for another woman:

> If I repudiate Tsendjehuty ... and if I am the cause for this harsh fate that will beset her, because I wish to repudiate her or because I prefer other women above her – except in the case the large crime that is (usually) found in a woman – I will give her two deben of silver and fifty sacks of grain.[109]

So Hunro was not the only woman to receive items from her husband following her divorce. However, the evidence we have about Hunro does not paint her in a particularly positive light, as before she was married to Hesysenebef, she was married to another workman, Pendua. They divorced as she had been unfaithful, again with Paneb.[110] However, Hunro's marital situation is complex, as the texts claim she was the wife of Hesysenebef but was only 'with' Pendua. The difference between these two relationship types is unknown, although it is suggested that being the wife (*Hmt*) of a man held higher social status than being 'with' someone.[111]

Paneb was married to the long-suffering Wa'bet, with whom they had more than ten children. Despite his philandering, she never chose to divorce him. It seems there were some other underlying problems between Paneb and Hesysenebef that may have fuelled the situation. Neferhotep was both Paneb's and Hesysenebef's adopted father, meaning they were adoptive siblings. Having intercourse with his sister-in-law may have been the result of a feud between Paneb and his adopted father's family. Paneb did not seem like an easy character to get along with, as accusations of his adulterous behaviour came from none other than his own son Aaphate who left Paneb's house and went to the doorkeeper declaring:

> I cannot bear with him; my father made love to the Lady Tuy when she was the workman Kenna's wife, he made love to the lady Hunro, when she was with Pendua and when she was with Hesysenebef. And after that he debauched her daughter too.[112]

For a son to make such accusations against his own father indicates there was little love lost between them. However, this accusation, and others, was recorded on Papyrus Salt, which was collated by Paneb's adopted uncle, Amennakht. He was a rather bitter man, as he believed his brother, Neferhotep, should not have passed his role to Paneb. As a blood relative, Amennakht wanted the job for himself. It is difficult to ascertain how many of the accusations have any element of fact about them, as Paneb does not seem to have been punished for them, although Amennakht would attribute this to corruption and bribery rather than innocence.

Sometimes in situations like this, the public took the law into their own hands and administered the justice they felt was justified. A papyrus currently in the British Museum (BM10416) records an event where punishment was administered to a woman following an eight-month affair with a relative of the 'mob':

> ... eight full months until today he is sleeping with that woman, though he is not (the) husband ... If he were the husband would he (then) not have sworn his oath concerning your woman?[113]

It seems they were indignant that the man remained with his wife while conducting a long-term relationship with another woman.

He should have divorced her and married the woman with whom he was having an affair. However, the group of people were also angry with this mistress: 'we are going to beat her, together with her people'. The group elaborated on this threat in a fragmentary letter (P. BM 10418 +10287) claiming: 'if we will not find her to beat her we will find Rta her little sister and we will find [...] ist also'.

This is a good indicator of the anger that can fester within a group, as such behaviour seems extreme for a consensual affair between adults. The narrator of the text, possibly the woman's son, tells the cuckolded husband to go to court with his wife to sort out the matter instead of succumbing to violence, adding: 'Really, even I held them back this time, I will not hold them back another time'.[114] Such mob rule seemed to be acceptable in this case, as there seems to be no consequences for the group beating a woman and threatening her family.

Even without such incendiary situations like adultery, maintaining a happy marriage was not easy. The wisdom text of Ankhsheshonq offers rather cynical advice on how a man can protect himself from the duplicitous nature of women. Ankhsheshonq appears to be a bitter man, and indeed he wrote the text in prison after conspiring against the king. Perhaps it was the betrayal of a woman that led to the arrest. He warns:

> Do not open your heart to your wife. What you have said ends up in the street.
> Do not open your heart to your wife or your servant. Open it to your mother. She is a woman to be trusted.
> Teaching a woman is like having a sack of sand with the side split open.
> What a wife does with her husband today she does with another man tomorrow.[115]

The Instruction of Ani, on the other hand, offers some more positive advice on keeping a wife happy:

> Do not control your wife in her house when you know she is efficient. Don't say to her 'Where it is? Get it!' when she has put it in the right place. Let your eye observe in silence, then you recognise her skill.[116]

However, marriages go wrong, and sometimes the only answer is divorce. As in the modern world, divorce happened due to infertility, incompatibility, adultery of either parties, or wanting a 'younger model'.

> It is like a cross-eyed woman who has lived for twenty years in the house of a man; but then he finds another woman and says to her 'I repudiate you, for you are cross-eyed!' And she replies: 'Because you have not found out during the twenty years I have lived in your house, I am the one who is mocking you!' (P. Bibl.Nat 198).[117]

It is also possible that cruelty or domestic violence was also a factor in divorce, as a twentieth dynasty marriage contract states: 'If I shall ever treat the daughter of Tenermentu unjustly again, I shall receive 100 strokes and be deprived of everything that I shall have acquired with her'.[118]

Divorce itself was an easy transaction if there was no dowry or contract. All that was needed was for the man or the woman to declare 'I divorce you', the man to declare 'I repudiate you' or the woman to state 'I will go'; and the marriage was over. Despite the potential ease of the divorce itself, it is thought that the complexity of some of the marriage contracts that stipulate the financial cost of divorcing meant that financial constraints may have prevented divorces being as common as they might otherwise have been.

Evidence suggests that men divorced women more than the other way around to a ratio of 12:3,[119] although there is evidence of female divorce. One woman drew up a marriage contract which claimed:

> If I repudiate you as my husband, if I take a dislike to you and want someone else, I shall give you two and a half kite (22 grams) of silver; and forfeit the third part of all and everything that I shall acquire together with you.[120]

A Middle Kingdom woman, Senet, appears to have divorced her husband, the vizier of Senusret II, and taken over their joint tomb in Thebes while her husband was buried near the king in the north of Egypt. Senet erased the images and titles of her husband in the tomb, and it can be assumed they were divorced.[121]

Generally in a divorce, the woman left her husband's house and either returned home to her family or set up a home on her own. Unfortunately, not all families were willing or able to accept a divorced daughter back into their homes, and one father, Horemwia, promised his daughter Tanetdjesere that should she get divorced she could stay in a room in his storehouse with the promise that 'no one in the land will throw you out'.[122] It is thought that as he was a workman at Deir el Medina, his house was owned by the state and therefore there may have been restrictions on who was able to live there, although it could simply be that there was no room for her there.

If some form of contract had been drawn up or gift had been given to the wife upon her marriage, then the wife was required to ask her husband to return this to her so she could start a new life. If he did not pay within thirty days, then he was obliged to pay her maintenance. If, on the other hand, the ex-wife did not ask for the payment of her 'wedding gift', then the husband was unable to legally make the payment or make maintenance payments.[123] Diodorus, writing somewhat later, did not approve of the arrangements Egyptian women had with their husbands:

> The wife lords it over the husband as in the deed about maintenance, the men agree to obey the wife in everything.[124]

Some people made a declaration of divorce at the *knbt* (court), in order to make it official throughout the community,[125] but this was not a legal requirement. There was no stigma for either men or women if they were divorced, and either could remarry. Evidence, however, suggests that any woman divorcing late in life (aged 30–35) was less likely to remarry than someone younger. Texts from the sixth century BCE indicate that one man upon divorcing his wife states:

> I am the one who has said to you; 'take yourself a husband'; I shall not be able to stand in your way in any place where you will go to in order to take yourself a husband there.[126]

This indicates that ex-husbands were sometimes happy for their ex-wives to remarry, and therefore when they chose not to, it may have been due to being financially self-sufficient, meaning they did not need a man to care for them, or they were considered poor wife material as they were potentially too old to bear further children.[127]

Whether divorce was complicated by children is unknown. Nowhere is it written who would normally gain custody in a divorce, and therefore we need to investigate individual cases and look for a pattern. Morton boldly claims that during a divorce the woman returned to her parents' home with the children in tow,[128] although he offers no supporting evidence for this. Moreover, the available evidence tends to support the opposite. The Deir el Medina workman Userhet swore an oath that following the divorce from his wife, Menat-Nakhti, his three children would not be taken from him. This indicates he was expecting custody and paid for the services of a wet nurse and a doctor in order to care for them.[129] The Stato Civile also shows that children stayed with their father following a divorce. Children are often listed in this text as having the same father but different mothers, which could indicate a step mother following a divorce or even the possibility of a polygamous family.[130] In the case of the divorce of Hunro and Hesysunebef, their daughter Wabet maintained a good relationship with her father, and is mentioned alongside him on an ostracon[131] following the divorce, although by this time she was married and it does not state whether she lived with him.

It is clear from the evidence presented that, for the vast majority of the Egyptian people, love, romance, marriage and possibly divorce happened in an undramatic and unrecorded manner. The records we have tend to be for the wealthy in the form of contracts or for unusual situations as in the Adoption Papyrus or the multiple accusations of adultery. For every record we have, there are hundreds of relationships going unrecorded. This goes some way to explain the gaps in the records and the assumptions that have been made. It is clear that for the ordinary people of ancient Egypt, love and marriage were an important part of everyday life, resulting in offspring who flourished and provided care for their parents in their old age. However, when you are dealing with people, things are not always simple, and families break up, either through adultery or broken relationship. In such situations, divorce and remarriage was possible.

For the royal family, on the other hand, divorce was not an option. There were more restrictions on their marriages than on an ordinary village inhabitant, and fewer records. In the next chapter, we will investigate the sexlives and marriages of royalty, and see how they differed to those discussed above.

3

SEX AND THE PHARAOHS

'[*She was*] beautiful in the heart of His Majesty
and he loved her more than anything'[1]

The pharaohs, like everyone else in ancient Egypt, had sex: within marriage, outside marriage, homosexual sex, and for religious or political reasons. Was royal sex in anyway different from non-royal sex? In practice, no, but the consequences of a royal dalliance could impact on the wider population of Egypt.

As discussed in previous chapters, there are very limited images of the intimate lives of the ancient Egyptians, and this is even more restricted for the royal family. The only exceptions can be found from the Amarna Period, where we have, for example, an image of Akhenaten and Nefertiti holding hands in front of their bed. Amarna art was renowned for being more realistic than other periods of Egyptian art, but while it appears that they are about to go to bed, it is more likely that there is some ritualistic element to this scene.[2]

Another image shows Nefertiti seated on the lap of Akhenaten, which is unprecedented in royal art. This naturalistic art was maintained by Tutankhamun, Akhenaten's son, and there are intimate scenes showing him with his wife Ankhesenamun and in one she hands him arrows while he is hunting in the marshes. The only other images of the king in intimate positions can be found in the harem building of Ramses III at Medinet Habu. He is depicted paying attention to the young girls, by chucking them under the chin and draping his arm around their shoulders. These scenes were only ever intended to be viewed by the king and the girls themselves and are not of a ritualistic nature. The harem will be discussed in more detail below.

Some of the most erotic scenes involving the sex lives of the royal family can be found in the divine birth scenes, which were a means for a king, normally with a tenuous claim on the throne, to prove his legitimacy to rule Egypt by highlighting his divine origins. The earliest example of these scenes belongs to Hatshepsut and is depicted on her mortuary temple at Deir el Bahri. As a woman, her claim to the throne was more tenuous than most.

All kingship rituals were two-fold, with the king carrying out the masculine element and the Great Royal Wife carrying out the feminine elements. Hatshepsut had therefore placed herself in the masculine role, meaning there was no Great Royal Wife to carry out the feminine rituals, which rendered them incomplete. To remedy this, her daughter, Neferura, took this role alongside her mother. As complicated as it is for the modern reader to understand, this idea was as complicated for the ancient Egyptians. While they were depicting the king Hatshepsut on temple walls as a typical male king, complete with false beard, in the accompanying texts there was confusion whether to refer to her as son or daughter of Re, his or her majesty, he or she. There was never a consensus, and in many texts about Hatshepsut both masculine and feminine pronouns were used with no apparent order.

Therefore, her divine birth scene added an element of legitimacy to this complicated state of affairs. The scene depicts the god Amun disguised as king Thutmosis I in order to have sex with queen Ahmosis, Hatshepsut's mother:

Amun found the queen in the inner rooms of the palace. When smelling the divine scent, she woke up, and she smiled at him. At once he proceeded towards her. He lusted after her, and he gave her his heart. He allowed her to see him in his real god's figure, having come close to her. She rejoiced at his virility, and love for him flowed through her body. The palace became inundated by the scent of the god, it smelled like in Punt [land of incense].

Thereupon the god did what he wished with her. She made him rejoice over her and she kissed him. She said to him, 'How splendid it is to see you face to face. Your divine strength engulfs me, your dew is all through my limbs!' The god once more did what he wished with her, and he said: 'Truly! Hatshepsut will be the name of the child I have placed in your belly, for this was what you exclaimed'.[3]

Amenhotep III also adopts this scene, although it is thought that, as he was a legitimate king, and the son of the king, it was unnecessary. Furthermore, by presenting his divine father as cuckolded by Amun, this scene devalued rather than strengthened his own legitimacy, even though the goddesses Hathor and Mut were present at his birth. The imagery is very similar with the knees of Amun touching those of the queen as he holds the ankh sign (eternal life) to her nose. This is believed to be the moment of orgasm when the child is planted in the queen's womb. The couple are held aloft by their feet by the goddesses Selket and Neith seated on a bed. Amun once more, disguised himself as the king in order to seduce the queen, but she recognised him by his aroma which was the scent of incense.[4] Although Amun is presented as the divine father of both Hatshepsut and Amenhotep III, it is Meskhenet, the goddess of the birthing brick, who announces their destiny as future kings (*see* chapter 4).

Ramses II was the third New Kingdom king to adopt the divine birth scene. Although he was the legitimate son of the king (Sety I), he was born a commoner, as he was born before Sety became king. He felt he needed to legitimise his right to the throne by claiming his father was none other than the god Amun. His divine birth scene was depicted at the Ramesseum in the chapel dedicated to his mother and at Karnak Temple. None of the images or descriptions are unique, and his mother can be seen touching knees with the god Amun who fills the room with his heavenly scent while Ramses is moulded on a potter's wheel by the creator god Khnum. Khnum was believed to be the deity who not only fashioned royalty on his potter's wheel but was additionally a benefactor of the ordinary people of Egypt. He governed the caves of Hapy, from which the annual inundation began, meaning Khnum was associated with the fertile soil upon which all the people of Egypt relied.

Ramses II is further depicted at Karnak being suckled by the goddess, further emphasising his divine status. Where Ramses does however make his divinity unique can be seen at Abu Simbel and Karnak from year 35, where his divine birth is referenced once more but with Ptah and not Amun as his divine father:

Words spoken by Ptah-Tatonne, he of the tall plumes and sharp horns, who begot the gods. I am your father, who begot you as a god to act as king of south and north Egypt on my seat, I decree for you the lands that I created, their rulers carry revenue to you.

They come to bring you their tribute, because of the greatness of [your renown].⁵

From the Late to the Roman Period, these divine birth scenes evolved into a structure called a mammisi, attached to temples such as Edfu, Philae and Denderah. These mammisi were built to celebrate the marriage of Hathor or Isis and the birth of their child, Ihy or Horus. Horus is then depicted as an adult avenging the murder of his father, reinforcing the traditions and the right to the throne of Egypt. As the king was the living incarnation of Horus, a king following the traditional religion was emphasising his connection with Horus and therefore his divinity and right to rule.

A further aspect of the divine birth scenes, introduced by Hatshepsut, took place during the Festival of Opet, which comprised a procession of the statues of Amun, Mut and Khonsu from Karnak to Luxor Temple either by boat or via the Sphinx Avenue. The temple at Luxor was dedicated to Amun in his form of Bull of his Mother, Kamutef. Once Amun was at the sanctuary at Luxor Temple, he was thought to meet with the king's mother in order to impregnate her once more with the king's ka,⁶ representing the king's (Amun's) ability to beget himself. Once this ritual act was complete, the king entered the sanctuary to receive his ka, once more reaffirming his role as the son of Amun. Between Karnak and Luxor temples, Hatshepsut constructed six-way stations for the barque bearing the god Amun to rest along the way.

Another means of celebrating the king's mother's role in the divine conception scenes was through their position of God's Wife of Amun. This was a prestigious role in the priesthood, only held by royal women and only presented to them by the king himself. Although the role changed somewhat (*see* chapter 8), the first holder of the title was Queen Ahhotep, the mother of Ahmose I. He presented this title to her in order to ensure that a senior royal female was in the top hierarchy of the cult of Amun as well as associating his mother closely with the god Amun, emphasising his own divinity.

As described above, in these divine birth scenes, Amun, disguised as the king, sneaks into the queen's bedroom in order to impregnate her with the new king. We are lucky to be able to visualise the scene in a little more detail due to the recovery of Amenhotep III's bedroom at the palace of Malkata giving valuable information on what a royal bedroom looked like.

The king's bedroom was part of a standard three-room apartment with a bedroom, dressing room and bathroom. In the bedroom he slept on a raised platform, which was no doubt covered in soft matting and blankets, although as was traditional he used a head-rest for a pillow decorated with images of deities who protected him as he slept. Such headrests were made of wood, ivory, bone or even stone, and comprised an upright stem with a curved T-bar across the top, which rested under the head. Above his head, the ceiling was beautifully decorated with repeated images of the vulture goddess Nekhbet, her wings outspread and holding a shen (eternity) sign in each claw. Beneath her wings were the cartouches of the king, indicating she was offering special protection to him. This goddess is often depicted protecting queen Tiye, the Great Royal Wife of Amenhotep III, as she is often shown wearing a dress of feathers, representative of the wings of the vulture goddess wrapped tightly around her thighs. Such a dress offered her protection but also emphasised her fertility and her role as a mother.[7] The image of the goddess on the ceiling may have ensured the longevity and fertility of the king.

On the wall of Amenhotep's bedchamber were images of the household deity, Bes, the dwarf god of fertility and childbirth, indicating the king spent the night here with his wives beneath this god's image, which protected him as he slept and offered him fertility. The royal wives each had similar apartments within the harem quarters, which were adjacent to the king's apartment, and they were no doubt summoned to the king's bedchamber when required.

Amenhotep III is attributed with a large harem of women and had three Great Royal Wives (Tiye, and his daughters Sitamun and Isis), two Mitannian wives (Gilukhepa and Tadukheba), two Babylonian wives and the daughter of the king of Arzawa.[8] The importance of any individual woman depended on her relationship to the king, rather than any personal familial relationships. Therefore, being the daughter of a foreign king placed her no higher in the Egyptian harem than a non-royal king's wife. In the Egyptian language, there was no word for queen, princess or prince. Everyone was defined by their relationship to the king; king's wife, Great Royal Wife, king's daughter or king's son. Therefore, while there were many king's wives, there was only one Great Royal Wife at any one time, a position coveted by many women in the harem and perhaps even outside it.

Should one of the women have a son who became king, she rose to the position of king's mother, another much coveted title. One such woman was the lady Isis, a secondary wife of Thutmosis II. She gave birth to Thutmosis III, who was to follow his father on the throne. The king's Great Royal Wife Hatshepsut had not borne a son, only a daughter, Neferure, so could not be called king's mother. Another example was the mother of Amenhotep III, Mutemwia, who was a king's wife but only featured in the records once her son came to the throne, when she then bore the title king's mother.[9]

Additionally, there were a number of low-born women, perhaps labelled as mistresses or concubines, who resided in the harem with no opportunity to participate in the theatre of the royal court[10] but were still essentially at the king's bidding.

As we have seen, the king was considered divine, the son of the sun god. He was additionally bestowed with the 'power of attraction' by Hathor, the goddess of love, sexual desire and fertility. The Pyramid Texts claim the king was 'the man who takes women from their husbands whither he will and when his heart desires'.[11] However, in order to maintain his attraction, it was necessary for him to perform rituals to the goddess. One ritual for Hathor, Lady of Drunkenness, recorded at Denderah is described thus:

> The pharaoh comes to dance,
> He comes to sing for you.
> O, his mistress see how he dances, O bride of Horus, see how he skips,
> The pharaoh whose hands are washed, whose fingers are clean,
> O, his mistress see how he dances, O bride of Horus, see how he skips,
> When he offers you this mnw-jar (with wine),
> O, his mistress see how he dances, O bride of Horus, see how he skips,
> His heart is sincere, his body is in order,
> There is no darkness in his breast.[12]

As the king renewed his virility and sexuality through this ritual, he was never short of a female entourage. However, marriage within the royal family was complicated, and marrying for love was not always considered to be politically astute. Protecting the throne of Egypt from being usurped and passing to another family always came before emotions.

Such political considerations sometimes led to incestuous marriages. Akhenaten (1350–1334 BCE) and Ramses II (1279–1212 BCE) both married their daughters, whereas Thutmosis II (1518–1504 BCE), Thutmosis III (1504–1450 BCE) and Tutankhamun (1334–1325 BCE) married their sister. There seemed little shame associated with Ramses II bearing a child with his daughter Bintanath or Akhenaten having children with three of his daughters. However, contrary to popular belief, such incestuous marriages were only considered appropriate for the royal family and the gods and, as discussed in chapter 2, was very rare among the ordinary populous.

Such incestuous marriages were justified for many years by the so-called heiress theory. This theory stipulated that the royal line passed through the women,[13] and a king who was ideally the son of a king, married the daughter of the king in order to reaffirm his claim to the throne. It was therefore believed that through the queen the right to rule was bestowed upon the king. However, as there were numerous queens who were not of royal blood (e.g. Tiye, Nefertiti, Nefertari), this theory has long been debunked. There was in fact a more practical reason behind marrying a sibling or other relative. This ensured that the king married a woman who had been raised as royal and knew her duties to her king and country. Such family ties also ensured loyalty to both her husband and her children, should the marriage produce offspring. Limiting the family gene pool also reduced the number of grandchildren and therefore potential claimants to the throne. The Egyptians gave further justification to incestuous marriages, as they mirrored the behaviour of the gods who were frequently married to siblings; Isis and Osiris, Nut and Geb, Shu and Tefnut (*see* chapter 9). Such behaviour further emphasised the divinity of the king.

As marrying one's sister may have been as distasteful to the Egyptian king as to anyone else, there were no limits to the number of wives he could have. The king could then choose which of his wives would become the Great Royal Wife and accompany him on a daily basis. This was not always a sister/daughter wife, but could be a non-royal wife as in the case of Tiye, the Great Royal

Wife of Amenhotep III, and Nefertiti, the Great Royal Wife of Akhenaten.[14] However, while a king could marry a commoner, the same was not generally acceptable for a royal princess.

In the New Kingdom, a princess could only marry a man of the same status or higher: an Egyptian prince or a king. This prevented over-ambitious sons-in-law claiming the throne should there be a dispute about succession, but severely limited the options for unmarried royal women who had little choice but to marry their brother, uncle or father. Prior to the New Kingdom, however, the threat was deemed negligible, and there were examples of princesses married to non-royal husbands. For example, in the Old Kingdom (sixth dynasty), king Tety's daughter, Seshseshet Waatetkhethor, was married to the vizier Mereruka, and she was buried in his mastaba tomb with him. In the Middle Kingdom (thirteenth dynasty), princess Reniseneb was married to a local mayor and she resided in his house rather than the palace.[15]

Polygamous royal marriages became in the New Kingdom, a common way of sealing alliances with the enemies of Egypt. Records show that Amenhotep III and Ramses II both married foreign princesses as part of peace treaties.[16] However, prior to the New Kingdom, there is no evidence of such international royal marriages taking place. This practice of foreign brides being used as political pawns was also represented in the mythology, once more reaffirming the king's divinity. The myth of the Contendings of Horus and Seth is discussed in more detail in chapter 8, but in summary, Seth murdered his brother, the king Osiris, and wanted to take over the throne of Egypt as his own. Horus, the son of Osiris, claimed that the throne was his by right. This dispute ended in an eighty-year tribunal before the gods, where eventually it was decided that Horus should take the throne. This led to the Egyptian throne passing from father to son as they were incarnations of Osiris and Horus on earth. The coronation of each new king was celebrated as part of the cycle of life, the rebirth of the son and the balancing of cosmic and social order.[17] Once the divine tribunal had made a choice in favour of Horus to rule Egypt, Seth was given compensation in the form of Anat and Astarte, two Asiatic goddesses, as wives.[18]

This myth, while essential for explaining the right of royal succession (from father to son), also contributes to the regalia of the king. The Pyramid Texts record that in the story Seth removes Horus' eyes, which were subsequently planted, growing into lotus flowers. As a counterattack to this, Horus removes Seth's testicles. These are represented in the two sceptres that the king can be seen carrying, one for each testicle.[19]

This myth therefore is important for many aspects of the divine kingship: succession, regalia and political behaviour. However, while as the myth makes clear, it is acceptable for foreign wives to be sent to Egypt, Amenhotep III made it abundantly clear to the king of Babylon: 'from the time immemorial no daughter of the king of Egypt has been given to anyone'.[20] Although the king of Babylon pursued his request by declaring:

Someone's grown-up daughters, beautiful women, must be available. So send me a beautiful woman as if she were your daughter and who will say 'She is not the king's daughter'.[21]

Amenhotep did not want to send a woman who could even be mistaken for his daughter and once more refused. This policy of not sending Egyptian princesses to marry foreign kings safeguarded the throne from usurpation.

The only evidence of an Egyptian queen offering herself in marriage to a foreign prince was the letter written by Tutankhamun's widow Ankhesenamun to the king of the Hittites. In the letter, she asks the king to send his son to Egypt to take over the throne to prevent her from being forced to marry a servant. Naturally, the Hittite king did not trust this unusual request from the Egyptian widow, but eventually sent his son Zennanza to Egypt. Unfortunately, the Hittite prince died before reaching the Egyptian border and his father, Supplilumas, chose to believe he had been murdered. This act led to a war between the Egyptians and the Hittites, where the Hittites accused the Egyptians of bringing plague to Hattusha (the Hittite capital), wiping out a large proportion of their population.

This letter itself, even if the content is not considered, sounds more like propaganda than fact and does not stand up to scrutiny. The main concern is that this letter has not been discovered in its original form. It is not even a copy of the original letter. Instead, it is quoted in a record from the Hittite capital commissioned by the brother of Zennanza who cites the letter as the start of events leading to a war between the Hittites and the Egyptians and their ultimate demise through the plague.

Would Zennanza's brother have seen this letter? He was a younger brother to the prince and was certainly not the intended recipient. Additionally, the comment that the widow Ankhesenamun does not want to marry a servant could be a foreign misunderstanding of the Egyptian hierarchy. The two potential husbands for the queen were Ay, her great uncle, brother to queen Tiye, and brother-in-law to Amenhotep III, a legitimate royal heir and vizier, or Horemheb who under Tutankhamun bore the title deputy king and had been named as the heir to the throne in addition to being the highest official in Egypt. Neither man was a servant. With Ay and Horemheb, and their respective loyal officials, it seems unlikely that this letter would have made it out of the palace, let alone to the Hittite king without the contents being made known to them. The whole request seems ludicrous. Furthermore, Ankhesenamun was of royal blood and was aware that such a request went against the rules of Maat and therefore would be unacceptable[22] if not treasonous. There are also no records of this request in Egypt. Evidence in the form of a ring bearing the cartouches of Ay and Ankhesenamun side by side suggests they married on his succession to the throne, although she thereafter disappears from the records and Ay is only ever depicted with one wife, Tiy.

For the princesses requested from foreign kings, life was uncertain. Once the request had been made, she was destined to marry the current king, not necessarily the king who made the arrangements. One of the Amarna Letters from the Mitannian king, Tushratta, regards a marriage between his daughter Tadukheba and Amenhotep III (EA22, 24, 25). Tushratta's sister, Kelukheba, was already married to Amenhotep III as part of an earlier agreement, and Tushratta wanted to reinforce the alliance. He lists the wedding gifts that would accompany Tadukheba to Egypt:

> It is all of these wedding gifts, of every sort, that Tushratta, the king of Mitanni, gave to Nimmureya [*Amenhotep III*], the king of Egypt, his brother and his son-in-law. He gave them at the same time that he gave Tadukheba, his daughter, to Egypt and to Nimmureya for marriage.[23]

Unfortunately, in the middle of the negotiations Amenhotep III died, and it is thought that Tadukheba was married to Amenhotep IV (Akhenaten) instead. Some people have identified this princess as Kiya, his secondary wife and mother of Tutankhamun.[24]

Once these foreign princesses arrived in Egypt, they were given the title of king's favourite and were sent to a harem, and only a few like Kiya raised themselves out of obscurity and into history.

Although such international marriages were born out of political necessity, there is no reason to assume there was no excitement at the prospect of the marriage from both parties. A letter from a Babylonian princess destined to marry Amenhotep III expresses her devotion to him:

> Say to my lord: so speaks the princess. For you, your chariots and your men, may all go well. May all the gods accompany you. In the presence of my lord I prostrate myself before you. My messenger brings you a gift of coloured cloth. For your cities and your household may all go well. Do not worry, or you will have made me sad. I would give my life for you.[25]

For the Egyptian king, the new people at court and the anticipation of the arrival of a new wife may have been an exciting prospect. Strangely enough, such eagerness and excitement is presented by Ramses II, better known for battles and pompous displays of power through his building works. In year 34 of his reign, following the death of his two Great Royal Wives, Nefertari and Isetnofret, Ramses commissions his marriage stela recording the marriage with the daughter of the Hittite king. This inscription was erected at Karnak, Elephantine, Amara West and Abu Simbel. The Hittite king had promised an enormous dowry to be sent with his daughter described as:

> ... greater will be her dowry than that of the daughter of the king of Babylon ... This year, I will send my daughter, who will bring also servants, cattle, sheep and horses.[26]

Unfortunately, once the dowry arrangements had been made, there was a delay on the princess's journey to Egypt. Ramses impatiently writes to the Hittite king demanding to know where she and the dowry were. He emphasises the dowry more than the bride by declaring poverty and a genuine need for all the wealth promised. The princess's mother, Padukhepa, replied to Ramses rebuking him:

> My brother possesses nothing? If the son of the sun-god or the son of the storm god has nothing ... only then have you nothing. That you my brother should wish to enrich yourself from me ... is neither friendly nor honourable.[27]

The princess still continued her journey to Egypt, where in southern Syria at the Hittite border post she was met by the Egyptian army to accompany her to Egypt. Ramses made offerings to the god Seth in order to prevent any further delays through poor weather and snow. Seth answered his prayers, and the Levant was unusually warm for the time of year and the royal entourage proceeded on their journey. It is at this point of the story that we have some indication of royal marriage rituals, as Ramses was required to send oil to the princess with which she would be anointed. Whether this ritual was simply a royal marriage ritual or also used by commoners is unknown.

When the princess arrived in Egypt, Ramses was delighted as she was 'beautiful in the heart of His Majesty and he loved her more than anything'.[28] Despite this apparent love, her true name was abandoned and she was given an Egyptian name, Maatneferura. The marriage stela, however, abandons all emotions and describes the transaction as little more than part of a tribute list from a lesser king to his master:

> Then he caused his eldest daughter to be brought with splendid tribute before her of gold, silver, much bronze, slaves, spans of horses without limit, and cattle, goats, rams by the myriad, limitless. Such were the dues they brought for Ramses II.[29]

Once married, Maatneferura was named as a king's wife on monuments and statutes along with her Egyptian counterparts Bintanath, Meritamun, and Nebettawi. This was an honour not often given to foreign brides. She was initially housed at the harem at the capital at Pi-Rameses and no doubt saw the king regularly. As she lost favour she was housed at the Gurob harem, Mer Wer. Her laundry list was discovered from this site and included a 28 cubit long piece of cloth, 4 palms by 4 cubits wide. It was not long before she disappeared from the records altogether, and it is thought she may have died. She bore Ramses at least one daughter, although, as she was in her forties or fifties when she was sent to Gurob, she is unlikely to have died in childbirth.

Her death meant that the alliance with the Hittites needed to be renegotiated, and another daughter and large dowry were sent to Egypt. However, this bride's name has not survived and where she was housed is unknown. In the Ptolemaic Period, the marriage between Ramesses and Maatneferura took on the form of legend and was used as an analogy for a better time when Egypt had been ruled by an Egyptian.[30]

The existence of a large harem demonstrated the wealth of the king, as only the wealthy were able to afford to keep multiple wives. Unfortunately, it is difficult to ascertain how many wives each king had in his harem. Records of Ramses II indicate he had over 100 children, maybe as many as 150, but from how many women is not stated. Moreover, at the temple of Sety I at Abydos, Ramses describes how his father gifted him a harem when he became heir to the throne: 'Throughout the land he selected women for me ... harem women and female companions'.[31]

It could also be assumed that Sety chose Nefertari as the Great Royal Wife of Ramses, knowing she would one day be queen and would bear the future king of Egypt. How this choice was made is unknown, but it seems likely they were married and had their first born child before Sety I died. Textual evidence suggests that Amenhotep III collected women for his harem almost by mail order, where he offered forty pieces of silver for each beautiful woman who was brought to him. The only stipulation made was that her voice was not shrill.[32] It would be interesting to compare this with the methods employed by Sety I when he was choosing women for his son.

The image we have of a harem as a place of sensuality and decadence is not accurate in regards to those of ancient Egypt. The Egyptian name was ipet nswt or xnrt, which has been translated as the royal harem, the royal women's quarters, the royal apartments, the royal granary[33], or place of seclusion[34]. The women residing in the harem were called the xnrwt, which translates as the secluded ones. They were not prisons, but rather a place where the royal women and their children could live safely. The harem was a noisy bustling place, with all royal wives and their children, king's sisters and aunts, women inherited from his father's harem as well as all the attendants and servants who accompanied the foreign brides.

Not all wives of the king necessarily met him or had the pleasure of bearing his children, especially if they lived in remote harems. This meant their status of king's wife could never improve. The king's favourite wives no doubt travelled with him while he inspected the land, and resided in the women's quarters at the main palaces. It is hardly surprising that some lower level royal wives were bored and frustrated, leading to ill thought-out plans and conspiracies. The most famous of these was known as the Harem Conspiracy.

The evidence of this conspiracy is in the form of legal papers from the court regarding the trial of thirty-eight conspirators who were all sentenced to death. The plot was hatched in the 'harem of the accompanying', which is likely to be the group of royal women who accompanied the king on his travels around the country.[35] The women forming this harem are likely to be those who were well favoured and therefore high up in the harem hierarchy, even if considered minor wives of the king.

The main protagonist was a secondary wife of Ramses III, Tiy, who wanted her son Penteweret (He-of-the-female-great-one) to be king, and she hatched a plot along with numerous members of the harem guard to murder the king and to push her son to the throne. Her son's name is likely to be falsified as a punishment in order to mask his identity. This was a common form of punishment, as to deny the repetition of someone's name ultimately sentenced them to eternal death with no hope for an afterlife.

Papyrus Rollin and Papyrus Lee tell us that the first attempt on the king's life was via the use of wax figurines designed to incapacitate him. Such figures have been named curse figures, and were often made of clay or wax and sometimes inscribed with the name of the enemy. Through manipulation of the figure, harm could be caused to the person represented, in this case, Ramses III:

And he began the ritual of consulting the divine oracle so to delude people. But he reached the side of the harem of that other great, expansive place, and he began to use the waxen figures in order that they be taken inside by the inspector Adi-ram for staving off one gang of men and spellbinding the others so that a few messages could be taken in and others brought out.[36]

An example of such a wax figure, currently in the British Museum, has a thread running through the centre, which may have some connection to the person represented and made the magic more effective. However, this is believed to be Roman in date. Such methods of incapacitating an enemy were considered common enough to appear in literary tales, and in Papyrus Westcar a man accused of adultery was thrown into the Nile with a wax figurine of a crocodile which became real and devoured him. In the case of the Harem Conspiracy, they were caught before the wax figurine could work, and it has been suggested that this was not actually a commonly used method, but rather a commonly feared method. Quirke compares it to the accusations thrown against witches in the European witch trials: more superstition than substance.[37] The Harem Conspirators' back-up plan was to kill the king when he was at a festival at his Theban temple of Medinet Habu. The attempt went ahead, and in 2012 a CT scan of the mummy of Ramses III showed that his throat had been cut with a sharp knife, perhaps as he slept, meaning the attempt was partially successful. The cut was 7 cm wide just under the larynx and is likely to have killed the king immediately, probably giving him little time to even cry out. The embalmers placed a wadjet amulet, or Eye of Horus, into the wound with the intention of magically healing it for the afterlife before wrapping the neck of the king in layers of bandages.[38] I say the attempt was only *partially* successful, as all the conspirators were caught and the king was succeeded to the throne by his intended heir Ramses IV and not the son of Tiy.

So what happened to the pretender, Penteweret? Studies of the mummy of Unknown Man E have shown it could be him. The mummy was discovered at Deir el Bahri, and for many years it was believed he was buried alive due to his unusual expression and the presence of a goat skin, which was considered ritually unclean. Examination of the mummy indicates he possibly died of suffocation, although the evidence of a gas build-up may have been due to natural decomposition.[39] DNA studies carried out at the same time as the examination have shown that he was related to Ramses III, probably his son, and places him as a good candidate for Penteweret, as the form of death and lack of proper mummification indicate he was being punished by being denied a proper burial and therefore an afterlife.

The Harem Conspiracy of Ramses III is by far the most famous due to the surviving trial records, but it was not the first. During the reign of Pepy I (2332–2283 BCE), something similar occurred, although we only have a snippet of evidence leaving us to wonder at the details. In the Abydos tomb chapel of Weni, he tells us of the royal wife, Weret-Yamtes:

> When there was a secret charge in the royal harem against queen Weret-Yamtes, His Majesty made me hear it alone. No chief judge or vizier, no official was there, only I alone ... Never before had one like me heard a secret of the king's harem; but His Majesty made me hear it, because I was worthy in His Majesty's heart beyond any official of his.[40]

This is made all the more intriguing when we realise that Teti, Pepy I's father, may also have been assassinated by his bodyguard. Did the plot come from the harem? We may never know. Such harem plots also appear in the literature, and the possibility that king Amenemhat was assassinated in such a plot is hinted at in the tale of Sinuhe, although, as he was succeeded as planned by his son Senusret I, this plot was also only partially successful. Sinuhe flees the city and ultimately Egypt because 'I believed there would be turmoil and did not expect to survive it'.[41]

Unrest and potential assassination attempts were the worst that could happen in the royal harem. For most of the women, life probably was quite boring, but safe, with the constant possibility of being lost and forgotten. A perfect case of a diplomatic bride going missing seems to be the case of the sister of the Babylonian king Kadashman-Enlil. He wrote to Amenhotep III stating:

> You seek my daughter for your wife and my sister whom my father gave to you is still there with you but no one has seen her now, whether she is alive, whether she is dead.[42]

Amenhotep encourages him to send an envoy who knows the woman: 'who can converse with her and identify her and let him converse with her'. When the envoy arrived, a woman was pointed out as the Babylonian princess, although she was not allowed to speak with him. When he left, he was uncertain of her identity.

It is quite likely that all women entering the royal harem, whether Egyptian or foreign, were controlled and any communication with the outside world was monitored if not restricted.[43] In a world where most women did not receive an education and therefore were illiterate, this may not have been that difficult to orchestrate. However, the foreign wives were not alone in the harem, as they often arrived with a large entourage of servants. The marriage scarab of Amenhotep III tells us that along with the foreign bride: 'Gilukhepa, the daughter of the prince of Nahrin Sutarna, and the members of her harem, some 317 women'.[44]

This indicates that with each foreign bride the harem grew by hundreds of women, which for the women already residing there may have been an exciting prospect. Amenhotep III also captured women for his harem, which included 323 daughters of Palestinian princes and 270 court singers.[45] These numbers, as a booty list, may be extremely exaggerated in order to emphasise the king's majesty, but it gives an indication of the numbers of women housed in the harem: hundreds if not thousands. Through studying the records, it is possible to estimate that, in addition to these Palestinian women and court singers, Amenhotep's harem comprised more than six hundred Mitannian women in addition to women from Syria, Asia Minor and Palestine.[46]

With such a large number of women and children, it is not surprising that there was more than one harem situated in different cities throughout Egypt. The further away the harem was from the capital and the main residence of the king, the less the king visited, placing the women firmly as secondary wives. However, whenever the king visited the harem, no matter how infrequently it was, the women's role was to entertain him, and wall reliefs show the harem ladies singing, dancing and playing board games before the king.[47]

A number of harem palaces have been discovered in the archaeological record, including one in the Faiyum at Gurob, called Mer-Wer. It was built by Thutmosis III and was in use until the late New Kingdom. This harem palace housed the senior royal ladies, their servants and officials. It also accommodated a large linen workshop manned by the royal women. Only the king's daughters, sisters and Great Royal Wife lived a life of luxury in the harem. The other women were expected to work, either in the linen workshop or as cooks, washerwomen, nursemaids, weavers or servants.[48] However, as royal wives, no matter how secondary and how hard they were expected to work, they wore the best clothes and lived in an element of luxury not available to ordinary women.[49] Those who worked were paid in rations of food, clothes and other commodities for their work. Of course, they also had time for relaxation, and eighteenth dynasty tomb images show Syrian women of Amenhotep III's harem dancing and playing musical instruments in order to entertain themselves and the other women,[50] and no doubt the king as well when he visited the palace.

The harem palace at Gurob, like most residential structures, was built of mud-brick and contained sleeping areas, pillared halls, a small temple and a large cemetery with at least one Ramesside prince buried there. In addition to the linen workshop, the palace also owned all of the surrounding land and earned income from their produce, and over its period of use, the harem had eleven married male administrators in charge of accounting and scribal activities in order to control this revenue. They lived in the surrounding areas, with the harem forming the centre of the community.[51]

Another harem was discovered at the palace of Amenhotep III at Malkata, in modern Luxor, which comprised four suites of rooms on either side of the main banqueting hall. Each of the suites consisted of four chambers, providing the women with a bedroom, dressing room, wash room and room for receiving guests. These were not far from the private quarters of the king (discussed above), enabling him to easily visit the female quarters or request one of his wives visit him.

The harem also housed the royal children, as is evidenced at the Great Palace at Amarna where the main columned hall led to six chambers with the remains of sleeping platforms. These may have been bedrooms of the six daughters of Akhenaten and Nefertiti. Adjacent to each bedroom was a small room that possibly functioned as a playroom, and a number of paintbrushes and pens stained with paint have been discovered here with traces of paint marks on the walls left by the little girls while playing. In addition to housing the six little princesses, there was a wider harem here with a pleasure garden leading down to the Nile.

By far the most complete harem is that discovered at the mortuary temple of Ramses III, which is situated in the gatehouse. The wall decoration on the third floor of the east side of the gateway shows Ramses III in intimate positions with the royal women. Some of the women are identified as daughters of the king, but that does not necessarily mean they were not also his wives (as discussed above). He is shown being offered flowers, food and drink by the women. In addition to embracing some of them, he is also shown playing senet, indicating this really was a recreational area.

The apartments here consist of two groups of three rooms, in addition to a roof complex with further small structures. While the gateway itself appears to be a traditional fortified gate, the large windows are more in tune with domestic architecture and indicate there was a semi-domestic role to the structure. The inscriptions in the gateway do not tell what the structure was used for, and the excavators of Medinet Habu believe that it is unlikely that the main harem would be placed so close to the enclosure wall where the women could be in danger. It is more likely that the gateway was seen as a temporary retreat where the women had a good view of activities, processions and rituals being carried out inside and outside the temple.

It is more likely that the royal women were permanently resident in the second palace at Medinet Habu, which was built near the end of the reign of Ramses III to celebrate his sed festival. The sed festival was an important festival of rejuvenation which the king was expected to participate in every thirty years, although often they would be performed at times of political instability as a means of emphasising the king's right to rule. The festival comprised a series of four runs in the presence of the gods, one carrying an oar, one with documents and another with the crook and flail as well as a race against a bull. In order to prove the king was able to continue ruling a unified Egypt, he needed to be successful in all of these runs. Initially, in the Predynastic Period, these races were an endurance test, and failure meant losing the throne, but in the Pharaonic Period they had developed into a demonstration of the king's abilities.[52] The palace was built to accommodate the people involved in the rituals and celebrations associated with the sed festival and enabled the king to receive dignitaries as necessary and prepare himself for the rituals and meetings.

At the rear of the palace there are three apartments that are comparable to the women's quarters at the palace of Amenhotep III at Malkata and the palace at Amarna. The apartments are reached by a maze of narrow corridors, which separate it from the public areas. This palace has two showers with a stone drain to remove the waste water and a pleasure garden with a pool and small garden structures. Could it be in this harem that the Harem Conspiracy was born?

For the ordinary people, the activities of the king and his numerous wives, concubines and mistresses was an unknown entity: something that took place in secluded areas of the palace. However, this did not prevent the people from speculating about the king and his sexual adventures. Graffiti near Deir el Bahri is a case in point, as it possibly shows Hatshepsut being penetrated from behind by a court official (Senenmut). It is thought that Hatshepsut and Senenmut were having a relationship, and the issue is still heavily debated today. The graffiti is quite basic, with the queen identified by a small nubbin at the forehead which could be a ureaus, and Senenmut is identified by an overseer's leather hat. As she is in the position of the nkkw (she who is penetrated), it presents her as weaker and to be scorned at as 'she could never dominate a man in the way that she is now being dominated'.[53]

The relationship between Hatshepsut and Senenmut is one that is more rumour and speculation than fact. A great deal, for example, is made of the fact that he appears to be unmarried with no children.[54] It was considered unusual in Egypt not to marry so he stood out, but whether this is enough proof to show he was having a relationship with the queen is debateable. Other, perhaps more compelling evidence can be found at his Gebel el Silsila shrine (no. 16), which in the absence of a wife and children, and the traditional funerary feast, depicts Hatshepsut being embraced by Sobek, the crocodile god, and Nekhbet, the vulture goddess of Upper Egypt (who we saw on Amenhotep III's ceiling). Senenmut held numerous titles including tutor to Hatshepsut's daughter Neferure, superintendent of the private apartments, superintendent of the bathroom and superintendent of the bedroom, which Winlock interpreted as meaning he helped with the more intimate details of her life. However, this is unlikely to be the case, as the titles are probably ceremonial and show his high status in the court rather than a mundane list of his daily duties.[55] His rapid rise through the palace administration and his subsequent burial at Deir el Bahri actually within the boundaries of Hatshepsut's mortuary temple are often also attributed to this relationship with the queen. There is definitely no doubt that they were close, and his representation of the queen in his own shrine and his own depiction behind a door at the temple at Deir el Bahri perhaps indicate they were closer than queen and courtier, or even friends. Personally, it is rather comforting that Hatshepsut was able to find love, loyalty and devotion in what was a political nightmare for her, as she was a woman ruling as king in a male-dominated world.

Another queen whose personal life caught the public imagination was that of Cleopatra VII, the last queen of Egypt before the Romans annexed Egypt incorporating it into the Empire. Unfortunately, the only evidence we have about Cleopatra is from the Roman viewpoint. They were extremely critical of what they viewed as an exotic and decadent lifestyle, and Lucan (39–65 CE) described her in his poem *Pharsalia*:

Having immoderately painted up her fatal beauty, neither content with a sceptre her own, nor with her brother her husband, covered with the spoils of the Red Sea upon her neck and hair, Cleopatra wears treasures and pants beneath her ornaments.[56]

This image of over-adornment led to further speculation about her promiscuity, especially in her public seduction of two great Roman leaders, Julius Caesar and Marcus Antonius. She was described as: 'a lecherous ... harlot queen of incestuous Canopus [*a Delta town*]'.[57]

The Roman records even go so far as to claim she was a prostitute, who killed her customers.[58] This connection with prostitution has continued through to the modern day, with modern prostitutes using a technique known as the Cleopatra Grip, to contract the vaginal muscles.

However, such a reputation is one of Roman propaganda, as the evidence shows Cleopatra had four husbands: two Egyptian kings Ptolemy XIV and XV, Julius Caesar and Marcus Antonius. Each marriage was legitimate and monogamous in nature as befitting a royal woman. However, as one of these husbands was an emperor and the other a powerful Roman soldier, she therefore threatened the foundation of Roman society and was reviled in the Roman-produced texts.

Sexually promiscuous reputations, were also formed of pharaonic kings, and speculation about the Egyptian king ended up in literary tales, such as the Middle Kingdom story of king Pepy II and General Sasanet (*see* chapter 5). This story explores the king's homosexual exploits with a soldier. Every evening the king was followed as he went to the general's house and knocked until a ladder was thrown down, enabling him to enter. For four hours he was with the general and did 'what he desired with him'.[59] The man following the king seemed to be irritated that the king was neglecting his duties for the sake of four hours of sex every night with someone of a lower class to him.

Another king who is also presented wasting time on frivolous sexual exploits is Sneferu in the Middle Kingdom Papyrus Westcar. He was bored in his palace and decided that in order to keep himself entertained he would go rowing on the lake. He called for:

> ... twenty women with the shapeliest bodies who have not yet given birth. Also let there be brought twenty fishnets and give these nets to the women to wear in place of their clothes![60]

These fishnet dresses may be in reference to the bead-net dresses which are depicted from the Middle Kingdom, which were generally worn over a white sheath dress and would not have been particularly revealing.[61] Without this white dress, however, it would be another story. There are only two of these dresses surviving, one in Boston and the other in the Petrie Museum, London. The latter comprises two breast caps measuring just 4.3 centimetres, and 127 mitre shells which are filled with little stones. Normally, it is believed dancers wore such shells, which rattled when they moved, but the Petrie examples do not make a sound and are more likely to be there to weigh down the hem of the dress.[62] Following the reconstruction, it was determined that this bead-net dress was designed for a child of approximately eleven years old, perhaps the age of the girls in the boat with the king. However, such a dress was impractical for rowing, and it is thought that instead they may have worn woven linen fabric with threads one quarter of an inch apart,[63] which when wet were transparent and when dry revealing enough to excite the king.

Obviously in the modern world, exploiting young girls in this way does not paint the king in a particularly positive light, especially if, as was normal, most girls were married and gave birth by the age of fourteen. However, how such an act was interpreted by the intended ancient Egyptian audience is unknown, but it is likely to be different. Perhaps the negative aspect of this story was the fact that the king was dictated to by one of these girls who refused to continue rowing when she dropped her fish pendant into the water. Even though he promised to replace it, she still refused and the king called upon the magician to help. The infallible power of pharaoh is certainly not displayed in this story, which may have been more derogatory than ogling young girls for entertainment. Or, as with the homosexual sex between Pepy and general Sasanet, Sneferu's actions could be considered a waste of time when he should be doing more important things.

But even kings need to unwind, and as with the general populace, no doubt falling into the arms of an attractive partner, or watching beautiful girls in revealing clothing, may have seemed like the perfect way.

4

CHILDBIRTH

'He slept with his wife at night; she conceived
and became pregnant'[1]

The result of the majority of marriages, whether for ordinary people from the villages or the royal family, was pregnancy and childbirth. Women married young, and therefore from the age of thirteen or so, and for most of their adult life, they were either pregnant, recovering from the trauma that was childbirth, or taking care of young children. Shortly after giving birth, a woman was expected to continue with her daily chores, and in the tombs of Menna and Montuemhet, a peasant woman is depicted carrying a child in a sling as she works. This was the expectation of all new mothers, although a king's wife was better situated than the wife of a peasant farmer.

Childbirth was a dangerous time for the mother and the baby, and it was not unusual for women to die in childbirth. It is estimated that 20 per cent of all pregnancies failed, 20 per cent of children died in the first year and 30 per cent died before reaching five years of age.[2] The most dangerous periods for both mother and the newborn baby were in the first few days of the baby's life, then after the first year and once more at three years when they were weaned. Although an Egyptian woman could hope to give birth to ten or twelve children, less than half survived into adulthood. The Instruction of Ani warns against complacency:

> Do not say 'I am too young to be taken', for you do not know your death. When death comes he steals the infant who is in his mother's arms, just like him who reached old age.[3]

There was very little difference between the rich and the poor in this situation, and it is estimated that at least 1.5 per cent of women died in childbirth.[4] This included royalty, and the wife of king Horemheb, Mutnodjmet, appears to have been buried with a foetus or newborn baby, and the mother or Tutankhamun, Kiya, is presented in the royal tomb at Amarna, lying dead in the birthing bed.[5] Perhaps because of the danger experienced by the mother during childbirth, they were greatly revered in society and the Instruction of Ani states unequivocally:

> Double the food your mother gave to you. Support her as she supported you. She had a heavy load in you but she did not abandon you. When you were born at the end of your months, she was yet yoked to you.[6]

Because of the danger that pregnancy and childbirth presented for mother and child, pregnant women and mothers turned to the gods for help. There were various deities associated with childbirth, labour and the protection of children, emphasising the importance and fear of this time of life for Egyptian women.

The most common deities were Bes, the dwarf, and Taweret, the pregnant hippopotamus. They were both invoked during labour, as they frightened away any demons intending to harm the mother or the baby in the womb.[7] Bes was represented as a dwarf with a lion's mane and ears and often wore a leopard skin. He is depicted face-on and carries the sa sign of protection, a knife, or a drum. At Lahun, Petrie found a cartonnage Bes mask, which was well used and had been repaired in antiquity. It is possible it was worn during childbirth by a magician or priest in order to represent the presence of the deity. During a difficult labour, a clay figurine of Bes was held at the head of the mother and a prayer was recited over this four times.

Bes was worshipped by pregnant mothers from all levels of society, and he is also depicted on the walls of the mammisi, which celebrated the king's birth as well as emphasising his divinity. This protection during childbirth is paralleled in the quest for rebirth, and he occasionally appears in the texts of the underworld holding a knife in a manner of protection. He was frequently depicted on household items such as apotropaic wands, headrests, mirrors and cosmetic items, fulfilling his role as god of fertility.

Bes is frequently depicted alongside Taweret, who was worshipped for her ferocious nature, as hippopotami were known to devour their young[8] but also go to violent lengths to protect them. She was depicted as a hippopotamus standing on her hind legs, with the legs of a lion and wearing a crocodile skin on her back. She has a protruding stomach and pendulous, human breasts, leaving little doubt that she is pregnant. She was also known as Opet, and there is a temple dedicated to this cult at Karnak Temple. However, there are no temples dedicated to Taweret herself. She had many functions within the realm of childbirth, and one of her titles was 'She Who Removes the Birth Waters', indicating her role at the start of labour.[9]

There are a number of faience vessels bearing her form, which probably held milk that was poured out through the nipple and therefore imbued it with fertility as well as protection against the child who drank it. She was recorded in magical spells as a protector of Horus, and, therefore should a child be stung by scorpions, the parents could invoke Taweret. As a goddess of fertility and childbirth, she was also naturally connected with Hathor and is sometimes depicted wearing Hathor's cow-horn headdress, or emerging from the western necropolis showing that her role overlapped into the realm of the dead.

A more practical deity can be found in the form of a birth-brick with a human head, known as Meskhenet. In the Book of the Dead, she is referred to as a cubit-with-head. Additionally, she was depicted with a uterus or a pesesh-kaf knife on top of her head. She was evoked during labour and delivery and was sometimes depicted alongside Renenutet, the goddess of harvest, nutrition and lactation.[10] Renenutet, whose name meant the 'nourishing snake', was generally a protector of the king and his linen, and therefore by default was a provider of mummy bandages.

She is depicted as a cobra, or a woman with a snake's head, and is at times depicted nursing the god Horus, in her role as a nurturer of children. In this role, she is connected with the divine mother, Isis, and in her role as a harvest deity, she is associated with the fertility of Osiris. She aids with the final stages of labour and encourages the child to live and, like Shay and Meskhenet (see below), proclaims the destiny of the child. There was a temple to Renenutet in the Faiyum, and in the later texts, she is said to have had a liaison with the creator god Atum, giving birth to Horus, therefore enabling her to fully take over the role of Isis.

Following the birth, it is generally Meskhenet who was responsible for proclaiming the child's destiny although other deities also held a similar role. As with all childbirth deities, she also held a funerary role aiding the deceased's rebirth into the afterlife in the same way she aided babies into the world. At times she is present in the Weighing of the Heart scene, which ascertained whether the deceased progressed to the afterlife after having their heart weighed against the feather of truth (Maat).

These three deities, Bes, Taweret and Meskhenet, were the most worshipped childbirth deities in ancient Egypt but there were no temples dedicated to them. But, as deities of childbirth, all mothers (royal or commoner) appealed to them, worshipped them and wore amulets bearing their images. As discussed in chapter 3, even Amenhotep III's bedroom wall was decorated with images of Bes, helping not only his fertility but protecting him while he slept. However, many more deities were associated with different stages of labour, fertility and sexuality.

For example, the frog deity, Heket, was essential for the final stages of labour. Frogs were believed to hold great powers of creation and formed part of the driving force behind the creation of the world (*see* chapter 8). Additionally, as the Nile receded after the inundation, the increase in frogs led the Egyptians to believe they self-created from the waters. This abundance of frogs also led to the tadpole forming the hieroglyphic sign for 100,000 and can often be seen in images of the king representing his longevity. Frog amulets were therefore worn for fecundity, longevity and protection during childbirth.

In Papyrus Westcar, Heket was the deity who encouraged the final stages of labour and therefore was an essential deity of childbirth, as well as representing a female counterpart for Khnum. Whereas he was responsible for creating man on a potter's wheel (*see* chapter 3), she was responsible for creating the child in the womb and breathing life into it.

Heket appears alongside Bes and Taweret on apotropaic wands, but also on a pair of ivory clappers that were thought to belong to a midwife. Unlike the deities discussed so far, there were temples dedicated to the cult of Heket: one at Qus in Upper Egypt and the other at Tuna-el-Gebel in Middle Egypt. Sadly these temples are no longer standing. As with most childbirth deities, Heket had a funerary role, although this was limited to helping the deceased king travel to the sky.

Having a healthy body during childbirth was essential, and therefore the mistress of the vulva, Nebet-hetepet, could be invoked in time of need. She was the female counterpart of Atum and was closely equated with Hathor.[11] She is believed to be the hand of Atum that grasped his phallus in the Heliopolitan creation myth creating the next generation of gods (*see* chapter 8). Therefore, she had integral creative characteristics and was a powerful though little-worshipped fertility deity.

Once the child was born, the mother may turn to the god of destiny, Shay, who allotted the lifespan of the child. However, he was only one of three deities of destiny. In the divine birth scenes of Hatshepsut and Amenhotep III, it was Meskhenet who announced their destiny to be king. In the story of The Doomed Prince, the Seven Hathors predicted the nature of the child's death, which in his case would be by crocodile, snake or dog.

While all predicted destiny, it was of a different kind; the Seven Hathors, predicted the mode of death, Meskhenet predicted social standing and Shay predicted the lifespan. Such an overlap of roles meant that Meskhenet and Shay were both represented as birth-bricks in the funerary Weighing of the Heart scene. Meskhenet can be seen hovering above the scales[12] and represented the social standing of the individual and how this controlled their good deeds that justified their admission to the afterlife.[13] Shay, on the other hand, was there to confirm that their allotted time was over.

One of the most popular deities in ancient Egypt was the goddess Hathor, the goddess of love, drunkenness and childbirth. Hathor's form changed depending on her role. In her human form she was the goddess of sexual love, and in her cow form she represented a mother and nurturer[14] of both the living and the dead.

At Deir el Bahri, an entire fertility cult arose around Hathor and hundreds of votive offerings were left here dedicated to her by both men and women. These votive offerings were in the form of phalli, breasts and fertility figures. Most were uninscribed, so the exact request is now long forgotten, but graffiti at the temple of Thutmosis III at the site, left by Paybasa, a priest of Mut, offers some insight into the sort of requests:

> Give to him love in the sight of every man and every woman. Cause
> that his phallus be stronger than any woman ... Give to him a good
> wife who will be his companion.[15]

Paybasa, was clearly single and believed, should Hathor improve his sexual performance, he would find a wife. Hathor was also invoked to ensure fertility and conception and prevent impotence:

> ... so that the goddess lets your wives bear sons and daughters,
> So that you may not be barren and you may not be impotent.[16]

Perhaps this song was only to be sung by priests celebrating the cult of Hathor, or perhaps it was well known and sung by her worshippers as well in the hope they would become pregnant.

Egyptian doctors were quick to recognise the signs of pregnancy (*see* chapter 7), the most obvious of which was when menstruation stopped. In the Story of Setne Khaemwast princess Ahwere announced: 'when my time of purification came I made no more purification', indicating she was pregnant. The images of pregnancy are limited to a handful of stylised images of queens with small bumps, and the texts are equally silent on the subject. In the literary tale of The Doomed Prince, we are told:

> He slept with his wife at night: she conceived and became pregnant. He recognised her in the recognition of a man. She became pregnant in the night with a small boy.[17]

This is often the only mention we have of pregnancy that of the moment of conception. The forty weeks that follow was generally ignored until the onset of labour and subsequently the birth. However, in the literary tale 'The Story of Setne' it appears that gifts were given at the announcement of the pregnancy rather than the birth of the child: 'Pharaoh had many things taken [out of the treasury] and sent me presents of silver, gold, and royal linen, all very beautiful',[18] perhaps the ancient Egyptian equivalent of a baby shower.

During the pregnancy, incantations were recited in order to ensure it ran the full term, and an example currently in Turin (Inv. No 1984) reads:

> We cause her to conceive male children and female children. We shall keep her safe from a Horus Birth, from an irregular birth and from giving birth to twins.[19]

Twins obviously were considered a disaster, health wise, as it doubled the danger the mother and subsequently the babies were in. Twins on the whole were not viewed in a negative light within the Egyptian community (chapter 5) and were generally believed to represent two halves of the same person. The 'Horus Birth' reference is a little more obscure and could refer to his premature birth described by Plutarch:

For this reason it is said that Isis, when she was aware of her being pregnant, put on a protective amulet on the sixth day of Phaophi, and at the winter solstice gave birth to Harpocrates, imperfect and prematurely born.[20]

As in the modern world, a premature baby is more at risk than a full-term child, and in ancient Egypt it is unlikely that a very premature baby would survive. However, in order to prevent such dangers, various deities attended the birth. An inscription on the sarcophagus chamber of Sety I at Abydos informs us of the protective goddesses who were present at his birth:

Then Isis and Nephthys stretched forth their hands towards Horus that they might receive him when Isis gave birth to him and he came forth from her womb.[21]

These protective goddesses were present at every birth in the form of midwives or the birthing bricks (see below). A hymn dedicated to the sun god further emphasises their role in his birth: 'Isis and Nephthys lift you up when you come forth from the thighs of your mother Nut'.[22]

Labour was a frightening time of any woman's life, as it could be extremely dangerous and there were many things which could go wrong. Naturally they turned to religion, invoking the gods and relying on amulets to provide protection. The tyet knot of Isis was a particularly powerful amulet used to prevent miscarriage. This amulet was in the form of a knot of cloth with the appearance of an ankh with the arms flopped down to the side. It was important to recite a prayer over it:

Incantation for the tyet of red jasper: You have your blood Isis ... for whomsoever this is recited the defensive power of Isis will be the protection of his body, and Horus, son of Isis will rejoice over him when he sees him.[23]

Trying to prevent a pregnancy from ending early indicated that the midwives were aware of the expected delivery date. However, although this information could be acquired through experience, the exact number of months has not survived in any medical text,[24] but it is hinted at in other written evidence. For example, a spell for speeding up labour states: 'her months have been completed according to the right number'. In the Instruction of Ani, he makes reference to: 'when you were born after your months'. Even in the literary tale, The Doomed Prince', his mother 'completed the months of childbearing'.[25] Although the months are not stated, these texts indicate that a birth was expected at a specific time.

The average gestation period for humans is 280 days or 40 weeks, and a sarcophagus currently in Berlin makes it clear they were aware of this: 'Your mother kept you until the first day of the 10th month'. A potsherd from Strasbourg is even more specific. There had been a trial wedding (*see* chapter 2), which lasted for 275 days. After this period passed, the bride swore she was not pregnant at the time of the marriage.[26]

While not necessarily offering anything to alleviate pain associated with labour other than burning resin near to or massaging saffron powder steeped in beer onto the abdomen, pain was regularly acknowledged in various texts. In the Satire of the Trades, the pain and wretchedness is compared: 'The mat-weaver in the workshop, he is worse off than a woman [in childbirth] with knees against his belly he cannot breathe out'.[27] A Deir el Medina workman, Neferabu, records that due to offending the goddess Meretseger she punished him with pain comparable to the last stages of pregnancy. Then she struck him blind.[28] Blindness

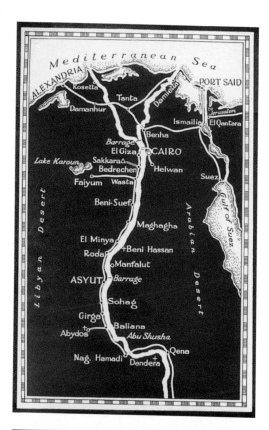

1-a. Lower Egypt.

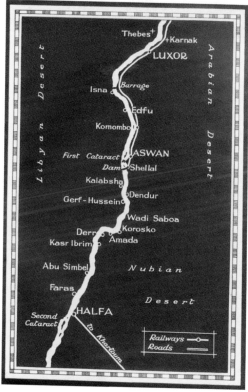

1-b. Upper Egypt.

Left: 2. Amun-Min, Karnak.

Right: 3. Cosmetic items beneath the chair of the wife of Remini, El Kab.

Left: 4. Sety I with Ramses II, wearing the side-lock of youth, Abydos.

Right: 5. Hathor stela showing the Hathor wig, Serabit el Kadim.

6. Noblemen wearing unguent cones, tomb of Khaemhat TT57, Luxor.

7. Khnum creating the king on a potter's wheel, Denderah.

8. Faience Bowl, Leiden Museum.

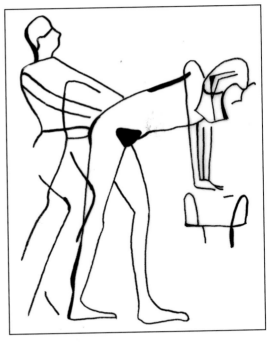

Above left: 9. Hathor nursing the king, Edfu.

Above right: 10. Graffiti of Hatshepsut and Senenmut, Deir el Bahri.

Below: 11. Throne room in the palace at Medinet Habu.

Above: 12. Harem at Medinet Habu.

Below left: 13. Bes, Denderah.

Below right: 14. Heket, the frog goddess of childbirth, Abydos.

15. Seven Hathors, Medinet Habu.

16. Weighing of the Heart with Meskhenet above the scales, Deir el Medina.

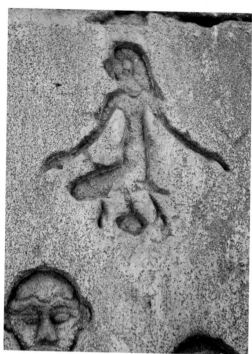

Left: 17. Hatshepsut's mother, Ahmosis, pregnant, Deir el Bahri.

Right: 18. Hieroglyph showing childbirth, Edfu.

Left: 19. Making offerings to Amun-Min, Karnak.

Right: 20. Niankhkhnum and Khnumnakht embracing.

Left: 21. Hathor holding a sistrum, Edfu.

Below: 22. Middle Kingdom birth-brick, Abydos.

23. Tutankhamun embracing Osiris with his ka behind him. Reconstructed tomb of Tutankhamun, Luxor.

Above: 24. Dancers from the Red Chapel, Karnak.

Below: 25. The sacred lake at Karnak.

Left: 26. Benben stone which represents the petrified semen of Atum, Cairo Museum.

Right: 27. Shu, the god of the air, Kom Ombo.

Below: 28. Nut giving birth to the sun-god, Denderah.

Above left: 29. Amun, Luxor Temple.

Above right: 30. Amaunet, Luxor Temple.

Right: 31. Sety I making offerings of incense, Abydos.

Above: 32. Bringing incense trees from Punt, Deir el Bahri.

Left: 33. Amenirdis, God's Wife of Amun, Karnak.

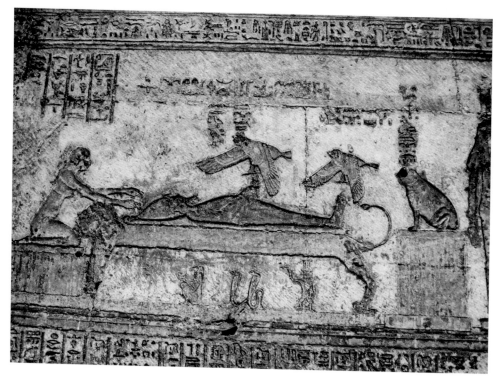

Above: 34. Resurrection of Osiris with Isis as a kite above him and Heket at the foot of the bed, Denderah.

Below: 35. Driving of the calves, Luxor Temple.

Left: 36. Sekhmet offers the menat to Sety I, Abydos.

Right: 37. Anukis, consort of Khnum the creator nursing Ramses II, Beit el Wali.

38. Scene from the Turin Erotic Papyrus showing the application of lipstick and use of external stimuli.

39. Ka statue of Djoser, Saqqara.

40. Cutting penises from the enemies during battle, Medinet Habu.

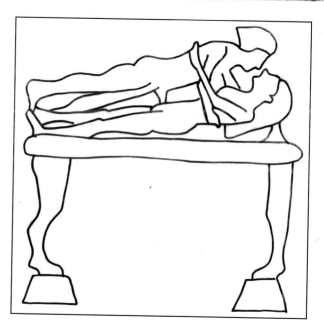

41. Hieroglyph of a couple making love, Beni Hasan, Middle Kingdom.

42. Hathor as a cow licking the hand of Hatshepsut, Deir el Bahri.

43. The Osireion, Abydos.

44. Banquet scene of Paheri, El Kab.

at Deir el Medina was not uncommon, as many of the workmen worked in the tombs that were dusty and therefore caused blindness. However, many of them attributed this affliction with their own behaviour in blaspheming or offending a deity.

Even queens complained of the pain of childbirth. In the divine birth scene of Hatshepsut (*see* chapter 3), queen Ahmosis appeals to Amun: 'Speed up the north-winds. The pregnancy has taken its time, it is painful the time has come ...'[29] Divine pregnancies were delivered in the same way as mortal pregnancies, and all the relief she may have received was beer: 'Happy is the face of the delivering person when she is drunk in response to the jug of the beer goddess'.[30] Not only could the alcohol numb the pain but the act of being drunk brought the woman closer to Hathor, the Lady of Drunkenness, who offered extra protection in her time of need.

In the gynaecological papyri, rather unexpectedly, there is no mention of the act of childbirth and how to ease the pain. It is thought this is because childbirth was not considered a disease or illness and therefore did not require medical help. It was believed to be the arena of midwives and wise women, not doctors. However, the evidence we have concerning midwifery as a discipline is virtually non-existent, and it can be assumed that as most women in ancient Egypt were illiterate, the skills required were passed on orally[31] and not recorded for prosperity.

Any assertions made about midwives and their craft are therefore speculation. It is believed that priestesses of Heket, the frog deity of childbirth, were possibly trained as midwives, as this would fit in with the role of the deity, but the evidence supporting this is not conclusive. There is only one female physician known from ancient Egypt, called Peseshet from the fourth dynasty. She bore the title 'lady overseer of the lady physicians', which specifies doctors rather than midwives. However, until the Ptolemaic Period there are no other female doctors recorded. However, her title indicates that there were more female physicians than the texts indicate, and it is likely they dealt with female ailments including labour and childbirth. In 700 BCE, the first temple to teach midwives was set up in Sais,[32] indicating that at this time it was considered important to have professionally trained women rather than the village-trained midwives who dominated the profession.

As the few images depicting childbirth are generally divine birth scenes, the midwives present are goddesses and do not provide any information about the realities of childbirth other than the symbolic number and position in which they stood. Papyrus Westcar is the only text that describes childbirth and discusses the birth of the fifth dynasty kings by the woman Ruddedet who was assisted by four goddesses:

On one of those days Ruddedet felt the pangs and her labour was difficult. Then said the Majesty of Re ... to Isis, Nephthys, Meskhenet, Heket, and Khnum: 'Please go, deliver Ruddedet of the three children who are in her womb ... These goddesses set out, having changed their appearance to dancing girls, with Khnum as their porter. When they reached the house of Rawoser, they found him standing with his loincloth upside down ... he said to them: 'My ladies, look, it is the woman who is in pain; her labour is difficult'. They said; 'Let us see her. We understand childbirth'. He said to them; 'Come in!' They went into Ruddedet. They locked the room behind themselves and her.

Isis placed herself before her, Nephthys behind her, Heket hastened the childbirth. Isis said: 'Do not be mighty in her womb you, whose name is Mighty'. The child slid into her arms, a child of one cubit, strong boned, his limbs overlaid with gold, his headdress of pure lapis lazuli. They washed him having cut his naval cord, and laid him on a pillow of cloth.[33] Then Meskhenet approached him, and said: 'A king who will assume the kingship in this whole land!'[34]

Although a work of fiction, it is believed that there was a lot of truth in the details. It is generally assumed that the lack of records about childbirth stem from the reality that men were not welcome in the birthing chamber, and this is supported by the tale on Papyrus Westcar. It is only in recent years in the West that fathers are expected to be in the room during the birth of their children, and therefore this idea of a female-only event is not that difficult to comprehend. That is not to say the ancient Egyptian men were not helpful at the time of childbirth, and indeed present at home, as one text claims: 'it was when I was in the house that you were born'.[35] The absentee record from Deir el Medina shows workmen were present at the time of childbirth, just not necessarily in the room: 'Kasa his wife being in childbirth and he had three days off'.[36]

The precise reason for the absence from work is not clear. It may have been in order to celebrate, although it is more likely that Kasa's wife was having a difficult labour and birth. He probably wanted to be with her in case she died. On another day, the entire Deir el Medina crew had time off for a birth. There was obviously something special about it to warrant the whole crew celebrating or mourning its passing.[37]

There are also records from Deir el Medina that show fathers often bought items for their wives to facilitate the birth. These included custom-made birthing beds with Bes-shaped legs as well as amulets useful during childbirth. Such items could have been kept for subsequent births and may have been valuable additions to the household inventory. These childbirth beds were probably used for the recovery period afterwards rather than the childbirth itself and call to mind the fertility figurines displaying a woman lying on a bed accompanied by a male child.[38]

There are a few artistic renditions of childbirth that include the divine birth scenes and show queen Ahmose, the mother of Hatshepsut, at Deir el Bahri, and Mutemwia, the mother of Amenhotep III, at Karnak, pregnant. The birth itself is depicted in a stylised way, and one scene in the Cairo Museum shows a woman squatting in a birth arbour being helped during the labour by two cow-headed deities.

A further image comes from the mammisi at Armant (50 BCE), and shows a child being born in a more realistic manner. The woman is kneeling on the ground and has her arms raised above her head. They are held by a woman behind her, as another kneels in front and receives or pulls the child out of the womb.[39] A text from Deir el Medina attests to this being the standard position for giving birth. A workman believed he was being punished by the goddess Meretseger and claimed: 'I sat on bricks like the woman in labour'.[40]

An unpublished papyrus in Berlin (P 15765a) also makes reference to birth upon birth-bricks:

> ... as to this noble god when he was delivered upon his birth-brick, his placenta came down and was put in the river (...) after his umbilical cord was cut off, the rope of his placenta with a knife of reed. It became [...] snake in a moment of 170 cubits.[41]

Squatting is seen by many modern health professionals as an excellent way to give birth, as gravity aids with bearing down,[42] although this would not be suitable in cases where there was a problem with the birth and medical intervention was required.[43] However, as the bricks elevated the mother's feet from the floor, it made the baby easily accessible to the helpers.[44] There is, however, one reference that makes no mention of birth-bricks. The Papyrus Brooklyn (47.218.2) dated to the seventh century BCE contains a

Spell for the protection of the bedchamber of the parturient: N born of N lies on a mat of reeds – another saying; a mat of *alfa* grass - while Isis is at her womb, Nephthys is behind her, Hathor is beneath her head, Renenutet is beneath her legs and Ipetweret [*Taweret*] makes her protection.[45]

This indicates that the pregnant woman was lying down surrounded by four goddesses. It is possible that these four goddesses and the four birth-bricks were in fact one and the same.[46] However, as an idealised position for childbirth, squatting is attested by the hieroglyph for a woman giving birth, which shows a kneeling woman with the head and arms of an infant emerging beneath her. This image also had spiritual meaning, as a woman on the birth-bricks with the head emerging between her buttocks was thought to represent the hieroglyphic sign of the horizon of the sun rising between two mountains.[47] This imagery therefore connected the new-born baby with the sun god.

One scholar suggests that the woman crouched on the floor, resting on her own buttocks,[48] although it is generally accepted that the pregnant woman had each foot resting on a birth-brick. There were at least two women helping the woman in labour, one behind to support her and one in front aiding the birth. A bowl of hot water was placed beneath the woman to ease the passage of the child.[49]

With a lack of evidence for the process of childbirth, it is sometimes necessary to turn to funerary evidence, as birth and rebirth rituals were similar. In the New Kingdom, four mud-bricks were placed in niches in the burial chambers of royal tombs, private tombs and the tomb of the Apis Bull. Each brick was associated with a specific deity – a jackal on a shrine, a mummiform image, a reed representing a flame and a Djed pillar, representing resurrection and stability. These bricks bore spell 151 of the Book of the Dead.[50] This text specifies exactly where each brick (and the associated deity) should be placed (north, south, east, or west). Despite this, they were not often found in the correct niche in the wall.[51]

The prayers inscribed on these magical bricks invoke protection from various demons including one: 'whose steps are backwards and whose face is hidden'. This bears a remarkable similarity to a demon that threatens children and is one: 'who comes in darkness and enters creeping, his nose behind, and his face backwards'. This makes the connection between these funerary bricks and those used in childbirth clear, as they obviously had a very similar function.[52]

It is thought that the four goddesses recorded in Papyrus Westcar could be represented by birth-bricks, and the number of bricks matches those discovered in the funerary context. It is thought these four bricks were stacked in two piles, one for each foot, or alternatively her feet and hands rested on the bricks,[53] perhaps giving her the appearance of the sky goddess Nut, spread across the vault of the sky. This in itself would be a powerful position for a pregnant woman to be in, as Nut was the goddess who swallowed the sun god every evening and gave birth to him in the evening. In the Book of Nut it states:

> The Majesty of this god goes forth from her hind part. He proceeds
> to the earth, risen and born (...) He opens the thighs of his mother
> Nut. He withdraws to the sky (...) He opens his amnion. He swims
> in his redness (...) The redness after birth.[54]

A woman giving birth in this position not only equates her with Nut but also the child with the sun god. The birth-brick, a representation of the goddess Meskhenet, whose name derives from the words meaning place of alighting,[55] indicates the purpose was to elevate the woman above the ground.

Only one birth-brick has been discovered in the archaeological record. It was discovered in an administrative building in Abydos, alongside an apotropaic wand and seals bearing the name of princess Reniseneb. It is unknown whether the brick belonged to her or a woman in the household.[56] The brick was made of Nile mud and measured 35 cm long by 17 cm wide, and there was an image of a woman with a baby with a Hathor standard on each side. As the brick was made of black alluvial mud, it added an extra level of significance to it in regard to fertility and birth.[57] However, it is thought that some bricks may have been made of bales of cloth,[58] which could provide an explanation for why so few have been discovered.

Where exactly the birth took place has been a subject of discussion for many years, with some scholars believing the box-bed structure in the first room of the house may have been used as a birthing bed. These structures were built into the wall, and some were painted with images of Bes and Taweret demonstrating a fertility function. In house NE11 at Deir el Medina, the box-bed was found to contain a limestone headrest and a fragment of a female statue, leading to the conclusion that it may have been a ritual place for sexual intercourse.[59] However, these box-beds were rather small (1.7 × 0.80 × 0.75 m3), and while it may have been possible to lie down in one and sleep, squatting in the traditional manner of ancient Egyptian childbirth would have been impossible as well as restricting the movement of the midwives at what was a critical time.

It is more commonly believed that childbirth took place in a special room or an external arbour known as a hrryt. Religious texts refer to a woman in labour giving birth in a 'fine pavilion'.[60] At the town of Tell el Amarna, one house had a small room beneath the stairs, which some have interpreted as a hrryt. In this small room there were two female figurines and model beds, in addition to a stela dedicated to Taweret. However, not all houses had such a permanent feature, as space was at a premium in these compact village houses and therefore most were thought to be temporary structures.

As these arbours were temporary, none has been found in the archaeological record and we have to rely on the artistic record for evidence. Some scholars believe that, as images of this birth arbour can be found in the first room of the houses at Deir el Medina, it is more likely they were somewhere secluded such as under the stairs (as at Amarna) or on the roof. The representations in the first room probably indicate that this room was where birth and fertility was celebrated rather than carried out.[61]

Images have been discovered on ostraca decorated with vines covering the arbour, which most scholars identify as the convolvulus leaf, although Harer[62] suggests it could be the *aristolochia*, which grows wild in Egypt. This plant is often used as a medicament for uterine contraction right up until the modern day, and in Greek the plant was known as 'excellent birth', leaving little doubt as to the purpose of the structure.

This temporary structure may also have been used by the girls in the house during menstruation as a means of purifying themselves.[63] In wealthy families, the absence of the women of the house for a week at a time for menstruation was perhaps not noticeable, as servants were present to carry out the household tasks. However, in the lower middle class families, such as those at Deir el Medina, this absence may have been more inconvenient. This goes some way to explain why some workmen at Deir el Medina took days off work because a woman in their family was menstruating. One can presume he was required at home during this time.

It is thought that during the birthing process there were numerous incantations and rituals designed to protect the woman in labour and the child. One instrument was used throughout the process; the apotropaic wand. These were often made of hippopotamus tusk, as once cut in half, it provided a flat and a convex surface, which was then decorated with carved images of Heket, Taweret and Bes (in his aggressive form as Aha), as well as amuletic symbols including the wadjet eye, the sa and the ankh. Most of the deities depicted are carrying knives, emphasising their role in chasing away threatening demons. Spells recited were designed for protection: 'Cut off the head of the enemy when he enters the chamber of the children whom the lady has borne'.[64]

When the owner's names were inscribed on these wands, they were normally those of the mother and a male child stating they were 'protected by day, protected by night'.[65] This indicates that the male child's name was inscribed on the wand following the birth, as they would not be able to identify whether the child was a boy or girl prior to the birth.

This has led to discussion regarding the time when a child was named, as it is often thought names were not given until much later in childhood. This assumption is based on the numerous child burials where they are simply referred to as the Osiris with no personal name. Some argue that the child was named at birth, as a name was important in order to know the true essence of an individual and was essential for the afterlife. To have no name was to be forgotten. The evidence, however, is inconclusive and possibly varied from family to family.

A number of these apotropaic wands have been discovered in funerary contexts, some of them ritually broken, which may have ensured that any harmful demons were unable to escape. Some have holes in them, indicating they were hung up when not in use.

The edges on some wands are worn away, and it has been suggested that part of their ritual use was to draw protective circles around the mother and baby in the sand. It is also suggested that the wand may have needed to be in contact with the woman during the birth, and perhaps it was rested on her stomach as the midwife chanted spells over her. However, with no supporting written evidence, these ideas are pure conjecture.

Once the birth was complete, the midwife used an obsidian knife to cut the umbilical cord. This knife is called the pesesh-kaf and was shaped like a fish tail and possibly represents a uterus. This knife was also important for rebirth in the afterlife, and was often included in the funerary equipment to ensure that the correct rituals were carried out in order for the deceased to be reborn in the afterlife.

Anything remaining after birth was preserved and often buried with the individual later in life. In the Myth of Horus, Horus finds the umbilical cord of his father and buried it at Hermopolis Magna,[66] as it represented part of his father's body. In chapter 17 of the Book of the Dead, the cutting of the umbilical cord was ritualistically associated with cleansing and therefore when it is cut, 'all the ill which was on me has been removed'.[67]

More important than the umbilical cord was the placenta, which was born at the same time as the baby and was considered to represent the ka (life-force) of the individual. It was therefore retrieved and preserved. Dried placenta appears as an ingredient in some magico-religious spells and was therefore kept in storage. It was deemed so important that there was an official title of 'Priest of the Royal Placenta', although his exact role is unclear. In the 1920s, women in Egypt buried the placenta under the threshold of their door or in a large bowl in order to bury it with food offerings under the floor. In this manner, the woman hoped to conceive again quickly. This ritual seems to be paralleled in the Middle Kingdom town of El Lahun, where large empty bowls were discovered alongside infant burials and associated food offerings.[68]

The birth was categorised according to its ease and therefore success, with 'Htp' being satisfactory, 'bnd' being difficult, and 'wdf' being protracted. In order to ascertain whether the child would live, the midwife listened to the baby's first cry. If it was ny, then the child would live, but if it was mb then the child would surely die. A new mother, following the birth, was in confinement for fourteen days along with the child. This was to ensure both the health of the mother who may be prone to infection and the new born baby. Images of the woman in confinement show a very distinctive hairstyle, which comprised a number of bunches tied on top of her head and falling down the side of her face.[69]

Following the birth of a child, there was also a celebration, which probably took place at the end of the fourteen-day confinement. A journal entry from Deir el Medina (O CGC 25521) simply announces 'his feast because of his daughter',[70] although whether his daughter was born or had given birth is not specified. Records indicate the birth was celebrated in the Place of Hard Drinking, which was connected to a religious structure and was therefore a means of thanking the gods while also getting drunk.

Another letter from Deir el Medina, refers to an unmarried servant girl who gave birth to the sculptor, Neferenpet's child. The recipient of the letter was encouraged to bring bread, meat and cakes, oil and honey to her. Perhaps, married women received these things automatically from their husband or family, but in this case the recipient of the letter obviously needed reminding.[71] Alternatively, it could be that this person was encouraged to bring food in order to participate in a celebratory feast.

Unlike some ancient cultures, while all couples preferred sons over daughters, girls were not exposed, murdered or abandoned. In the Roman Period however, this changed, and in Oxyrhynchus Papyrus 744 (1BCE) a man tells his wife: 'if it is a girl, expose it'. However, in the Pharaonic Period all children were raised with the expectation that they would care for their parents in old age. However, girls, as discussed in chapter 2, moved upon marriage to the home of their husband, but boys, on the other hand, stayed at home and their wife moved in, providing another person to help in the household. Boys were also expected to take over the family business in the sense of taking over the role of their father once he retired or died.

Once the child was born, it was traditional for the mother to nurse it for up to three years. Not only did this ensure safe and healthy food for the baby during the most vulnerable time of their lives but also acted as a contraceptive allowing the mother to space out her pregnancies. According to the instruction texts, breastfeeding was a noble thing, and Papyrus Lansing (a schoolbook) compares it to the pleasure of writing:

> ... more enjoyable than a mother's giving birth, when her heart knows no distaste. She is constant in nursing her son; her breast is in his mouth every day.[72]

The connection between the mother's health and the quality of her milk was well known, and therefore, should the child be ill, the medicine was fed to the nursing mother, with the belief the child would receive the benefit in the milk. Ensuring there was enough quality milk was obviously a concern of the doctors, and the Ebers Papyrus advises: 'To induce milk in the woman breastfeeding a child, the backbone of a fish to be baked in oil and rubbed on her back'.[73]

Other means of inducing milk was via sympathetic magic, through invoking Taweret, the hippopotamus goddess of childbirth. In Berlin, there are three statues of Taweret, two of which have removable clothes. The third statue has holes in the breasts, and it is thought this vessel was filled with milk in the hope the mother could produce good milk for her baby.[74]

However, not all milk was considered good enough quality, and it is stated that with bad breast milk 'you shall perceive that its smell is like the stench of fish'.[75] Presumably, in this situation the mother should refrain from feeding her baby. In a situation like this, or one where the mother was not producing milk, the mother died, or the family could simply afford it, an alternative was to hire a wet nurse to feed the child.

Having a wet nurse was considered a status symbol in the New Kingdom, especially if your wet nurse had also fed the influential. Some officials called themselves milk-brother to the king in order to show they had a shared wet nurse. Wet nurses were almost as revered as mothers, and from the Middle Kingdom, their names were included on funerary stela alongside other members of the family.

In some cases, the contractual expectations have survived between a wet nurse and the family. The child fed by the wet nurse should be inspected by the mother regularly in order to monitor its health and growth, and the wet nurse could only feed her own child and the employers' children. Should the nurse have sexual intercourse or indeed fall pregnant while feeding the child, then her contract would be terminated.

The most common image of a nursing mother shows the goddess Hathor or Isis nursing the king, emphasising his divine nature. While goddesses are shown in this position, it is very unusual for a queen to be shown breastfeeding. A bronze statue from the Second Intermediate Period is one of the few depictions of a royal woman nursing. The image depicts princess Sobeknakht breastfeeding her son. Both figures have the ureaus on their brow, clearly identifying them as royal. The title of the statue identifies her as 'hereditary noblewoman', which is an unusual title. It appears elsewhere on a scarab alongside the title 'king's daughter', clearly identifying them as the same woman. Although given earthly titles, the representation shows her as divine performing the role of a mother goddess.

There are a handful of images showing ordinary women breastfeeding, including one from house SE1 at Deir el Medina. In the first room, there is a wall painting of a woman breastfeeding, indicating perhaps this was the room within which the women resided. In house C7, in the first room an image shows a female grooming with her attendant, and in house NW12 a woman is depicted on a papyrus skiff. All these images indicate that the first room was a feminine, sexualised space[76] and may have been where the women carried out their daily tasks. Often the women depicted breastfeeding are nameless, and perhaps represent 'ideal' mothers rather than individuals. For example, in New Kingdom tombs, nameless peasant women are shown suckling as they continue their daily chores, or there are vessels in the form of a woman holding a child. Although rarely is the child shown nursing, the woman is sometimes shown cupping her breast in preparation. It is likely that these jars contained milk and represent 'spiritual' wet nurses, as they have hairstyles that are distinct from those of pregnant women and new mothers. The main body of hair falls down the back, and there are two long, thin locks hanging down on either side of the face.

Unfortunately for many children, despite being breastfed for up to three years, they died in infancy. There were numerous infections that could be contracted, and in the absence of antibiotics these were incurable. Many children were buried in jars or boxes beneath the floors of the houses and many were unnamed, simply referred to as the Osiris to demonstrate their rebirth (*see* chapter 9). However, one stela, belonging to the child Isemkheb, survives from the twenty-first dynasty:

> I worship your ka, O Lord of the gods
> Though I am but a child!
> Harm is what befell me
> When I was but a child!
> A faultless one reports it.
> I lie in the vale, a young girl.
> I thirst with water beside me!
> I was driven from childhood too early!
> Turned away from my house as a youngster
> Before I had my fill in it!
> The dark, a child's terror engulfed me,
> While the breast was in my mouth![77]

At Deir el Medina, the lowest region of the eastern cemetery was dedicated to the burial of foetuses, neonates, and infants as well as the detritus of childbirth including placentas, viscera and blood-soaked cloths. Each burial comprised a shallow pit, less than a metre deep. They were placed in a variety of vessels including amphora, baskets, boxes or even coffins with a small array of grave goods such as food and beer. Later, in the New Kingdom, these child burials were incorporated into the tombs of the adults.

Childbirth must have been a terrifying and traumatic time for the women, as there were so many things that could go wrong endangering their lives and those of their new-born baby. Some of these dangers have been recently outlined, albeit in a study of a Roman cemetery in Egypt, which is much later than the period covered in this volume. Two of the children who died at eighteen months old both suffered broken clavicles during childbirth, which was due to pressure passing through the birth canal and accounts for 90 per cent of trauma in modern childbirth. Two other individuals suffered breaks to their humeri, possibly caused by rotation or hyperextention of the arm during birth, which is also reflected in modern birth trauma.[78] Breech births are also represented in this cemetery, where the cervical vertebrae were broken as a result of forcing the birth. The researchers suggested that this part of the cemetery may reflect a 'particularly rough midwife or possibly that females linked to this part of the cemetery had problematic obstetric dimensions'.[79]

The traumas experienced by these children are still experienced in the modern world, and therefore is likely to have been suffered by those in the Pharaonic Period. It is difficult to imagine the upset of these women who lost child after child while knowing that it was an accepted part of life and one they could do nothing about.

5

HOMOSEXUALITY

'How beautiful are your buttocks, how vital!'[1]

In previous chapters, we have investigated heterosexual relationships, essentially those that ended in marriage and children. However, the homosexual lives of the ancient Egyptians is a little more complex, as there are even fewer records because such relationships never ended in marriage or some other documented agreement. So the question is, did homosexuality occur in ancient Egypt? The simple answer is yes, but a more important question is how was homosexuality expressed in ancient Egypt?

Trying to identify and subsequently discuss homosexuality in ancient Egypt is a difficult task, and not just because the evidence is lacking, but also because the concept of homosexuality, as we understand it, did not exist in the ancient past. Terms such as 'gay', 'lesbian' or even 'homosexual' are modern terms associated with modern contextual constructs and cannot be applied to the ancient past, and indeed none of these words existed in ancient Egypt. Furthermore, there was no word for sexuality, as the concept did not exist in the same way. To give an idea of the modernity of the terms, the word 'homosexual' was only introduced in the 1860s CE.[2] As such modern terminology generally used describes modern constructs, ancient sexuality is often misread, as we can only interpret it within the boundaries of these constructs.[3] Moving away from these terms, and their associated meanings, is however extremely difficult. So, how do we discuss such relationships in the past? Meskell suggests that the only appropriate term to use is 'same-sex relations',[4] but even this neutral term is not one that was used by the ancient Egyptians themselves.

In the modern world, the terminology we use describes the person, for example, 'N is gay', whereas in ancient Egyptian the sexual act was referred to more than the person. Homosexual relationships were categorised according to who was penetrat*ing* and who was penetrat*ed*. The former had no specific label or title, whereas the latter was known as *nkkw*, he who is penetrated, or *Hmiw*, back-turners or cowards, which is related to the word *Hmt*, wife, indicating this passive element of homosexuality.[5] In the Old Kingdom, there was a broader element of abuse and aggression attached to the term nkkw, which changed in the New Kingdom to simply refer to passivity of the act of being penetrated.[6] A rather controversial term, *Hmt-T3y* is used in the Instruction of Ptahhotep, and there has been much debate about the translation as it combines male and female sexuality. It has been translated as woman boy,[7] vulva boy,[8] the wife and a man[9] or, more commonly, a woman who has intercourse with a man (*see* chapter 2). The section in the text is discussing the effects of greed, which naturally are negative:

> It embroils fathers and mothers, with mother's brothers.
> It entangles the *wife and the man (Hmt T3y)*.
> It is a levy of all evils, a bundle of all hatefulness.[10]

Some have even suggested that this term refers to a male prostitute who is acting as a means of expelling such homosexual/abnormal feelings.[11] However, it is not the same-sex relationship that was opposed in ancient Egypt, but rather the passive role of being penetrated. There was rarely complaint or negativity about the instigator of homosexual sex, only the recipient of it. It was this passivity that defined the person in a negative way, not their homosexuality.[12]

Anthropological studies have clarified the opinion held by the ancient Egyptians to a certain extent. In Latin America, homosexual relationships are viewed in a similar way, where those who penetrate are considered the gendered male and those who are penetrated are the gendered female.[13] In most cultures, males being gendered female due to particular behaviour is considered negative, and therefore the social associations are often enough to encourage them to avoid the 'female' behaviour.

This was likely the case in ancient Egypt, as men invariably describe themselves using the word *nht*, which means power/strength or erection. In the Ptolemaic Period nome-list[14] at Edfu, the god Min is described as 'boasting of his *nht*' and is a clear play on words, as he is always depicted with an erect penis. He could be boasting of his erection or overall masculine strength. The same word-play is used in a dream book where dreaming of an erection (*nht*) is the portent of victory (*nht*) over an enemy.[15] The phallus, in text or illustration, was not just a display of sexual power but general masculinity and male power in society. It is clear that a man would prefer to be labelled as *nht* rather than *Hmiw* (back-turner), and homosexual relationships are often presented as an expression of power rather than desire.[16]

This therefore indicates that avoiding homosexual relations was more for social than religious or legal reasons. In ancient Egypt, everyone was expected to marry and produce children, although evidence shows that not everyone did this. If wives appear to be absent in tombs (which is often the only means of identifying the existence of such relationships), it is often used as evidence that the tomb owner was divorced, celibate, widowed or homosexual.[17] However, being unmarried did not necessarily prove homosexuality, in the same way that marriage did not prove heterosexuality. Studies done on 93 eighteenth dynasty tombs show that only three did not show any evidence for a wife.[18] This does indicate being unmarried was an unusual state of affairs, and therefore it could be suggested many homosexual men were in fact married.

In addition to the negativity surrounding the penetrated man in a homosexual relationship, relationships were expected to be procreative, and therefore any in which this was not possible was considered a waste and actively discouraged.[19] There were also more far-reaching concerns, as such unproductive relationships also hindered rebirth into the afterlife.[20] Fertility, conception and birth were all important elements in the rebirth of an individual (*see* chapter 9) and were governed by the ability to produce children. Moreover, anything that deviated from this accepted social norm in regard to sexual relations was considered taboo.[21]

Therefore, adultery, while being a form of taboo sex, was considered more socially acceptable than a homosexual relationship, as an adulterous relationship could result in offspring. The wisdom text of Ankhsheshonq reinforces this idea when he states: 'Do not take a young man for your companion'.[22] As he does not explicitly mention intercourse, he could be referring to the wider sense of a relationship, excluding all women. These ideas are further emphasised in chapter 125 of the Book of the Dead, the so-called Negative Confession which states: 'I have not done wrong sexually or committed homosexuality'.[23]

In this chapter of the Book of the Dead, homosexuality is associated with adultery (done wrong sexually), which strongly indicates they were viewed in the same way: a deviation from Maat but not necessarily a crime.[24] The Negative Confession is a complex text, which can be misleading when trying to identify levels of criminality or disapproval, as trivial misdemeanours (adultery) are listed along with serious crimes (murder) almost on equal footing, making it difficult to assign the level of acceptability. The act of homosexuality as described in the Book of the Dead refers to the act of instigating such a relationship as the literal translation is 'I have not *nkd a nkk(w)*' or 'I have not had penetrative sex with a man upon who penetrative sex is performed'.[25] Such an act is seen as an act of aggression against another person and makes no reference to the emotions or desires involved. This is further emphasised in the Coffin Texts (spell 635) where the deceased states:

Re has no power over N.
[It is N] who takes away his breath.
Atum has not power over N
N *nks* his backside (CT VI 258 f-g).[26]

The aggressive element of penetrative sex between males is emphasised by a single case of male-rape recorded in the Turin Indictment Papyrus. It is a 'charge concerning the violation done by this sailor Panakhtta [... to ...] a field labourer of the estate of Khnum, Lord of Elephantine'.[27] The outcome of this charge was not recorded. Neither are the social connotations associated with being a victim or perpetrator of male rape.

Female rape is recorded in the literary stories of Petese from the third century BCE, where there is a tale about the rape of a woman called Hatmehit:

He [Psemmut] was the servant while his wife [Hatmehit] poured drinks for the men. It happened one day that the Prophet of Horus [of Pe] saw Hatmehit and he desired her very much. He had her brought to his home by force. He slept with her ...[28]

The situation gets a little confusing as Hatmehit convinces the priest to bring her husband Psemmut to the house. Obviously, he confronts the priest, resulting in his imprisonment, as the priest refuses to allow Hatmehit to be taken from him. As the end of the tale is missing, we do not know what punishment if any was administered to the Prophet of Horus-of-Pe. The penalty for rape generally was said to have been amputation of the sexual organs,[29] or possibly even death,[30] although whether the penalty was the same for male and female rape is not recorded. The act, however, is naturally condemned, and in one nobleman's autobiography he states: 'There was no citizen's daughter whom I misused'.[31]

Later in the Negative Confession, it states the deceased did not *nk* a *Hmt-T3y* or 'have penetrative sex with a married woman' (should that be the correct translation of *Hmt-T3y*), indicating such taboo sexual acts were on a par with one another.[32] However, as with most things in ancient Egypt, attitudes towards sex changed over time, and these clauses only appear in the Negative Confession after the eighteenth dynasty, which could suggest that prior to this the attitude was more positive.[33]

As time progressed, the attitude towards homosexuality deteriorated further, and a text from the Heracleopolitan Period (2160–2040 BCE) from Abydos indicates there were legal repercussions for homosexual behaviour:

I did not wish to love a youth. As for the respectable son who does it, his (own) father shall abandon him in court.[34]

As with all the texts that are interpreted as mentioning or referring to homosexuality, there is some doubt as to the exact nature of the term 'love a youth' and why this would necessarily end up in the court. However, some of the Goedicke interpretations are often refuted, and a more likely translation of this text reads:

> I haven't aimed my desires at a married woman I haven't desired
> the beloved of a citizen.[35]

Although this translation is not about a homosexual relationship, it is interesting that adultery and homosexuality are confused in the ancient texts, suggesting perhaps socially they were considered equal. The Teaching of the Vizier Ptahhotep offers additional advice on such behaviour:

> May you not have sex with a woman-boy, for you know that what
> is opposedwill be water upon his breast. There is no coolness (i.e.
> relief) for what is in his belly (i.e. his appetite).[36]

The meaning of this paragraph, however, is not totally clear, and the translation is open to discussion. This interpretation suggests that succumbing to desires like same-sex desire will bring no relief and therefore should be avoided. However, Goedicke translates the last line in a completely different manner: 'there is no calming to one who is in his bowels'.[37] He takes this to have a more graphic representation and very clear condemnation of penetrative sex between two men.

The issue of interpretation can once more be viewed in the twelfth dynasty text 'The Dispute Between a Man and his Ba'. One translation of the paragraph in question states:

> Lo my name reeks,
> Lo more than that of a sturdy child,
> Who is said to belong to one who rejects him.[38]

This is a sad commentary on a rejected child, and the associated taboos, reactions and emotions associated with this. However, Goedicke translates the same verse with a homosexual spin: 'A valiant lad against whom it is said: "he belonged to the one whom he hates"'.[39]

According to this translation, the text is of a sexual nature and laments giving oneself sexually to someone despised, presumably a homosexual man. The homosexual act here is not the problem, but rather the lack of mutual satisfaction and consent. However, as the translations are so very different, can they really be said to reflect social commentary on homosexuality in ancient Egypt? Or, do these differing translations reflect the views of the Egyptologists? With such a subject, which is difficult to prove one way or another, these linguistic debates will no doubt continue far into the future.

Regardless of how it was accepted in society, homosexuality or same-sex relationship was a part of Egyptian life, so much so that it was included in religious texts, literary texts and poetry. However, as mentioned, homosexuality did not have the necessary lifestyle choices or associations that it does in the modern world, and Parkinson has suggested that to ancient Egyptians: 'Sexual preferences were acknowledged but only as one would recognise someone's taste in food'.[40]

Some love poetry is believed to discuss same-sex desire, although as the narrators are never identified it can be difficult to identify whether they were male or female. However, it has been suggested that in this poem, where the narrator has fallen in love with a young charioteer, the obstacle is the same-sex nature of the relationship:

On the way I met Mehy on his chariot, with him were his young men.
I knew not how to avoid him. Should I stride on to pass him?
But the river was the road, I knew no place for my feet.

My heart you are very foolish, why accost Mehy?
If I pass before him, I tell him my movements.
Here I'm yours I say to him. Then he will shout my name,
And assign me to the first ... among his followers.[41]

While the narrator does not specify why he feels he cannot approach
Mehy, it could be because of the taboo nature of same-sex desire.
According to the Instruction of the Vizier Ptahhotep (32nd maxim),
homosexual desires were a natural weakness of man and something
to be overcome or ignored:

Let him not spend the night doing what is opposed;
He shall be cool after renouncing his desire.[42]

Just as the Egyptians were advised to avoid acting on their desires,
such suppression is also evidence in the interpretations of modern
Egyptologists. Therefore, should two men be depicted together in
unusually intimate positions, they are identified as twins rather
than entertain the idea they were in a homosexual relationship.[43]

Depictions of men embracing is not particularly unusual in a
royal context, and in the Middle Kingdom temple of Senusret I and
the White Chapel at Karnak the king is shown numerous times
embracing the god, oftentimes the ithyphallic deity Amun-Min.
This particular deity was important to the king for the continuance
of his reign, and he would often perform the sed festival before this
god, the rejuvenation ceremony to show his suitability to continue
ruling Egypt (*see* chapter 3). In these scenes, the god is completely
covered in a cloak with only his erect penis protruding from the
front, indicating this was an important element of the cult.

It also needs to be considered that such temple and chapel images
were only accessible to men. Therefore, with an intended male

audience they could be considered as homoerotic although not necessarily homosexual.[44] These images essentially demonstrate the king (a male) worshipping the fecundity of an erect penis. This was in fact a theme that was popular from the Predynastic Period until the second century CE and the destruction of such images by the Coptic Bishop Schenute.[45]

The earliest ithyphallic images can be found with the colossal statues found by Petrie at Koptos of the god Min. He is shown as an upright standing figure, holding his erect penis in his hand, although the penis is now missing. Unfortunately, many of these ithyphallic temple images of Amun-Min have had the penises chipped away either in anti-pagan campaigns or by people believing that the scenes held restorative or aphrodisiacal properties and therefore ground out the stone in order to consume it.[46]

In Middle Kingdom tomb chapels, which also had an intended male audience, male bodies were over-masculine with clearly defined muscles. It was clearly important to be considered impressive to other men, but not necessarily desirable to them. There was a fine-line between homoeroticism and homosexual desire, which may not have been very clear in a world where the sexes were often segregated by role and position, meaning men worked and socialised with men and women with the women.

From a young age, boys would have been aware of homosexuality, as it was considered such a normal if not necessarily acceptable part of everyday life, that it was a prominent element in religious mythology. The myth known as the Contendings of Horus and Seth is the tale of the conflict between Seth, the god of chaos, and his nephew, Horus the god of order. Seth wanted to take the throne of Egypt, following the murder of his brother Osiris, from the rightful descendent, Osiris's son Horus. This conflict ends in an eighty-year tribunal, and in various incidents, including sexual, between the two deities. The homosexual encounters that took place between Horus and Seth are always instigated by Seth, the god of chaos, with Horus as the recipient:

> Seth said to Horus, 'How beautiful are your buttocks, how vital! Stretch out your legs'. Horus said, 'Wait that I may tell it.'... Horus said to his mother Isis, 'Seth wants to know me'. She said to him, 'Take care. Do not go near him for that. Next time he mentions it to you, you shall say to him; It is too difficult because of my build, as you are heavier than I am. My strength is not the same as yours'. She says 'When he has aroused you, place your fingers between your buttocks ... the seed which has come forth from his penis without letting the sun see it'.[47]

Isis' response is surprising, as rather than condemning the action, she advises Horus what to do once he has been aroused. She indicates Seth is the problem, as he is instigating homosexual intercourse as a display of power which even Seth states is the 'work of a male' or 'warrior'.[48] This presents Horus as the weaker rival in the activity, and therefore places him in the inferior position.[49] Isis believes Horus should use his youthfulness and weakness as an excuse to repel Seth. However, the act of penetrative sex while being an embarrassment for Horus, as the *nkkw,* was for Seth 'sweet to his heart'.[50] Montserrat, on the other hand, interprets the act of intercourse as more equal than the religious and moral commentary suggests, with Seth making the propositions but Horus willingly agreeing to them anticipating that he would enjoy the experience.[51]

In order to retaliate against Seth, Horus sprinkled his semen over the lettuce garden of Seth. Seth ate lettuces every day and therefore unbeknown to him became the penetrated agent in this homosexual encounter. Returning once more to the tribunal, Seth explains to the gods that he has penetrated Horus. They react with contempt towards Horus, the weaker individual in this scenario, but Horus retaliates and claims that the situation is in fact reversed. He summons his semen as proof:

> Then Thoth, lord of script and scribe of truth for the Ennead, put his hand on Horus's shoulder and said: 'Come out, you semen of Seth' ... Thoth put his hand on Seth's shoulder and said: 'Come out, you semen of Horus'. Then it said to him: 'Where shall I come from?' Thoth said to it: 'Come out from his ear'.
>
> Thereupon it said to him: 'Is it from his ear that I should issue forth, seeing that I am divine seed?' Then Thoth said to it: 'Come out from the top of his head'. And it emerged as a golden solar disk upon Seth's head. Seth became exceeding furious and extended his hand(s) to seize the golden solar disk. Thoth took it away from him and placed it as a crown upon his (own) head. Then the Ennead said: 'Horus is right, and Seth is wrong'.[52]

As Seth had consumed Horus' semen after it had been sprinkled over his lettuce garden, it placed him as the one who had been dominated and was therefore, in the minds of the gods, worthy of contempt.[53]

It should be taken into consideration that this myth is not intended as a piece of political or social commentary but is a literary tale with the ultimate objective of identifying the laws of accession for the throne of Egypt. This is reflected to a certain extent the variance in ancient transcriptions of the story. For example, the Old Kingdom Pyramid Texts (1036) indicates the act was reciprocated with both Seth and Horus penetrating the other: 'Horus insinuated his semen into the backside of Set and Set insinuated his semen into the backside of Horus'.[54] In the Middle Kingdom Petrie Papyrus fragment (UC 32158), a softer approach is taken where Seth instigates the exchange with what is said to be the first chat-up line in history[55]: 'How beautiful are your buttocks, how vital!' This is in fact a parody of the traditional greeting of 'How fair is your face!'[56] Papyrus Chester Beatty I, from the twentieth dynasty, however, states Seth took his penis and 'inserted it between the thighs of Horus', indicating the act was instigated by Seth, more as a show of power than reciprocal desire. Could these changing approaches to the act of Seth and Horus reflect a change in social attitude? It is something that is difficult to prove based on a literary tale.

However, it is not only Horus and Seth who engage in homosexual activities in the religious mythology. In the Coffin Texts Geb, the god of the earth honours the deceased by stating: 'his phallus is between the buttocks of his son and his heir' (CT VI 333h). It is thought that here Geb is the son and the penis belongs to the dead man.[57] The actual function of this act is not made clear.

So, while homosexual acts were present in religious texts, and instruction texts advised against such sexual activity as abnormal and socially unacceptable, how widespread was homosexuality within the population of Egypt? In order to identify this, especially in the life of the elite, the most obvious place to look is in the tombs and funerary monuments. However, the evidence, as patchy as it is, is ambiguous and raises more questions than it answers.

Unlike most other aspects of Egyptian social life, there is no evidence from Deir el Medina of homosexuality, which could mean it was so common that it was not recorded or that as it did not result in any legal cases there was no real need to record it. If homosexuality was similar to adultery, then a so-called paper-trail is counterproductive with secrecy. However, other sites have produced scraps of evidence. For example, a twelfth dynasty faience funerary figure from Lisht came under scrutiny when it was identified as a 'male concubine' figure for a male tomb owner.

The figure apparently depicts a squatting male wearing a patterned kilt with a 'gross obscenity'[58] or an enormous erect penis. Riefstahl offers various interpretations of the figure, including that it was a symbol of the tomb owner's homosexuality, and once it was placed in the tomb it would be: 'a forbidden pleasure which the Egyptian of Tomb 315 ... had enjoyed in this this world or hoped to enjoy in a better world to come'.[59] However, further examination of the piece has debunked this theory, as the so-called erect penis is now identified as the stand of an offering table.[60]

A more promising piece of evidence is a thirteenth dynasty stela from Abydos, dedicated to a harpist called Neferhotep, son of Henu, which mentions no wife or children. The more interesting aspect is that the stela was commissioned by 'his friend whom he loved, the brick-carrier, Nebsumenu'. Generally such stelae are dedicated by family members, so this is unusual. Unfortunately, it is impossible to speculate as to what kind of friend Nebsumenu was: a work colleague, a friend, or a lover,[61] but one that was close enough to commission such an intimate funerary item.

Another ambiguous stela was donated to the deity Upwawet at Asyut by two military men Ramose and Upwawetmose. Neither man holds a title, but the latter was called: 'the greatly praised' and 'organiser of pleasure'. However, it was clear from their kilts that they were low-ranking military men. What is rather intriguing is that the stela depicts a number of *ba* figures of Amun-Re connecting the inscription with male potency or fertility. If the stela depicted a married couple, this fertility connection would not be so unusual, but as they are two men, their relationship is questioned. Are they brothers, twins or possibly lovers?[62] However, it seems rather unusual for brothers or twins to appeal to a god for potency without their wives depicted, but conversely, if they were in a same-sex relationship, potency and fertility would not be an issue as they would be unable to produce children.

Another stela, currently in the British Museum (826), is the eighteenth dynasty stela of Suty and Hor. They were more than likely twin brothers due to the unambiguous statement that: 'But my brother, my likeness, his ways I trust, he came forth with me from the womb on the same day'.[63]

They are thought to be the only documented twins from ancient Egypt.[64] However, it does not specify that he came from the same mother and therefore they could simply have the same birthday. However, they were both overseers of the works of Amun under Amenhotep III,[65] and the phrase 'my likeness' really indicates they were indeed twins. They were also named after the gods Seth and Horus, who while not twins are the polar opposites of each other (chaos and order). What is rather intriguing is that their figures have been erased from the stela as have most examples of their names and titles, indicating they fell out of favour at some point, although why is unknown.

The most commonly discussed potential evidence of homosexual relationships is the fifth dynasty mastaba of Niankhkhnum and Khnumhotep in Saqqara. Since its discovery in the 1960s, the nature of their relationship has been discussed widely. Both men were manicurists of the king, and inspectors of manicurists of the palace during the reign of king Neuserre (2453–2422 BCE). These titles have fuelled the discussions regarding homosexuality due to modern twenty-first-century stereotypes that a male manicurist must be homosexual. In reality, the position of manicurist to the king was a revered position and ensured they were in close proximity to the king on a daily basis.[66] Moreover, it is suggested that rather than the king needing two people to do this job of manicurist, they both performed the job of a single person,[67] rather like a job share.

The unusual depictions of the two men together, holding hands and embracing, has fuelled discussions about a possible homosexual relationship. It was unusual for couples (male/female) to embrace completely, as normally the woman embraced the man, rather than embracing each other.[68] Khnumhotep in particular is depicted in what is traditionally considered feminine poses and perhaps indicates there was a male/female duality to their relationship.[69]

For example, Khnumhotep is depicted smelling lotus flowers, which in the Old Kingdom was normally reserved for women. Men smelling lotus flowers became more common in the eighteenth dynasty,[70] but he is one of only three men in the fifth dynasty as a whole shown in this position.[71] It is clear that stylistically Khnumhotep is holding the position of 'wife' in this tomb,[72] and in one scene Niankhkhnum leads Khnumnakht into the tomb by his hand. This representation is paralleled in the mastaba tomb of Mereruka, who leads his wife Seshseshet Waatetkhethor into the tomb in exactly the same way.[73] One image opposite the false door in Niankhkhnumn and Khnumhotep's tomb shows the men face-to-face, nose-to-nose and even the knots on their belts are touching. It is clear they are kissing rather than simply embracing and this is unprecedented in any other tomb depicting two men together.[74] The level of affection they show to each other in the form of embracing, touching faces and holding hands is something normally demonstrated by only married couples,[75] and therefore must make some reference to their relationship together.

Beneath the banquet scene in the tomb, there is an unusual but intriguing image of musicians, which comprised a conductor leading three singers and two harpists. He directs the musicians to 'play the one about the divine brothers', which can only refer to the story of Seth and Horus (discussed above). It is interesting to consider which aspects of the Horus and Seth mythology was sung about for the two men. Normally, banquets were steeped with erotic symbolism anyway, and there is no reason to assume it was different when the banquet was overseen by two male friends rather than a married couple.[76]

The wives of both Niankhkhnum and Khnumhotep are represented in the tomb, and presumably also buried there. They are, however, not shown in the same intimate positions as seem to be reserved for the two men. This in itself was rather unusual, as when wives were shown, they were normally holding hands with or embracing their husbands.[77] However, rather unusually, in one banquet scene Niankhkhumn's wife has been erased, and all that is visible is the shadow of her hand on his shoulder. In this scene, Khumnhotep's wife was completely omitted.[78] Although the wives are represented, it is disproportionate to the representations of the two men together, with the wives shown three or four times, whereas Niankhkhnum and Khnumhotep are depicted more than thirty times.[79] This in itself has been used to show how the relationship between the men and their wives was marginalised. The omission of a man's wife in his tomb does not necessarily mean he was unmarried, divorced or homosexual in the same way that the depiction of a wife and children in the tomb does not exclude the possibility of same-sex relationships before or after marriage.[80]

A study of artistic trends throughout the Dynastic Period shows that in the Old Kingdom it was not common to show the wife in the tomb anyway. Wives appeared in the tombs only in the fourth dynasty[81] and were depicted once or twice throughout the tomb, significantly less frequently than the male tomb-owner. In the middle of the fifth dynasty, wives disappeared from the tombs altogether until the beginning of the sixth dynasty, although they still only appeared in two-thirds of tombs. Nearly 40 per cent of Old Kingdom tombs do not include images of the wife, showing this was not unusual.[82] This study does therefore indicate that the few representations of Niankhkhnum's and Khnumhotep's wives were within the normal range of representation, and in fact revered them by representing them at all.

So what is the nature of the two men's relationship? The most accepted theory is that they were twins[83] and therefore closer than average siblings as emphasised by their exaggerated displays of affection. However, even Baines, the pioneer of this theory, states that it is 'unprovable'.[84] Such embracing has been compared to the images of the king embracing his ka (spirit) in tomb images, and the ka is sometimes even referred to as the twin of the deceased, emphasising their closeness and their necessity to be together to aid rebirth (*see* chapter 9). These scenes normally transmit the ka to the deceased, either by a god passing it to the king or a parent to a child. Yet in this tomb, as they are embracing each other, they are potentially passing their kas to each other. O'Connor had an even more extreme theory to explain their tight embraces; they were co-joined twins.[85]

Although neither of the men's parents are named in the tomb, their similar names and titles could indicate they were at least brothers.[86] Some scholars believe that the choice of the god Khnum to be the men's namesakes further proves their status as twins, as Khnum is a creator god who moulds a person and their ka (twin) on a potter's wheel[87] However, nowhere in the tomb do they refer to each other as brother, although relationships between people are not always recorded in tomb inscriptions. This could be because claiming one is the brother of another places them into an inferior position, which is acceptable if they appeared in each other's tombs, but unacceptable in a shared tomb.

It is possible that their parents are depicted in the tomb, although not clearly identified as such. There is a row of figures depicted comprising a male and female couple at the front, two men, three women and three men. The two men bringing up the rear are holding hands and are identified as Niankhkhnum and Khnumhotep, and the procession is led by a ship's captain. It is thought the couple at the front could be the parents of both men or one of them, but unfortunately none of the people have any identifying text.[88]

Another suggestion is that they were metaphorical brothers, where, as they had the same titles and role, they may have been friends who had the same influence and values, resulting in being considered equal in the afterlife.[89] In the fishing and fowling scene, an important event in most tombs to aid the deceased in rebirth, Niankhkhnum is shown fishing and Khnumhotep is shown fowling. Normally, the tomb owner would perform both tasks, but it is suggested they were considered to be one person and therefore should one perform a ritual task the other benefitted from it in the afterlife.[90]

It is unfortunate that, should these men have been twins, as some believe, they made no reference to this as Suty and Hor did on their stela, meaning such an assumption is not based on firm evidence. Baines even suggests that there was some taboo against twins in ancient Egypt, which he believes is expressed here through non-verbal expression but hinted at through intimate depiction.[91]

However, both of these theories of brotherhood or twinship can be thrown into doubt. The dominance of Niankhkhnum in the tomb, and the so-called feminisation of Khnumhotep, could be because Niankhkhnumn commissioned the tomb. It appears that Khnumhotep died first, leaving Niankhkhnum in control of the decoration. Some scenes show Khnumhotep with a curled divine beard being honoured by the 'great god', whereas Niankhkhnum bears more human epithets and does not have a curled beard.[92]

If the assumptions are correct and Khnumhotep died first, then it is impossible they were co-joined twins, as it is unlikely that Niankhkhnum could have survived separation surgery at this time in history. However, does that prove they were simply brothers or twins? Baines comments that as twins they were likely to have been treated as a single person rather than two independent individuals.[93] However, this may appear to be the case in their own tomb, but it is only in their tomb that they are depicted side by side and in intimate positions. In the tomb of the vizier Ptahshepses at Abusir, both Niankhkhnum and Khnumhotep are depicted but in isolation of each other, indicating they were not viewed by everyone as one person and were able to function separately. In the earlier part of Ptahshepses' tomb, Khnumhotep, the barber of the great house, and ka servant, is depicted on his own. It is thought this may be the same person in his role prior to becoming the manicurist to the king. As there is no mention of Niankhkhnum at all, this could represent a time before they met each other. Surely, if they were twins, it is likely they would always be depicted together, even if they had different job roles.

The conundrum of their relationship could be solved if the bodies of Niankhkhnum and Khnumhotep had survived. Without them, we are left purely with the images that strongly support a same-sex affection unprecedented in any other Egyptian tomb. It may never be possible to categorise this relationship as just good friends, brothers or a homosexual relationship.

As the evidence for homosexual relationships among the elite is difficult to prove irrefutably, it is even more ambiguous to identify such relationships among royalty. Imagery in royal tombs and on monuments was more regimented than for the elite, with more rules to be followed. This means that such personal choices as those made by Niankhkhnum and Khnumnakht, and Neferhotep, son of Henu, were not represented in the royal funerary monuments. Kings were unable to represent personal relationships, but that is not to say they did not have same-sex relationships. Proving it, however, is the problem.

The only stela that has raised a question of a possible homosexual relationship between a king and another man was the Pase Stela, currently in Berlin (17813). However, there are so many unanswered questions about this stela that a conclusion regarding the true interpretation has never been reached. The stela was dedicated by a soldier, Pase, and depicts two men affectionately embracing. The stela, dating to the Amarna Period, appears to show two kings, Akhenaten wearing the crowns of Upper and Lower Egypt, and next to him, what appears to be another king wearing the blue crown. Unfortunately, all of the cartouches on the stela were incomplete, adding fuel to the debate. Percy Newberry in 1928 identified these kings as Akhenaten and his co-ruler Smenkhkare:

> The two royal personages here are undoubtedly Akhenaten and his co-regent Smenkhkare. The intimate relations between the Pharaoh and the boy as shown by the scene on this stela recall the relationship between the Emperor Hadrian and the youth Antinous.[94]

In 1973, John Harris refuted this theory using the number of cartouches to prove the stela did in fact depict a king (Akhenaten) and his queen (Nefertiti), despite the kingly crowns. There were two cartouches by the solar disc intended for the Aten, two behind the king's head, intended for Akhenaten, and three in front of the pair. If these were two kings, this bank of three should in fact be four to incorporate the throne name and birth name of the king. Therefore, Harris concluded these three were intended for the two names of Akhenaten and one of Nefertiti, his wife.[95] The uncertainty surrounding this small stela is due to the ambiguity in artistic representation of his period and the elevated position of Nefertiti in the court of Akhenaten.

One of the most discussed texts regarding the king and homosexuality is a Middle Kingdom literary tale recorded on three fragmentary sources: an eighteenth dynasty writing board, a twentieth dynasty ostracon from Deir el Medina and a twenty-fifth dynasty papyrus from Thebes. This story had clearly stood the test of time, as these sources span over 650 years. Although these sources are all from the New Kingdom, it is believed to have been written at the end of the Middle Kingdom and tells the story of king Pepy II (2278–2184 BCE) and his relationship with the general Sasanet.

The story tells of a man from Memphis who was attempting to speak out about the general and possibly the king at the palace but was mocked when he tried to speak or drowned out by court musicians. Tjeti is informed of the affair and becomes the 'first recorded amateur detective',[96] as he follows the king on his nocturnal trysts:

> Then he noticed the Person of the Dual King, Neferkara going out at night, all alone with nobody with him. Then he removed himself from him without letting him see. Hent's son Tjeti stood thinking; 'so this is it! What was said is true. He goes out at night'. Hent's son Tjeti went just behind this god – without letting his heart misgive him – to see all that he did.
> He [Neferkara] arrived at the house of the general Sasanet. Then he threw a brick and kicked the wall so that a ladder was let down

for him. Then he ascended. Hent's son Tjeti waited until His Person returned. Now after His Person had done what he desired with him, he returned to his palace with Hent's son Tjeti behind him.

When His Person returned to the palace, Tjeti went back to his house. Now his Person went to the house of general Sasanet when four hours had passed of the night [i.e. 10pm], he had spent another four hours in the house of general Sasanet, and he entered the palace when there were four hours to dawn [i.e. 2am]. And Hent's son Tjeti went following him each night – without his heart misgiving him; and each time after His Person entered the palace Tjeti went back to his house ...[97]

The ending of the tale is unfortunately missing, as are so many of the papyri from ancient Egypt. It is probable, however, that the tale ended with the king abandoning his relationship[98] and the man is heard in the palace. Tjeti is clearly distressed by the nocturnal activities of the king, although the reason is questionable.

The way the king enters the house of Sasanet is presented in a less than regal way, as it is secretive and somewhat sleazy. Perhaps this is part of the Tjeti's concern: that the king's relationship is with someone of a much lower class than him, meaning the king is in an inferior position to the general in the sense he is the one waiting outside, whistling and waiting for the ladder to be lowered. Not the behaviour of a god. It is suggested that role reversal could in fact be the message of the text. In addition to the king's role being reversed, so is that of the general. Normally the general subdues enemies in the battle field, whereas in this relationship he is the one being subdued.[99] It is made very clear that in the act of intercourse the king is in the superior position, 'His Person had done what he desired with him' rather than the position of the *nkkw*.

It does not appear that the king is criticised necessarily for having a homosexual relationship but rather for the neglect of his royal duties while spending four hours every night in homosexual carnal pleasures. As Montserrat claims, 'the sexual nature of what they do is not important; what is emphasised is that they like it too much and do it too often'.[100]

The relationship itself seems to be a continuous one, where each man is the sole interest of the other.[101] Sasanet is said not to be married, although the king's marital status is not stated, but it can be assumed he was married with a harem of wives. It is not made clear whether Sasanet's single status was a result of his homosexual desires or another cause.[102] As discussed above, homosexuality was not viewed in a positive light but was on par with adultery: something that was not recommended, indeed frowned upon, but was an inevitable part of life.

During the Ptolemaic Period, there is further criticism of a king for inappropriate behaviour, aimed at Ptolemy IV. He was criticised for a lack of self-discipline especially when it came to his homosexual lover Agathocles. He was also criticised for his excessive devotion to the cult of Dionysus (Osiris), which he demonstrated by being tattooed. It is not so much the actions that are criticised but how this took him away from his kingly duties.

However, like adultery, homosexuality was secret by nature and therefore considered taboo. This idea of secrecy features a great deal in the discussions on homosexuality, including this tale of the king and Sasanet, as Tjeti and the man from Memphis want to expose the relationship of the king and the general but due to the taboo nature of the relationship they were prevented from revealing his 'secret'. This idea of secrecy is also echoed in the Contendings of Horus and Seth, as Horus threatens Seth with,

'Watch out; I shall tell this!' However, just because something is secret and therefore taboo is not the same as illegal and was more than likely accepted as an inevitable part of daily life.

All of these discussions of course only refer to same-sex relationships between men, as same-sex relationships between women do not receive the same attention either from the ancient Egyptians or modern Egyptologists.

As discussed, the tomb of Niankhkhnum and Khnumnakht has received great interest due to the intimate scenes between the two men, whereas banquet scenes of groups of women holding hands and feeding each other mandrakes (an erotic symbol discussed in chapter 1), which appear in the majority of non-royal tombs, do not receive the same scrutiny.

It is assumed that women spent the majority of their time in the company of women and, as women are generally more affectionate than men, they were closer to their female companions than they were with men. Manniche, for example, states:

> Without exactly accusing them of being lesbians it is obvious that women enjoyed being touched by other women.[103]

However, the same argument is never applied to men. Men also spent the majority of their time in the company of other men, and even in modern Egypt it is not unusual to see men holding hands or resting their hands on each other's knees. Such relationships, while not necessarily representing homosexual relationships, certainly demonstrate a homosocial relationship.[104] Such relationships are readily accepted for women in ancient Egypt but not for men.

If women are depicted as being intimate with each other, it reflects friendship, whereas if men are shown as intimate with each other, a debate ensues regarding their relationship as brothers, twins, father and son or lovers. These interpretations are more a reflection of the Western Egyptologists discussing the images than the ancient Egyptians.

If, as the discussion above shows, relationships between intimate men are to be analysed in great depth, then female representations should be analysed likewise. If homosexual relationships between men existed in ancient Egypt, then homosexual relationships between women also existed. However, as the vast majority of tombs are designed by men and the majority of religious texts, letters, and documents are written by men, the personal intimacies of women are not necessarily depicted or discussed. Therefore, much of the evidence is possibly lost with the exception of the banquet scenes, which could be hiding same-sex relationships in plain sight.

The ancient Egyptians themselves acknowledged women in same-sex relationships, in particular, in the dream interpretation books, which offered a positive or negative interpretation for any dream. Papyrus Carlsberg states: if a woman 'dreams that a woman has intercourse with her she will come to a bad end'.[105] However, this alone cannot be used as evidence that female homosexuality was considered negative, as Papyrus Carlsberg XIII, currently in Copenhagen, lists a number of sexual dreams of women, the majority of which were considered a negative omen. The only positive sexual dreams were

If a ram has intercourse with her, Pharaoh will be benevolent towards her,
If a wolf has intercourse with her, she will see something beautiful,
If an ibis has intercourse with her, she [will] have a well-equipped house.[106]

The question arises as to whether this female dream book was written by a man, and if so were these dreams actual dreams experienced by women. Needless to say, they are rather unusual dreams and modern psychiatrists would no doubt read something telling into them. Even a woman dreaming of having sex with her husband was considered a bad omen:

> If a woman dreams that she is married to her husband, she will be destroyed. If she embraces him, she will experience grief.[107]

According to the standards set by the dream interpretations books, women dreaming about sex with humans, male or female, was seen as a bad omen and therefore does not really reflect any views of homosexual relationships between women.

A potentially interesting text is the Negative Confession on the papyrus of Nestanebtasheru, which states: 'I have not had intercourse with any woman in the sacred places of my city god'. As the papyrus belongs to a woman, it could be a reference to lesbianism, although Manniche claims it is likely that the text was copied badly from a male's Book of the Dead[108] or it could have been an 'off the shelf copy' where the name of the deceased was simply added. However, as discussed in chapter 9, when texts are copied for female usage, the masculine terminology is often kept, as it is the masculine that aids with rebirth. Therefore, although readily dismissed as badly copied, these textual oddities may in fact be deliberate.

However, in Nestanebtasheru's copy there are no masculine pronouns (e.g. he, his), so it is not a badly copied text but rather an accurately copied text that either was not adapted for a woman or was chosen because the woman was homosexual.

It is an interesting and frustrating situation that, while it is inevitable that same-sex relationships happened in ancient Egypt and there is enough circumstantial evidence to support this, it is impossible to identify the finer details of these relationships. Parkinson believes 'ancient Egypt was, regrettably, a repressive society towards gays'.[109] However, the evidence does not really support such an opinion. While being the recipient of homosexual penetrative sex was considered a weakness or a taboo, there is no evidence that anyone was treated like a criminal or beaten because of it. Moreover, in the other form of taboo sex, adultery, it only became a crime when the injured party prosecuted (chapter 2). In a consensual homosexual relationship, there was no injured party, and therefore no crime.

Considering the language does not include terms to express the modern concept of homosexuality and the artwork is open to misinterpretation, we are limited to exactly what facts can be proven. Baines, while discussing the artistic representations in the tomb of the two men Niankhkhnum and Khnumhotep, stated: 'little can be said about their meaning beyond the fact that they express publically the close involvement of the two men'.[110] Despite all the theories and discussions about their relationship, this is essentially all we can genuinely ascertain from the evidence. They were close: so close that above the entrance to the inner rooms of the tomb their names were joined together to read Niankh–Khnum–Hotep, meaning it could be read from left to right or right to left. The same could be said of Neferhotep and his friend, Nebsumenu, who commissioned the funerary stela for him. They were obviously close and wished to continue their friendship and intimacies into the afterlife.

6

PROSTITUTION

'Here you are spending all your time in
the company of prostitutes'[1]

It is often stated that prostitution is the oldest profession in the
world, and therefore one would expect prostitutes in ancient Egypt.
However, it was not until the Graeco-Roman Period that there are
clear records of this profession in the form of ostraca regarding
income tax and papyri recording the leasing and taxation of
properties for prostitution.[2] This evidence suggests that prostitutes
could openly tout their trade, and buildings were provided for use
as brothels. In order to encourage men into these brothels, the
prostitutes wore sandals with enticements formed by nails on the
soles. As the prostitute walked through the streets, her footprints
read such things as 'follow me', signposting the customers to the
brothel.[3]

It is clear that prostitution was a recognised, if not necessarily
well-recorded, part of everyday life in Graeco-Roman Egypt.
Visiting a prostitute was not considered a negative thing for
bachelors, soldiers and men away from home for an extended
period of time. The main concern was that it was not considered

a useful way of spending time[4]. In chapter 5, homosexual sex was viewed in a very similar way in the Pharaonic Period: a waste of time and therefore to be avoided.

The Pharaonic evidence we have suggests that intercourse with a prostitute was accepted as an inevitable aspect of life and was even included in a calendar of lucky and unlucky days from Tanis, in the Delta. This calendar states that on the twenty-third day of the third month of inundation (9 October) it was taboo to be found 'fornicating with a fornicator, male or female'. This is translated as having intercourse with a prostitute, male or female, which suggests that both men and women acted as prostitutes at this time. Another inscription at Edfu claims: 'having intercourse with a prostitute, over the entire country' would only result in heartache.[5] One man, writing a letter (P.Leiden 1, 371, 38) to his deceased wife, Ankhiry, tries to prove his faithfulness to her memory by claiming he had remained single. Furthermore, he finished the letter with 'And then: the sisters in the house, I have not entered any one of them'. Some scholars take this to mean he has not visited prostitutes,[6] whereas others believe they were servants in his home.[7] It was believed that there were three types of women in ancient Egypt: wives, mothers and prostitutes.[8] Whereas the first two were honourable and greatly revered, the third was not, and this man may have wanted to disassociate himself from them.

The risk of young men engaging with prostitutes was considered such an inevitability that the instruction texts warned against it:

Here you are spending all your time in the company of prostitutes, lolling about ... Here you are next to a pretty girl bathed in perfume, a garland of flowers around her neck, drumming on your belly, unsteady, toppling over onto the ground, and all covered in filth.[9]

Papyrus Lansing (a schoolbook) takes a similar stance encouraging the student to avoid prostitutes and beer and instead concentrate on studying:

> You follow the path of pleasure; you make friends with revellers. You have made your home in the brewery, as one who thirsts from beer. You sit in the parlour with the idler. You hold the writings in contempt. You visit the whore. Do not do these things! What are they for? Take note of it![10]

While this young man was advised against paying for intercourse, Ankhsheshonq, a rather embittered priest, writing in prison boldly states: 'Man is more anxious to copulate than a donkey. What restrains him is his purse'. Whether Ankhsheshonq was being literal by suggesting more men would visit prostitutes if they could afford it is unknown, but it does indicate visiting a prostitute was not an unusual pastime,[11] perhaps even an expected element of a man's life.

So who were the prostitutes? Naturally we do not know of individuals in the profession, but Strabo provides an insight into their age. He refers to a very young prostitute who 'has intercourse with whoever she likes until the purification of her body takes place'.[12] This particular prostitute was sent to the temple of Amun or Zeus, and it was here that she performed the role until her menstrual cycle started when she would then get married and have children. This does raise a number of questions, especially in regard to how prostitutes were received by the populous. Perhaps being a temple prostitute held a higher status than a village prostitute because the actions were sanctioned by the god. If once the prostitute reached puberty she was no longer eligible for temple prostitution and could become a wife then, this indicates she would not be shunned by the community and would be considered acceptable wife material. However, the likelihood of child prostitutes in the temple is up for debate, as Strabo may have simply been told things that his informant believed would interest him regardless of whether the information was factually correct.

Prostitutes as a group were generally not considered to be honourable women, and while their profession does not seem to be criticised as such, it was considered dangerous to become involved with them. Ankhsheshonq suggests that 'He who makes love to a woman of the streets will have his purse cut open'.[13]

This idea of prostitutes being untrustworthy is attested by other texts. For example, a man, Sopolis, petitioned Ptolemy IV (222–205 BCE) about the prostitute Demo, who apparently tricked his son out of 1,000 drachmas. Regardless of how she managed to coerce the money from him, the idea of a dishonest prostitute is more of the issue. In the New Kingdom, a woman who conned someone in a similar way was called a *kat tahut* (*kat* meaning vulva and *tahut*, prostitute), showing that the connection between prostitutes and dishonesty was a long one.[14]

Could this mistrust of prostitutes be due to their sexual freedom and lack of supervision by a man, whether her husband or father? However, some men believed not only prostitutes were untrustworthy but women in general. For this we return once more to Ankhsheshonq, who clearly mistrusted all women and offered a great deal of advice regarding this:

Let your wife see your wealth but don't trust her with it.

Never confide in your wife – what you say goes straight into the street.

What she does with her husband she will do with another man tomorrow.

When a man smells of myrrh, his wife is a cat in his presence, when a man is suffering, his wife is a lioness in his presence.

Do not rejoice over your wife's beauty, her mind is on her lover.
Teaching a woman is like having a sack of sand with the side split
open.[15]

The only woman he claims is trustworthy is your mother:

Do not open your heart to your wife or servant. Open it to your
mother. She is a woman to be trusted.

It is difficult to know how common Ankhsheshonq's ideas were
among the general population of ancient Egypt, but as they formed
part of the genre of wisdom texts, the opinions voiced may not
have been considered too outlandish. It is believed that he was
aiming his advice at a lower social stratum than other instruction
texts, and therefore his opinions may reflect those of the poorer
man, describing lower-class women who were wont to steal and
be untrustworthy.

It is clear, however, that visiting prostitutes was considered a
poor use of a man's time, and this doubled when applied to the
king. The connection between a king and prostitution was used
as a literary tool in order to blacken their reputation. Herodotus,
travelling to Egypt in the fifth century BCE, had been told two
tales of royal prostitution, which he eagerly recorded in Book 2 of
his *Histories*.

One tale concerns king Cheops (Khufu), the builder of the Great
Pyramid at Giza. Apparently this king, who had a reputation as a
tyrannical ruler, was said to have forced his own daughter to take
payment for sex to boost the royal coffers:

But no crime was too great for Cheops: when he was short of money,
he sent his daughter to a bawdy-house with instructions to charge a

certain sum – they did not tell me how much. This she actually did, adding to it a further transaction of her own; for with the intention of leaving something to be remembered by after her death, she asked each of her customers to give her a block of stone, and of these stones (the story goes) was built the middle pyramid of the three which stand in front of the great pyramid. It is a hundred and fifty feet square.[16]

This central pyramid is believed to belong to queen Meritetes, who was in fact the daughter of Sneferu and the wife of Cheops (Khufu). Could the people talking to Herodotus simply have made a mistake regarding the relationship between Khufu and Meritetes? It needs to be taken into consideration that Herodotus was writing some 2,000 years after the pyramids were built, and the story may have been pure propaganda, or even at this point, a legend about an unpopular king.

The second tale of enforced prostitution has a more cunning, less materialistic element to it. King Rhampsinitus was searching for a thief and was not having any success following traditional methods. Therefore,

He sent his own daughter to a brothel with orders to admit all comers, and to compel each applicant, before granting him her favours, to tell her what was the cleverest and wickedest thing that he had ever done.[17]

Through this method the princess was likely to find out the information that the king required. Even Herodotus did not believe this far-fetched story but it is rather similar in plot to the Late Period story of Setne and Tabubu. In this literary tale, the son of Ramses II falls in love with Tabubu, the daughter of a priest of Bastet. After making initial contact with her, he decides to visit her at her home, with the hope that she will agree to have intercourse with him.

Each time he approached her, she responded with: 'Return to your house. I am of priestly rank. I am not a low person. If you desire to do what you wish with me you must ...'; what followed was a task to demonstrate his desire, which included providing her with a deed of maintenance which was also to be upheld by his children, and the requests escalated until he actually killed his children in his desire to have sex with her. Although Tabubu is not a prostitute, but a high ranking daughter of a priest, her requests for 'payment' before she had sex with the prince is reminiscent of Rhampsinitus's daughter requesting information.

However, such tales may say more about man's nature and how 'man is more anxious to copulate than a donkey. What restrains him is his purse'.[18] These tales show a manipulation of this nature in order to gain what is required: whether blocks of stone, information or property.

Another classical story about the royal family and a courtesan has an element of exoticism rather than duplicitousness about it. Herodotus recorded the story in the fifth century BCE, and then Strabo elaborated on it in the first century BCE in the form of a poem. Although much of her story is clearly fictionalised, it is believed that she was in fact a historical character.[19]

> By birth a Thracian, the slave of Iadmon the son of Hephaistopolis
> of Samosa and fellow-slave of Aesop the fable writer.[20]

It is clear that this slave, Rhadopis, is a character of legend considering her connections with Aesop. After some time, she was freed from slavery at great expense by the brother of Sappho, the lyric poet, and then turned to prostitution:

> Having in this way obtained her freedom she remained in
> Egypt and succeeded by her great beauty in amassing a fortune

which – for her – was a considerable one, but certainly not sufficient enough for building a pyramid ...[21]

Herodotus does not believe that a courtesan was able to gain enough money to build such a pyramid, although Strabo attributes Menkaura's pyramid to her. It is thought that the story of Rhadopis was based partially on the myth of the daughter of Cheops, as discussed above.

Strabo, however, in his poem, seems to have been the instigator of the Cinderella fairy tale, as he describes how Rhadopis lost her sandal, which was picked up by an eagle and dropped into the lap of the king:

> When the eagle arrived above his head, it flung the sandal into his lap; and the king, stirred both by the beautiful shape of the sandal and by the strangeness of the occurrence, sent men in all directions into the country in quest of the woman who wore the sandal; and when she was found in the city of Naucratis, she was brought up to Memphis, and became the wife of the king.[22]

Herodotus does not mention this element of the story, and it can be assumed to have been an embellishment of Strabo, and went some way to explaining the fame of this courtesan throughout the Hellenistic world:

> The prostitutes of Naucratis seem to be particularly attractive; for not only did Rhadopis live there, and become so famous that every Greek was familiar with her name ...[23]

The difference in status is clearly an important part of the tale, hence the king ends up marrying a courtesan, indicating there was a huge social difference between the two: not just the poorest of the poor, even denied liberty, but also morally poor, making money from her looks and sexuality. However, as discussed in chapter 3, it was not unusual for the king to marry non-royal women, although perhaps a Thracian slave-turned-prostitute may have been a little lower down the social scale than was usually expected.

However, on a thirtieth dynasty stela currently in the Metropolitan Museum of Art, New York, a story is recorded where the goddess Isis is forced to dwell with prostitutes, showing social class systems could be overcome. In the story, Isis and her son Horus were travelling along with seven scorpion goddesses and needed somewhere to sleep for the night:

> At last I got to the house of the prostitutes. As soon as the Lady had seen me from afar, she closed her door to me. This annoyed my companions [seven scorpions]. They deliberated on it and put their poison together on the sting of Tefenet [one of them].
>
> A harlot opened her door to me, and we entered the shabby dwelling. But Tefenet had crept under the door and stung the son of the Lady. A fire broke out in the house, and there was no water with which to put it out. The skies rained into the house of the Lady, although it was not its season.
>
> Because she had not opened her door to me, she was distressed and she did not know whether her son would live. She walked about the town and cried, but no one heeded her cries.[24]

It seems that in the house of the prostitutes, one wealthy woman had closed the door and it was her son who had been stung by the combined sting of the seven scorpion goddesses. Another prostitute in the brothel, however, had opened her door to Isis, and it was in view of her kindness that Isis cured the child of the scorpion bite. Isis was viewed as the ultimate doting mother, and although the wealthy woman had been unpleasant, Isis could not watch an innocent child die. In thanks, the wealthy woman gave all of her worldly goods to Isis. The similarities between this story and the Biblical story of Mary and Joseph looking for somewhere to stay cannot be overlooked, with the result that Isis and Horus stayed in the lowest form of accommodation at the time.

As we can see, the textual evidence of prostitution is scant and primarily comes from the later periods of Egyptian history. The pictorial evidence we have is earlier but difficult to interpret. The most discussed pictorial evidence is the Turin Erotic Papyrus, produced in Thebes at some time between the nineteenth and twentieth dynasties. It was found in 1824 but was not published for many years due to the inappropriate content.[25]

The papyrus contains two different forms of illustration, one showing a number of animals participating in human activities and is thought to be a representation of well-known folklore. The other form of illustration is what interests us here as it includes a number of scenes showing men and women engaged in sexual intercourse.

It was initially thought these scenes recorded the adventures of a Theban priest of Amun and a prostitute although as each man appears to be at varying stages of balding and possesses different facial hair it is likely to be a number of men. All of the men are wearing simple, undecorated kilts common to lower-class men such as servants, field labourers and workmen and all have 'a huge phallus which swings pendulously between the couple'.[26]

The women also appear to be different with varying wigs, hip belts, jewellery, make-up and occasionally a lotus flower in their hair, although it could be the same woman adorned differently. Their lower regions are emphasised, as each has a narrow waist and large hips, but their breasts are small showing that the ancient Egyptians found the hips more sensual than breasts (*see* chapter 1).

The images appear to be a series of unconnected scenes, and Manniche boldly states that there 'can hardly be any doubt that we are experiencing a unique glimpse behind the screen in a whorehouse at Deir el Medina'.[27] Each of the images is accompanied by short texts demonstrating the conversation held by the copulating couple, and although severely damaged includes phrases like: 'Oh, sun, you have found out my heart, it is agreeable work,' or 'Come behind me with your love,'[28] 'I make your job a pleasant one. Do not fear' or the question, 'What would I do to you?'[29] The couples are depicted in seven different positions, three of which are from the rear, in addition to scenes of the women seducing the men, dancing and applying cosmetics.[30]

There also appears to be a reference to the literary tale 'The Tale of the Two Brothers', which would be well-known to the intended audience. In one image, the girl supports her weight on a cushion and the man is holding a sack over his shoulder perhaps in reference to the scene in the story when Bata was carrying a sack of grain impressing the sister-in-law greatly. In the story, she asks Bata: 'How much is it that you have upon your shoulder?' and he answers that he is carrying three sacks of wheat and two of barley to which she replied, '"You are very strong ... Every day I see how strong you are". And she desired to know him'.[31]

Some scholars have suggested that this man on the Turin Papyrus could be a client in a hurry who did not have time to even put down his belongings before continuing with the business at hand.[32] This interpretation seems unlikely, as it takes little effort to drop the sack to the floor and would make the activity with the woman easier. Other scenes that have sparked creative interpretations include the scene where a couple are together in a chariot which is pulled by two young girls. A smaller unkempt man is running away, and while some believe he is a servant, others suggest he is the owner of the chariot and the woman is cuckolding him with another man.[33]

Not everyone is convinced this is a depiction of a Theban brothel, and alternatively suggest it could a sex manual, of the type popular in the Far East,[34] pornography or an orgy with numerous partners.[35] Others look for more spiritual elements to the papyrus, believing it is a satirical commentary on well-known religious images. For example, excessive drinking and sexual activity were known aspects of numerous religious festivals at Deir el Medina, and one image shows a couple having sex in exactly the same position as the gods Geb and Nut found on papyri and coffins representing the creation of the earth. The Turin papyrus is also peppered with images of sistra, the bronze rattles sacred to the goddess Hathor,[36] and therefore could represent the celebration of the New Year's Festival.[37]

While it is evident from the literary sources that prostitution was a profession in ancient Egypt, albeit one discouraged, there is no archaeological evidence of such establishments as brothels. The Turin Papyrus is therefore the closest thing we have to represent a brothel, and even that is not accepted by all.

One scholar, however, has made the assumption that house SE VIII at Deir el Medina, was in fact a brothel. This has been based purely on the decoration discovered in the first room of the house, which comprises a feminine theme including an image of a female musician. However, the material culture from within the house are identical to artefacts discovered in other houses in the workman village, and in no way sets the house apart as one solely inhabited by women, let alone prostitutes.[38]

The same scholar became intrigued by a section of the cemetery at Deir el Medina preserved for the burials of unattached women and their children. She states there are documents from Deir el Medina naming such women who were not wives or mothers as 'others', which she believes hints at a class of prostitutes.[39]

In a village dominated by working men and family units, unattached, independent women were conspicuous unless they provided a service or were attached to an established family. Graves-Brown has suggested that these unattached women here were either unmarried or divorced.[40] Generally, women were buried with their husbands or, if unmarried or divorced, in their father's tomb. Having a section of the cemetery, especially in the poorer part, separates them from the rest of the community in death and no doubt in life as well. Bruyère initially thought they were the burials of dancers and female musicians[41] who were often equated as being prostitutes, which may have influenced Manniche's convictions concerning them as 'others'.

Dancers and musicians are often thought to be prostitutes, although this is not something that can be identified from the pictorial record alone.[42] However, as they are invariably the only adult women displayed naked, there is an aura of eroticism surrounding them. However, dancers only appeared naked in non-royal tombs in the middle of the eighteenth dynasty,[43] indicating there may have been a change in status or in the perception of the dancer in noble society. The Turin Papyrus includes sex with a singer and the text identifies her as such (*Hsyt*).[44] There is clearly a connection between musicians, dancers, music and sex, and their associated deities of Hathor and Bes further perpetuate this association (*see* chapter 1). Hathor is addressed on the pro-pylon at Philae as:

... the lady of the dance, the mistress of the songs and dances accompanied by the lute, whose face shines each day, who knows no sorrow.[45]

There were also a troop of temple dancers known as *xnr*, who from the Old Kingdom performed at processions, funerals and temple rituals and were closely associated with Hathor. There is also a curious Late Dynastic or Ptolemaic figure that has been entitled an 'erotic music lesson'.[46] This title is on account of the image of a man with a huge erect penis with a small female harp player seated on the tip in addition to odd markings on the statue, which may be musical annotation.[47]

The discovery of blue faience fertility figurines in tombs was interpreted as Nubian dancing girls: 'in order that their spirits might while away the time of the Theban grandees in the tedious hours of eternity'.[48] It was believed that, when found in the tomb of men, these dancing girls provided sexual entertainment for the deceased, but their function was as servants when discovered in the tomb of women. Neither of these theories stands up to scrutiny, as the depictions of the figurines show hairstyles worn by Middle Kingdom court ladies rather than those of servants or Nubians. In fact, there is nothing about the figurines that indicate they may be Nubian other than the cowrie shell belts, which have also been discovered in Middle Kingdom Egyptian burials of royal women. The geometrical patterns depicted on these figurines are the same as those on C-Group Nubian fertility figurines as well as those discovered tattooed on the mummies of Egyptian priestesses of Hathor (*see* chapter 1). However, Winlock identified these mummies as dancers, ignoring the revered site of burial within the royal complex at Deir el Bahri and their priestly titles.[49] Perhaps as part of the role of priestess of Hathor, these women may have danced in processions but this does not indicate they were full-time dancers or by association prostitutes.

The association, however, between singers, dancers and prostitution is not one of modern construction as Papyrus Anastasi IV states:

You have been taught to sing to the pipe, to chant to the flute, to intone to the lyre, and to sing to the *nTh*. Now you are seated (still) in the house and the harlots surround you. Now you are standing and bouncing. Now you are seated in front of the wench, soaked in anointing oil, your wreath of *tStpn* at your neck, and you drum upon your belly, anointed with dirt.[50]

This idea has developed over the centuries, and connections are now automatically made between dancers or women bearing tattoos and prostitution. For example, one image (Leiden) shows a musician with a tattoo of Bes on her thigh, and as he is the god of fertility and childbirth, it has been interpreted as the sign of a prostitute, and could protect against venereal disease like gonorrhoea.[51] This seems like a huge leap of faith, as Bes was a patron god of all mothers, young children and fertility, and as we saw in chapter 3, adorned the bedroom wall of Amenhotep III. This surely muddies the water if trying to identify prostitutes by their connection with Bes tattoos.

Even connecting prostitution with tattoos is problematic, as both men and women wore tattoos, which were often the insignia of being a member of the priesthood. The most reported evidence of a female mummy bearing tattoos belong to the priestesses of Hathor discovered at Deir el Bahri (Chapter 1). While her status alone does not exempt her from being a prostitute, a number of women at Deir el Medina held the same priestess titles and were highly respected in the community and were married to high-status members of the village.[52] Therefore, they were clearly not the unattached 'others', segregated from the community that Manniche wishes to identify as prostitutes. She claims there are documents naming the 'others' but does not provide references, and an expert on Deir el Media texts has been unable to identify them among the available texts.[53]

However, this lack of evidence regarding the identity of these segregated, un-attached women does not exclude the possibility of a brothel at Deir el Medina. However, when considering this possibility, it is essential to consider the purpose for building the village in the first place. Deir el Medina was originally constructed to house the workmen who built the Valley of the Kings and their families. Therefore, all of the houses were inhabited by people with a function on the construction of the royal tomb. Would the government consider a brothel an essential use of space within the small village? It seems rather unlikely. It is more likely that transient sex-workers may have passed through the town as and when they were needed, although no written evidence on sexual services being bought in the village survives.[54] This in itself need not be considered as absence of activity. Visiting a prostitute was considered inappropriate and one that the man would prefer to keep secret, so it is unlikely he would write a receipt or journal entry marking the event.

This is essentially the problem with identifying prostitution prior to the Graeco-Roman Period. At this time, prostitution was taxed and records were kept as a means of monitoring activity. However, prior to this period prostitution was a non-taxable profession and therefore no records were kept. The records we have from towns like Deir el Medina are items like receipts or legal cases, and it is unlikely that in such a small village any man (or woman) would want to bring a case to the court where they were conned or abused by a prostitute. These were private transactions, and as much as possible they wished to keep them secret from friends, family and in the future prying archaeologists.

7

SEX AND MEDICINE

'Instructions for a lady suffering in her pubic region'[1]

Egyptian doctors were known all over the ancient world for their superior medical skills, and it was not unusual for Egyptian kings to send their doctors abroad to help foreign rulers. Herodotus records that the Persian king asked the pharaoh to send an eye doctor to him immediately. Although an honour and a great indication of his skills and ability, the doctor did not appreciate being: 'torn from his wife and family and handed over to the Persians'.[2] He was so embittered that he encouraged the Persian king to invade Egypt in 525 BCE.[3]

Despite being world renown, to a modern observer, Egyptian medical practice was a combination of brilliant science and observational skills, with many of the medicines used forming the basis of modern medicine, and superstition with the potential to cause more harm than good. On the one hand, the long practice of mummification enabled Egyptian doctors to gain an insight into the workings of the human body, which other cultures did not have, but on the other, a dead body is very different from a living one. There were many ailments caused by things they could not physically see, and therefore they were unable to ascertain what the cause was. It was in these instances that the doctors were more likely to turn to magic and superstition, although there was little difference in the mind of an Egyptian between religious incantations and practical medicine. They were both required if a patient was to be successfully cured.

The types of ailments to affect women can be found on a number of papyri including the Kahun Gynaecological Papyrus, discovered in the Middle Kingdom city of El Lahun (Kahun). The most common concern of women was fertility, and of thirty-four cases in the papyrus, seven (20.5 per cent) were concerned with determining female fertility.[4] As discussed in chapters 2 and 8, having a family was the most important aspect of an adult's life, and therefore a prayer inscribed on a scarab expressing the hope that 'your name may last, children may be granted to you,'[5] indicates this was a particular worry of adults in ancient Egypt.

The majority of the medical needs of women were difficult to treat, as the causes were often unseen and doctors prescribed according to their presumptions about the female body and how it worked. The main presumption was that female pelvic organs were not static in the abdomen and were free to move. It was this movement that caused the majority of ailments, and they would be cured once these organs were drawn back to their natural position. In order to do this, fumigation was considered the most effective remedy. Records show that such serious illnesses as a prolapsed uterus were treated with a fumigation of excrement and frankincense and a wax figure of Thoth[6] or pessaries of vegetable matter and beer[7] inserted into the vagina.

All female health was dependent on keeping these mobile pelvic organs in place, and in the Kahun Gynaecological Papyrus, one remedy is specifically for 'Causing a woman's womb to go to its place'. This travelling of the pubic organs not only caused general ill health but could damage the organs themselves:

> Instructions for a woman whose womb has become diseased through journeying. You should proceed to ask her: 'What do you smell?' If she answers 'I smell fries, you should declare about her, 'This is a disorder of the womb'. You should prescribe for it; fumigation over everything she smells as fries.[8]

However, a woman suffering from a stiff neck or painful eyes was also believed to be suffering due to wandering organs, and it was diagnosed as a 'discharge of the uterus in her eyes'. The treatment was not pleasant and comprised rinsing her eyes with goose leg fat, washing her vagina with incense and fresh oil and eating the fresh liver of a donkey.[9] Almost everything was attributed to this ailment, and the Kahun papyrus even describes an ear infection:

> Instructions for a woman suffering in her neck, pubic parts and ears;
> She does not hear what is said to her.
> You should say about her: 'This is a disturbance of the womb'.
> You should prescribe for it the same prescription as that for driving out discharges of the womb.[10]

Obviously, as wandering organs could cause ear infections or a stiff neck, they had a major effect on fertility. To be fertile, it was important to have a clear passage from the vagina to all parts of the body, and fertility tests often involved testing for blockages. If such a blockage was evident, then the woman would not conceive. There did not appear to be a method of clearing the blockages, just identifying them. Sometimes it seemed to be possible to identify these problems through a simple examination of the skin:

> After having anointed the patient with fat on the preceding night, if in the morning her flesh is green [or if the vessels on her breast are fresh?] she will conceive happily; if it is wet like her flesh [or if the vessels are sunken?] the delivery will be difficult; if they are fresh [or dark green?] already at night she will conceive with difficulty.

Changing characteristics of the eyes were also observed:

> If you find one of the eyes similar to those of an Asiatic, and the other like that of a southerner, she will not conceive.

Finally the breasts were examined:

> If the vessels on her breasts are turgid, she will conceive; if they are flat, she will conceive with difficulty.[11]

However, sometimes more interactive tests needed to be carried out. One test was for the woman to crouch over a mixture of beer and dates. If after some time she vomited, it was clear there were no blockages and she would conceive. Furthermore, the number of times she vomited was an indicator of how many children she would have. If she did not vomit, then she was infertile and would not conceive.

Another fertility test was recorded on the Berlin Papyrus:

> To ascertain whether or not a woman will have a child; the herb *bededu-ka*, powdered and soaked in the milk of a woman who has

borne a son. Let the patient eat it ... if she vomits it, she will bear a child, if she has flatulence, she will not bear.[12]

A more invasive test involved inserting an onion into the vagina:

You should cause the bulb of an onion to spend the night in her flesh until dawn. If the odour appears in her mouth she will bear children. If it does not, she will never [bear children].[13]

Once fertility was confirmed, fertility aids were used in order to speed up conception. A simple approach for a woman wanting to conceive was to eat lots of lettuce. It was thought to be an aphrodisiac due to the long ithyphallic shape, and when cut, a thick, white liquid came out which resembled semen. It was also the sacred vegetable of the fertility god Min,[14] and appeared in the myth of the Contendings of Horus and Seth as the receptacle for the semen of Horus which impregnated Seth (*see* chapter 8). Surely, if a lettuce aided in the pregnancy of a man, the power over a woman's reproductive organs would be excellent. With such connections with sex and fertility, lettuce was also seen as a cure for impotence and, infertility and was used as an effective aphrodisiac.

Impotence was not an unusual ailment in ancient Egypt, which concerned men greatly. In the Ebers Papyrus, the cures came under the title: 'weakness of the male member', and in a British Museum hieratic papyrus similar remedies are labelled for: 'reviving the limb of one dead' in reference to a 'dead' penis.

The remedies were all in the form of a poultice applied to the penis, and one doctor on Papyrus Rameses V number XII, suggests applying a poultice comprising 'leaves of Christ thorn, 1; leaves of acacia, 1; honey, 1; grind (the leaves) in this honey'.[15]

If the medicinal remedies were not successful, it was possible to turn to a magic ritual instead. A prayer from 1000 BCE was to be recited, presumably over the penis:

> Hail to you, great god, who created the upper class. You Khnum who established the lower class. May you test the mouth of every vulva, be erect, be not soft, be strong, be not weak … you strengthen testicles with Seth, son of Nut.[16]

Even if a man should not be suffering with impotence, not all men were confident when it came to women. These men seemed to have also approached the local doctor or wise woman to get help in enticing women to have sex with them. Some of the remedies were of a practical nature, with a potion to administer to the object of desire. As long as she was unaware of the ingredients, perhaps such a love potion may have worked:

> Take dandruff from the scalp of a dead person who was murdered, and seven grains of barley, buried in the grave of a dead man, and crush I with 10 *oipe* of apple pips. Add the blood of a tick from a black dog, a drop of blood from the ring finger of your left hand and your semen. Crush it to a compact mass, place it in a cup of wine and add 3 *outeh mut* [unknown] which you have not yet tasted and which has not yet been used for offering. Recite the said formula over it seven times and let the woman drink it. Tie the skin of the tick in a piece of linen and tie it in a knot round your left arm.[17]

Obviously, a potion like this necessitated the man knowing the woman well enough for her to drink wine with him. Perhaps this was a means of spicing up a dying relationship rather than instigating a new one.

Another remedy designed for a husband to be able once more to attract his wife to his bed includes grinding acacia seeds with honey: 'rub your phallus with it and sleep with the woman'. The alternative, however, was even more bizarre and stated: 'Rub your phallus with the foam of the mouth of a stallion and sleep with the woman'.[18] Unsurprisingly a man's virility was often associated with such animals of strength. In one of the New Kingdom love poems, it states:

> Oh that you would come to your sister,
> Like a stallion of the king,
> Chosen from among a thousand horses,
> The finest of the stable.[19]

Horses were associated in particular with virility, and in the Graeco-Roman Period Horus himself was shown riding a horse to emphasise his mastery of warfare and horsemanship. A statue from the Ptolemaic Period discovered at Saqqara shows a man riding a horse while holding his enormous phallus. This emphasised the man's rather than the horse's virility, but nonetheless associated the horse with sexual prowess.[20]

If the practical medicine was not working, alternatively, the desperate men simply appealed to the gods for help in bringing the women to them:

> Hail to Re-Horakhty, father of the gods! Hail to you, Seven Hathors, who are adorned with bands of red linen! Hail to you, gods, lords of heaven and earth! Come [make] So-and-So (fem) born of So-and-So come after me like a cow after fodder; like a servant after her children; like a herdsman [after] his herd. If they do not cause her to come after me, I will set [fire to] Busiris and burn up Osiris.[21]

Unsurprisingly, there were very few remedies of this type (practical or spiritual) aimed at women hoping to entice men into enjoying intercourse. This could be for one of two reasons. One is that women requiring such help no doubt went to a woman in the village who would know the ingredients without the need for a reference papyrus. The second reason could be that the medical papyri were written by men, and as they held the view that women should only require intercourse with their husband, and therefore if not married they would not be participating in such activities. It was also quite likely that it was considered unseemly for a woman to entice a man into her bed through trickery, whereas it was acceptable for a man to do this.

The only remedies that aided a woman in anyway were those aimed at harming another individual. On Papyrus Ebers, there is a remedy to make the hair of a woman fall out, although who the intended audience of such a negative concoction is not specified:

Another remedy to make hair fall out; burnt lotus leaves are to be steeped in oil and placed on the head of a hated woman.[22]

Could this be for women with philandering husbands wishing, not necessarily to make themselves more attractive, but making the competition less attractive? However, the remedy itself is rather suspicious and may not be a genuine recipe for hair loss. The doubts are cast by the ingredients, as the lotus was a symbol of sexuality and the flower was often worn on the head as a head band (*see* chapter 2). If the lotus could genuinely be used to cause hair loss, it is unlikely that the Egyptian elite (both men and women) wore them as adornments,[23] as it would be too risky.

Additionally, most of the beauty remedies that appear in the medical papyri concern the reversal of such tragedies. A common solution to prevent the hair from falling out involved a mixture of

ochre, collyrium, Ht-plant, oil, gazelle dung and hippopotamus fat, and rub the mixture on the head.
Mix crushed flax seed with an equal quantity of oil, add water from a well, and rub the mixture on the head.
Boil a lizard in oil and rub the oil on the head.[24]

Another remedy to make the hair grow involved

the fruit of the castor-oil plant, pounded and kneaded into a lump; the woman must then put it in oil and anoint her head with it.[25]

Whether this was to help the hair to grow once it had fallen out or to speed up hair growth is not stated. Cleopatra VII, who is reputed to have written a cosmetic book, also includes a recipe for curing baldness, which comprised powdered red sulphate of arsenic and oak gum applied to a freshly shaved head.

If this remedy did not work, there were others, and the sheer number of remedies for this problem gives some indication on how widespread the concern was. One could always apply equal parts of burnt domestic mice, burnt horse teeth, burnt vine, bear grease, deer marrow, and reed bark dried mixed with honey or the head could be rubbed with the fir oil or fat from lions, crocodiles, hippopotami, ibex, cat or serpents: so-called powerful animals. The body parts of any black animals were believed to be useful for grey hair, or using hedgehog spines as a sympathetic remedy for baldness: a clear case of the properties of the animals being transferred to the individual. Once hair was in abundance, it was important to keep it strong and beautiful and the best means of doing this was a 'donkey's tooth crushed in honey'.

On the other end of the scale, people also may have approached the doctor for help with hair removal, as it was important to be as hair-free as possible in order to prevent lice as well as to remain clean and smelling fresh. Hair removal cream was recommended, which was heated in a similar way to modern hair-removal wax. It was then placed on the hair and ripped off once it had cooled down. However, instead of wax the mixture comprised boiled and crushed bird bones, fly dung, oil, sycamore juice, gum and cucumber.[26]

Going to the doctor to halt the ageing process was as prevalent in ancient Egypt as it is in the present day. In the absence of cosmetic surgery, the ancient doctors were somewhat limited to what they could do to aid an old man who wished to look young again, for example. It was recommended that he took fenugreek seeds ground into oil, and boiled in water.[27] The Ebers Papyrus claims to get rid of wrinkles with a poultice:

> frankincense, gum, wax, fresh balanites oil and rush-nut should be finely ground and applied to the face every day. Make it and it will happen![28]

Another similar recipe included: 'gum of frankincense, wax, fresh oil, and pounded cypress kernels and mix with milk'. It was important to maintain the treatment for six days in order to see any results. It is likely this acted as a moisturiser, and while making the skin smoother, probably did not make much, if any, difference to the wrinkles.

Another ageing concern, this one specific to women, was dealt with in the Ebers Papyrus, where they include a group of spells 'to prevent the breasts going down', which presumably means to prevent the breasts sagging. The cure was to smear the breasts, stomach and thighs with the blood of a woman whose menstruation has just started,[29] with the mentality that her youth and vitality would be transferred to the ageing woman.

One of the main signs of ageing was the inability to get pregnant and the ending of the menstrual cycle. Pregnancy was a major part of life for an Egyptian woman, and she spent most of her adult years pregnant or breastfeeding. For many poorer people in society, a trip to the doctor to confirm pregnancy may have been too expensive, and they relied on local women as well as signs in their own body. The richer members of the community, however, would visit the doctor for a pregnancy test. The most obvious means of identifying pregnancy was calculating when menstruation had stopped, and in the story of Setne Khaemwast, princess Ahwere says: 'when my time of purification came I made no more purification'. This makes it clear that the Egyptians took this as a sure sign of pregnancy.[30]

However, they understood that not all irregularities with menstrual cycles were due to pregnancy:

> If you examine a woman who experiences pain in one side of her vulva you should say concerning her. It is an irregularity of her menstrual period.[31]

The Edwin Smith Papyrus comments on amenorrhoea (missed periods):

> If you examine a woman who has spent many years without her menstruation coming; she spits out something like *hebeb*. Her belly is like that which is on fire. It ceased when she has vomited. Then

you shall say concerning it/her; it is a raising up of blood in her uterus.[32]

However, missed periods for many women were due to pregnancy, and the doctor would carry out a pregnancy test. The Berlin and Carlsberg VIII Papyrus provide the details of the test. The woman's urine was poured over barley and emmer seeds. If neither of the seeds sprouted, then the woman was not pregnant, but if they did sprout then she was. They doctor also went one step further claiming that should barley sprout first the baby was male, and if the emmer sprouted it was female.[33] These gender specifications are connected more with linguistics than science, as barley was masculine and emmer feminine in the Egyptian language.[34]

In 1968, scientific experiments were carried out in order to test this pregnancy indication using forty-eight urine samples; two male, six non-pregnant and forty pregnant women. The samples were poured over barley and emmer seeds. As would be expected with the male and non-pregnant samples, neither seed grew, but in twenty-eight of the forty pregnant samples there was growth from one or both seeds. These seeds, however, did not accurately predict the sex of the baby, and was only correct in seven of the twenty-eight cases.[35] Although it was clear if the seeds sprouted the woman was pregnant, pregnancy could not be eliminated should neither have sprouted.

Once it was ascertained that a woman was pregnant, it was imperative that she should be protected against miscarriage. As miscarriage appeared to have an unknown cause in order to prevent it, it was necessary to approach the deities for help, and therefore a combination of magic and medical practices was used. For example, when women anointed their bodies with a particular oil, it was essential it was stored in the correct type of vessel. These vessels were often in the form of a naked pregnant woman, although despite her nakedness she was shown without genitalia: 'if a woman's body is closed up without an opening, she cannot miscarry'.[36]

A more common prevention was to recite spells over a piece of knotted fabric, which was then placed inside the vagina. This prevented blood flow during the pregnancy and therefore miscarriage. The spell recited over the fabric prevented blood from soiling it.[37] Another remedy to prevent miscarriage can be found on the Ebers Papyrus:

> To prevent miscarriage: the dried liver of a swallow with a sticky liquid from fermented drink to be placed on the breasts, abdomen and all other parts of the body of a woman.[38]

It is not exactly clear how this was expected to work, other than perhaps calm and relax the pregnant woman.

Following a successful birth, it was quite plausible for the woman to develop an infection, and an inflammation of the perineum is recorded in the Kahun Papyrus:

> Instructions for a lady suffering in her pubic region, her vagina and the region of her vagina which is between her buttocks. You shall say concerning it: very swollen due to giving birth. You should then prepare for her: new oil, 1 henu (450 ml) to be soaked into her vagina.[39]

Very little else was offered by means of remedies to ease pre- or post-childbirth infections, pains or trauma.

While it was clearly important for the baby not to come too early, when the time was right, a quick and trouble-free labour was desired. There are a number of spells that appear in the medical papyri from which it is not clear if they are for aiding labour when the time came, or for encouraging an abortion in an unwanted pregnancy. These spells are entitled 'for loosening a child', for 'causing a woman to give forth on the ground', to 'draw out the blood of a woman' or to 'separate a child from the womb of its mother'. For most of the spells, it is difficult to know for sure whether it is for a quick birth or an abortion, although one such spell dedicated to Hathor encourages her to attend the birth:

> Rejoicing, rejoicing in heaven, in heaven! Birth giving is accelerated! Come to me, Hathor, my mistress, in my fine pavilion, in this happy hour.[40]

There is no ambiguity here, as the spell is to speed up the birth, which is viewed as a joyful occasion. However, some of the ingredients in other remedies include date palm and acacia, which can produce anti-fertility substances,[41] or pine oil and juniper berries, which can cause uterine contractions and are normally avoided during pregnancy.[42] Moreover, the Ebers Papyrus claims sherds of a new henu-jar ground in oil and fat would: 'cause all that is in a woman's belly to come down'.[43] This could potentially cause injury and coupled with other remedies for: 'releasing a child from the belly of his mother', which include fly excrement or fresh salt from Lower Egypt that could cause infection or at best sting. Such remedies were applied either as pessaries, oral medication or bandaged to the stomach of the woman.

Other remedies could induce menstruation, although whether this was used on women reaching the menopause or for unmarried pregnant women[44] wishing for an abortion is not clear. Marjoram oil was the main ingredient, and was applied to the vagina as a poultice. When mixed with honey, it could be used to sooth feminine pains and other 'conditions of the vulva',[45] as could the application of henna oil.

How well abortion was received by the wider community is not known, although there was a complaint letter which discusses: 'death from the removal of a pregnancy', although they could be equally angered by the death or the removal.[46]

Egyptian doctors understood about the menopause and the effect it had on the menstrual cycle, and Ebers 833 comments: 'if you examine a woman who is many years old and her menstrual period does not come ...'[47] This indicates they were able to tell the difference between pregnancy and menopause, although it would seem to be by age alone.

For women who had not yet reached the menopause, it was natural that they should want to concern themselves with rudimentary family planning. Sex in ancient Egypt was intended purely for procreation, although homosexual sex (*see* chapter 5) and sex with prostitutes (*see* chapter 6) were for pleasure. With many women marrying at perhaps twelve or thirteen years of age, they started having children early and some women wanted to space their pregnancies out, if not for convenience then to allow their bodies to recover from the trauma of childbirth (*see* chapter 4). There were numerous problems that could occur following childbirth, and there seems to be at least one record from the medical papyri of a fistula (small channel or tear) between the rectum and the vagina. It is rather vague but makes reference to 'a lump of faeces as something which has gone down the vagina of his mother'.[48] The eleventh dynasty princess Hehenhit appeared to have died due to infection caused by a vesicovaginal fistula, something which is mentioned in the Kahun Gynaecological Papyrus:

Prescription for a woman whose urine is in an irksome place: if the urine keeps coming ... and she distinguishes it, she will be like this forever.[49]

The most common form of birth control was prolonged breastfeeding to prevent pregnancy. It was common, for practical reasons, to continue breastfeeding for three years, as milk was safer for the child than the food and water available. Mother's milk was considered to be a powerful substance, and there was a goddess of milk, Hezat, who was able to cure her son Anti after his flesh had been ripped from his bones, by simply pouring her milk over him. Milk was considered such a staple to live that it was called 'beer of Hezat'. However, in the remedies recorded in the medical papyri, it sometimes specifies cow or human milk, normally from a mother who has borne a male child. For example, for an eye infection the prescription was: 'black eye-paint, fat of goose, milk from one who has borne a male child, antyu-resin; both eyes painted with it'.[50]

If breastfeeding was not reliable enough, then medicinal contraceptives were utilised. On the Ebers Papyrus (783), there is no ambiguity in the expected results of using the mixture of acacia, carob, dates and honey, which was placed onto a bandage and placed into the vagina:

> Beginning of the prescriptions prepared for women/wives to allow
> a woman to cease conceiving for one year, two years or three
> years.[51]

One contraceptive is recorded on the Ramses IV Papyrus as well as the Kahun Papyrus, indicating it was a popular one, and included a mixture of 'crocodile dung, chopped over *hesa* and *awyt* liquid'.[52] This was inserted into the vagina as a tampon, allowing the dung to act as an absorbent sponge.[53] It is more likely to have worked as a deterrent to a potential suitor.[54]

Less odorous and possibly more effective was the use of honey, which contains spermicidal properties. The Ebers Papyrus suggests a pessary of plant fibre soaked with acacia fruit, colocynth, dates and honey. If fermentation of these ingredients occurred, it produced lactic acid, which dissolved in water. This is used in modern contraceptive jellies and could have had positive results.[55] Another potentially effective oral contraceptive was a mixture of beer, celery and oil, heated up and consumed for four days. Scientific studies indicate it could have antifertility effects.[56] The Berlin Papyrus appears to have a 'morning after' pill, which comprised fat, maatt herb (mandrake?), sweet ale, all boiled together and swallowed by the woman for four days in order to 'get rid of it'.[57]

Although sexuality and fertility were thought to be the responsibility of the man, with the woman acting purely as a vessel for his seed, there are no contraceptives in the medical papyri to be used by a man. It is likely, if a man did not want to impregnate his partner, he would employ *coitus interruptus* or *coitus per anum*.[58]

As discussed in chapter 1, the breasts of a woman were considered essential to her image of a fertile mother, as they were associated with breastfeeding and providing nourishment for the children. However, in ancient Egypt as in the modern world, women were afflicted with breast cancer, something for which there was no cure in the ancient past. It is difficult to identify cancer from the medical papyri alone, and with ever-increasing technology it is becoming easier to identify this in the surviving human remains. Recently, an Old Kingdom woman from Saqqara was identified as having breast cancer that had accelerated enough to spread to the bones (bone metastases), causing lesions on the cranium and one of the vertebrae. It is likely she survived for many years with the condition, requiring a great deal of home care in the final stages.[59]

One aspect of sexual activity that could not be prevented in ancient Egypt was sexually transmitted disease. As discussed in previous chapters, men had active sex lives with wives, lovers or prostitutes and used no protective barrier like modern condoms. Even women, if the texts are to be believed, were sexually active, having affairs and getting divorced and remarried. This suggests that sexually transmitted diseases may have been common, but unfortunately these are not easily identified in the archaeological record and therefore symptoms need to be matched with those discussed in the medical papyri.

One of the most discussed sexually transmitted diseases from ancient Egypt is gonorrhoea, although there is no conclusive evidence to support the theory of its existence. Manniche believes that the Bes tattoos (*see* chapter 2 and 6) present on the thighs of musicians and dancers was apotropaic, as protection against gonorrhoea,[60] although she does not expand on this theory or discuss the potential evidence for it. Ghaliounghi takes the theory further and claims it would have been prevalent in villages like Deir el Medina or Amarna.[61] Symptoms of gonorrhoea appear in the Ebers papyrus, which include leucorrhoea (a white or yellow discharge from the vagina) and burning micturition (burning sensation when urinating). The cure is a medicine made of balanites oil, honey, stibain and flakes of copper, which is said to be 'excellent to expel purulence'.[62]

Examination of the genitals of male mummies have identified small legions that some have identified as genital warts or genital herpes,[63] although studies have not shown any evidence of syphilis. Until more accurate tests are carried out on the human remains to try to identify sexually transmitted diseases, we will never know for sure how common they were.

As with many texts from ancient Egypt, the medical texts are open to interpretation, which means that sexually transmitted diseases as well as other ailments that affect the soft tissues are difficult to identify. It is essential to try to match symptoms described in the papyri with symptoms of known diseases. However, such a system is open for error and the ingredients in the remedies are often unidentifiable. That is not to say, in the future, as our knowledge of the human remains and development in the language improves, then our knowledge of the sexual health of the Egyptians will also improve.

8

SEX AND RELIGION

'He heard our pleas, he hearkened to his prayers'[1]

In our journey behind the bedroom doors of the ancient Egyptians, it is clear that sex had a purpose: to procreate. Procreation, however, was not always easy, and sometimes help was required from the gods. Therefore, sex and religion were closely intertwined. As sex was a part of everyday life and so was religion it is hardly surprising that they overlapped.

From a young age the Egyptians were familiar with religious mythological stories, and sex features in them in a number of ways; in tales of creation, sex as a form of rebirth and sex as a display of power.

Observations of the environment, especially after the inundation and the emergence of newly fertilised land, gave rise to a number of creation myths that not only explained how the world came into being but involved the gods in this annual cycle of inundation and fertility. There was no homogenous story believed by all, as each cult had their own idea regarding the Supreme Deity and his role in the creation myth.

The most important creation story was that of the Ennead of Heliopolis, which almost forms the foundation of all creation stories, with later additions being tacked onto the beginning, rather like a prequel, giving the later god supremacy. This myth took place at Heliopolis, just outside modern Cairo, and describes the creation of the Ennead (*psDt*), which were the first nine gods to exist. Very little has been exposed of this major solar city, although excavations of the temple of Ra indicate the site was bigger than Karnak.

The earliest records of the myth of the Ennead can be found in the Pyramid Texts of Unas (2375–2345 BCE). Before creation, the world comprised a primordial soup of darkness and waters personified by the deity Nun. Atum, the creator god laments:

> Not finding a place in which I could stand or sit,
> Before Heliopolis had been founded, in which I could exist;
> Before the lotus had been tied together, on which I could sit;
> Before I had made Nut so she could be over my head and Geb could marry her.[2]

Every temple in Egypt had a representation of the primordial water in the form of a sacred lake, and this was where the priests purified themselves before entering the temple. There are not many scenes showing this purification ritual, but two blocks depict the God's Wife of Amun standing ankle deep in water with signs for water above her head and in front of her. Her dress is very tight fitting and the hem is not visible, giving the impression that she was in fact naked, although it is possible the linen was good quality, and therefore transparent.[3] The accompanying text makes it clear that this purification ritual occurred prior to entering the temple:

> Going down to be purified by the God's servants (priests), and the God's Wife, God's Hand in the Qebehyt pool, in order to proceed into the temple.[4]

Although from these waters all creation began, the waters always threatened to once more engulf the world if certain rituals were not carried out. All that protected the earth from this was the vault of the sky (Nut) and the earth (Geb), which joined and created a sphere, outside of which was the primordial water (Nun).

This water was very powerful with the ability to create and to destroy, and in Papyrus Chester Beatty IV a prayer states:

> Fertile fields made pregnant by Nun,
> Thereafter to sprout good things in endless number,
> As sustenance for the living.[5]

The water itself was full of creative power, and a small mound of land rose from it providing somewhere for Atum to rest. This mound was Heliopolis. The image of a mound was familiar to all Egyptians, as every year the Nile flooded from July until October throwing the land into a watery world similar to the time before creation. When the flood started to abate small mounds of fertile land emerged from the swirling waters. This mound was also represented in all temples in the form of the sanctuary, which was always the highest point of the temple. Medinet Habu, on the other hand, had a temple dedicated to Kom Djeme, the mound of creation, and was believed to have been one of the mythical burial places of Osiris. This mound temple was surrounded by the primordial waters of Nun, and for the Decade Festival the statue of Amun–Re was carried here every ten days in order to rejuvenate his spiritual powers.[6] How this was done is not depicted, presumably as it was too sacred to represent, so it is impossible to know what sexual rituals (if any) were carried out.

Once the mound emerged from the primeval waters, the solar deity, Atum, began his own creation and rose as the first dawn. He was able to self-develop by simply desiring it: 'It was as I wished, according to my heart that I built myself'.[7] As a creator god he was androgynous and produced offspring without the need of a female counterpart:

> Oh Atum-Kheprer, you became high on the height, ... you spat out Shu, you coughed up Tefnut, and you set your arms about them as the *ka* symbol, that your essence might be in them.[8]

There are, however, alternative records of this monumental event. Papyrus Bremner-Rhind states:

> I made every form alone, without another having developed and acted with me ... For my part, the fact is that I acted as husband with my fist, I copulated with my hand, I let fall from my mouth by myself, I sneezed Shu and spat Tefnut.[9]

The petrified form of Atum's semen is believed to have formed a pyramid shape which was known as the benben stone. The original was housed in the Temple of the Benben at Heliopolis, and this shape later formed the capstone of all pyramids. The two deities born from the bodily ejaculations of Atum were Shu, the god of air or atmosphere whose name meant empty or void, and his sister Tefnut, the goddess of moisture. Both of these deities took their place in the void created by the sky and the earth.

Shu is generally depicted standing with his arms raised supporting the sky goddess Nut, or sailing between the sky and the earth god Geb in a boat. He is identified by a feather upon his head. He was also visible to the people on earth in the form of clouds, which were used by the king to ascend to heaven.

Tefnut's name means to spit, and she was the goddess of moisture. The Pyramid Texts claim she produced pure water for the king's feet from her vagina connecting the king with creation and also emphasising the importance of the deity's bodily fluids. The visible sign of Tefnut's presence could be witnessed in the morning dew.

As the first male/female couple, Shu and Tefnut conceived in the traditional way, and Tefnut gave birth to the next generation of gods, Geb, the god of the earth, and Nut, the sky goddess. Nut became important in the solar mythology, as every evening at dusk she swallowed the sun god. He travelled her body at night, and she gave birth to him in the morning amidst a flood of birthing blood stretched across the sky at dawn.

Geb was not as essential to the mythology other than his role in creation, and was shown in human form, sometimes with green skin representative of vegetation. The papyrus of Ten-Amun (twenty-first dynasty) shows Geb's body decorated with Nile reeds in flower, and other images show barley sprouting from his ribs. Therefore, he was closely associated with agriculture and vegetation.

These two deities were visible all the time to the ancient Egyptians as they formed the protective sphere around their world. However, they were a sombre couple, and their laughter could spell disaster; earthquakes were caused by Geb's laughter and thunder by Nut's.

The coupling of Nut and Geb was also visible to the population in the form of the horizon blending into one another. In illustrations, Nut is depicted stretched over Geb as he reclines close to the earth. The imagery of Nut in this position suggests her hands and feet touch the four cardinal points of the earth. The cenotaph of Seti I at Abydos explains:

Her right arm is on the north-western side, the left on the south-western side. Her head is the western horizon, her mouth is in the

western horizon, her crotch is the eastern horizon ... With her rear
in the east and her head in the west.[10]

The deities from the Heliopolitan myth explained the environment
to the populace by placing human values and relationships to
it. However, it was the next generation of gods, the offspring of
Geb and Nut, which were considered more important, as they
explained the foundation of kingship ideology. Nut and Geb gave
birth to Osiris, Isis, Seth and Nephthys, who are all part of the
mythology of Osiris and Seth. Seth, as the god of chaos, is said to
have ripped himself from the womb of Nut,[11] which is the only
reference to the actual birth of the gods. Osiris and Isis then gave
birth to Horus, cementing the ideas of rebirth and fertility (*see*
chapter 9). As the king was believed to be a living incarnation of
Horus, this mythology ensured he could trace his genealogy back
to the sun god, emphasising his divinity and therefore right to rule.

Although the Heliopolitan myth was the foundation creation
myth, others soon developed favouring a local deity over those
in the Ennead. One such myth was that from Middle Egypt from
the site of El Ashmunein, near Amarna. Their creator deities were
known as the Ogdoad of Hermopolis. Hermopolis was the cult
centre for the god Thoth, the ibis-headed god of writing, education
and knowledge, as well as the Ogdoad until the time of Alexander
the Great. The eight deities of the Ogdoad comprised four couples,
with female snakes and male frogs, although sometimes they are
depicted as baboons. They resided in the primeval waters of Nun,
and each represented a different divine concept present in the
primordial chaos before creation. Nu and Naunet represented
primeval waters, Heh and Hekhet represented flood force, Kek and
Kauket represented darkness and Amun and Amaunet represented
concealed activity.

The frantic activity of the divine couples in the water, forced the mound of creation, known as the Isle of Flame, out of the water, which played host to the first dawn:

> The fathers and the mothers who came into being at the beginning, who gave birth to the Sun and who created Atum.[12]

Although these eight deities were fundamental for all the other creation myths, which all took place on this mound, six of the eight deities slip into obscurity and are not referred to again. Heket, the frog goddess of childbirth, maintained a fertility role and aided women during the last stages of labour and was discussed in chapter 4. Amun and Amaunet also maintained their divine status and became the focus of their own cult. Amun took a new form of a snake rather than the primeval frog. Snakes represented rebirth due to the ability to slough its skin without dying. The cult of his form of Amun-Kem-Atef grew, and instead of simply being one of the eight creator deities, he was promoted to the one who created the Ogdoad. He was one 'who fashioned himself' before the existence of the Ogdoad and was 'the father of the fathers of the Ogdoad'.[13] By the eleventh dynasty, these primordial associations were mostly forgotten, as his cult developed further until he was the god of Thebes. However, the primeval form of Kem-Atef was not totally abandoned, and the statue of Amun from Karnak was carried to the shrine at Medinet Habu in procession to greet his ancestor in the form of 'he who has completed his moment'.[14]

The two deities separated, so Kem-Atef was no longer a form of Amun but was considered to be his ancestor. Furthermore, Luxor Temple is dedicated to the creator aspects of Amun as a nod to his primeval origins, where he is entitled the 'Bull of the Ennead,' and 'the creator who begets himself and all beings'.

This creator element of Amun becomes essential in his connection with the king, and he holds the title 'Bull of his Mother', indicating that he was the creator and the created, an epithet also adopted by the king. Amun's connection with the creation myth was further emphasised in his role of 'The Great Honker', where he is represented as a primeval goose, whose voice instigated the activity in the primeval waters, which subsequently started creation.

The bodily fluids of Amun, as with other deities, also have a creative function, and he claims: 'I brought the gods into being from my sweat; and people are from the tears of my eye'.[15] The sweat of the god was considered a special and beautiful thing, and often incense is referred to in this way. Egyptian priests particularly favoured terebinth resin, olibanum (frankincense) and myrrh for temple use in order to represent the god's presence.

One of the most famous forms of incense known was kyphi and was used throughout the Pharaonic Period to the modern era. Over the centuries, the recipe changed although the earliest ingredients included honey, frankincense, mastic, genen of niuben tree, pine kernals, cyperus grass, camel grass, inektun-herb and cinnamon.[16] By the reign of Ramses III, raisins were also added, and by the first century CE fragrant wine was a key ingredient. Kyphi was used to treat snake bites as well as for fumigation. Lighting incense in a space sanctified it and enabled those in the room to experience the god. Plutarch claims the incense was lit as often as three times a day. He also adds that there were certain narcotic characteristics about it:

The [ingredients] emit a sweet breath and a beneficent exhalation
by which all is changed, while the body, being moved by the whiff
softly and gently acquires a temper that seductively brings on sleep,

so that without intoxication it relaxes and loosens the chain-like sorrows and tensions of daily cares.[17]

Temple and tomb walls are covered with depictions of the king and priests giving offerings of incense to the gods. This was not simply a royal prerogative, as in the Book of the Dead the deceased also offered incense and burners, as have been discovered in the tombs.[18]

Incense was an expensive commodity as it was imported, and scenes at Deir el Bahri depict incense trees being carried into Egypt. They are thought to represent frankincense and myrrh which Hatshepsut was hoping to plant these trees and make them a commodity of Egypt. The level of success of this plan is difficult to gauge, although there are two tree pits currently visible at the temple indicating they were planted here. Evidence suggests that these trees formed part of a garden within the enclosure wall of the temples, which also comprised T-shaped pools.

The cult of Amun became such an important one that the temple of Karnak became the most powerful in Egypt, and in the Third Intermediate Period, the High Priests of Amun had enough power to take over the throne of Egypt. A particularly unique aspect of the cult of Amun was that he was furnished with his own 'harem' comprising a group of priestesses known as the God's Wives of Amun.

Priestesses were generally supporting roles for priests in most cults, and were responsible for singing, dancing and playing instruments in religious processions and the daily worship of the cults. Roles with more responsibility were normally only held by priestesses of the cults of goddesses such as Hathor, Mut or Isis. However, the role of God's Wife of Amun held the same status as the king within the temple.

This role was introduced in the Middle Kingdom when the title was held by two women; one was the God's Wife of Min of Akhmim, and the other with the cult of Amun-Ra at Karnak. By the eighteenth dynasty the title was held only by royal women: the daughter, sister or the Great Royal Wife of the king. The first holder was Queen Ahhotep, the mother of Ahmose I, and the title was given to her in order to ensure a senior royal female was in the top hierarchy of the cult of Amun. The role of second prophet of Amun, a title normally held by a man, was held by Ahmose-Nefertary, the daughter of Ahhotep.[19]

It was clearly impractical at this point for the role to be a celibate one, but as time progressed the title holders were always unmarried. They chose and named their successor in the same manner as a childless king named his. There was only one God's Wife at any one time, and once they adopted their successor, she was trained on the job. Unfortunately, the criteria for this adoption are not clear. The king may have been involved in the adoption process, as he often gave one of his unmarried daughters to the God's Wife in order to take up the position.[20] Their initiation into the position upon the death of the previous God's Wife was a spectacular one with a river procession as well as: 'every ceremony as was done for Tefnut in the beginning'.[21] This connection with Tefnut, one of the Ennead of Heliopolis, does suggest there was a creation or fertility aspect to the role.

The role fell into disuse at the end of the eighteenth dynasty, and was not revived again until the reign of Tawosret (1187–1185 BCE) who used it when she ruled alongside Siptah. However, it reached a powerful high point in the Third Intermediate Period. In the twenty-fifth and twenty-sixth dynasties, the God's Wife of Amun was more powerful than the High Priest of Amun at Karnak and was essentially the head of the cult. In the twenty-sixth dynasty, Nitocris became the God's Wife, and it is recorded at Karnak that she travelled from the Delta to the Thebes by river procession accompanied by a large dowry,[22] exactly as if it was a wedding (*see* chapter 3).

The role of God's Wife was a complex one as they were responsible for rituals that reinforced the king's legitimacy to rule as well as the maintenance of Maat throughout the whole world. They were often depicted in closer proximity to the god than the king ever was. The god Amun was often represented holding hands or embracing the God's Wife, showing the intimacy of a husband for his wife. From the twenty-first dynasty, the God's Wife adopted a second cartouche for her own name,[23] something only normally given to kings and sometimes Great Royal Wives.

There were three titles connected to the role and its hierarchy; the senior position of God's Wife, of which there was only one; the God's Adoratice, who was the heir to the senior role and the God's Hand, which seemed to be an intermediary position somewhere between the two.[24] This latter title could be in reference to the creation myth where Atum masturbated to create the next generation. However, there is no evidence that there were any sexual relations with the gods or the priests of Amun.[25] A further suggestion is that this title of God's Hand or Hand of the God could refer to the role as a female counterpart of the king, as often she performed rituals alongside him.[26]

However, there was a sexual or fertility element to the title. The initiation of a new God's Wife was presented as a marriage to the god and this idea of a marital union between the priestess and the god could represent the divine conception of the king[27] as depicted in the divine birth scenes (*see* chapter 3). Initially, the cult was associated with the cult of the ithyphallic deity Min, and this cemented the idea in the minds of Egyptologists that there must have been a sexual aspect to the role of God's Wife, as they were responsible for arousing the sexuality of the god.

Moreover, evidence suggests there were sexually oriented rituals, although the exact nature of them is unclear. One such ritual follows the Decade Festival, where every ten days Amun-Ra visited Kom Djeme (mound of creation) at Medinet Habu for rejuvenation. When he returned to Karnak, the God's Wife participated in the two-day divine re-entrance ritual. During this ritual, Amun was represented as 'He whose hand is holy' and 'Bull of his Mother', showing the fertility aspects of this re-entry. Two statues representing these gods were placed in shrines and carried in procession by four priests each. The only women at this ritual were the God's Wife and her entourage.[28] Although the sexual aspect of the role is unclear, in the divine birth scene of Amenhotep III at Luxor temple, Amun is called 'pre-eminent in his harem',[29] indicating that, like the king, the god had a number of women to pleasure him at his will.

There were other festivals that celebrated divine marriage, including the Festival of the Beautiful Valley, which also saw a procession of the god Amun travelling to the west bank of the Nile at Luxor and resting overnight at the temple of Deir el Bahri. Here he celebrated a ritual wedding night with the goddess Hathor. Hathor of Denderah also featured in a similar festival where she began a journey from Denderah to Edfu for the summer Festival of the Beautiful Embrace,[30] which was a form of sacred marriage. On the day of the new moon, she arrived at Edfu and was met by Horus. They were both presented with an image of the goddess of truth, Maat, before retiring to the temple of Horus at Edfu for a marriage that was celebrated for two weeks with additional feasting.[31] It is quite likely that married couples saw these festivals as an excellent time to conceive a child as it was a great time of fertility instigated by the divine coupling occurring in the temples.

Whereas these festivals required a male/female deity in order to re-enact a sacred marriage, this was sometimes unnecessary for Amun, as he was a creator god in his own right and therefore contained fertility characteristics of both male and female within himself.

This is one of the most characteristic aspects of any creator god, as it was their androgynous nature that enabled them to recreate themselves and then others. The king was also, at times, presented in this androgynous form in order to demonstrate his divinity and his fertility. Most displayed themselves with the title Kamutef (Bull of his Mother). This title emphasised the fertility of the king and his ability to self-create through the act of impregnating his mother with himself. How this act comes about is never explained, but that further demonstrated his divine fertility.[32]

One king, Akhenaten, took this idea one step further, and adopted the androgyny of the creator gods in his artwork, presenting himself as both masculine and feminine. The statues of Akhenaten from the Gempaaten temple at Karnak show him with breasts, large hips and a sagging stomach. Over the decades, there has been a great deal of debate about these representations, with theories ranging from realistic representation of potential deformities, hermaphroditism, or even that the images are Nefertiti.[33]

The most popular theories are those regarding realistic representation of possible diseases, which include Frolich's Syndrome (Dystrophia Adiposogenitalis), a condition that leads to obesity; Marfan's Syndrome, which is a hereditary disease where the sufferer grows very tall and thin; or Klinefelter's Syndrome where the male sufferer has breasts, small testes, very long legs, a high pitched voice and limited facial hair growth. Without a clearly identified body of Akhenaten, it is impossible to know whether he suffered from anything and therefore the theories will continue to be discussed *ad infinitum*. It is more likely, however, that the representations have a ritualistic element to them and he is representing himself as a creator god, in essence the mother[34] and father of the people of Egypt. This would fit in with his religious ideals, where all of the gods of Egypt had been abandoned to be replaced by himself.

Aside from the creation myths, of which here only two have been discussed, the most obvious religious tale to discuss ideas of fertility, birth and rebirth is the myth of Osiris and Isis. Osiris, the king of Egypt, was murdered by his brother Seth and cut into fourteen pieces. These were scattered throughout Egypt except for the penis, which Seth threw into the Nile. The grief experienced by Osiris' wife Isis manifested itself annually in the form of the inundation of the Nile, which was believed to be started by her tears. According to later Greek records, the tears that started the inundation were in fact tears of joy at her later pregnancy.[35] The inundation was a time of great fertility throughout Egypt, because when the flood waters abated, rich silt was deposited across the land fertilising it for the following year's crops. Therefore, this act of grief instigated the rebirth of the land and was something the population of Egypt greatly relied on.

In her grief, Isis travelled the length and breadth of Egypt collecting the pieces of her husband Osiris in order to resurrect him. Plutarch records:

> The only part of Osiris which Isis did not find was his male member; for no sooner had it been thrown into the river than it was swallowed by the *lepidotus*, the *phagrus* and the *oxyrrhyncus* fish ... In its place Isis shaped a dummy and consecrated the phallus to whose honour the Egyptians celebrate a feast to this day.[36]

This phallus, formed from Nile clay, is steeped in sexual imagery. Not only was Isis able to resurrect Osiris by re-forming his penis but she was also able to impregnate herself upon it, with Horus.

Even the fish that ate the phallus of Osiris were considered sacred, and it was forbidden to catch them and eat them in life. However, these fish are often depicted in non-royal tombs in the fishing and fowling scenes (*see* chapter 9). The deceased is depicted with these fish on the end of his spear, and they transfer fertility and eternal life onto him.

The artistic representations of Osiris's resurrection show an ithyphallic Osiris lying on a funerary bier with his hand around his erect penis. Above, Isis in the form of a kite lowers herself onto it. Combined with her ability to later protect her son in the marshes from the dangers of snakes and scorpions, Isis was attributed with the power of healing and was approached to cure fever and burns as well as bites from venomous snakes and crocodiles. The healing elements can be found within her bodily fluids and she states: 'water is within my mouth and a Nile flood between my thighs'.[37] This is a common element in religious myths, as not only do the tears of Isis start the fertile floods, but the bodily fluids of the creator god Atum were enough to instigate the creation of the entire world.

The primary element of the Osiris myth is fertility, in the form of Osiris' resurrection and his subsequent rebirth. And there is no better symbol of fertility than the phallus. The phallus of Osiris features in the scenes of his resurrection but was also associated with the fertility gods Amun, Min and from the Old Kingdom the baboon deity Baba. In Coffin Text V 92, Baba begets human children and calves,[38] presenting him as a minor creator deity.

In later times, Osiris was associated with the Greek god Dionysus, and Herodotus records a festival of Osiris of the ithyphallic form of Dionysus:

> In other ways the Egyptian method of celebrating the festival of Dionysus is much the same as the Greek, except that the Egyptians have no choric dance. Instead of the phallus they have puppets, about eighteen inches high; the genitals of these figures are made almost as big as the rest of their bodies, and they are pulled up and down by strings as the women carry them round the villages. Flutes led the procession and women as they follow sing a hymn to Dionysus.[39]

This festival was thought to be one associated with the harvest and the themes of fertility and rebirth that accompany it. Osiris, in addition to being the god of the dead, was also closely associated with the harvest.

His myth recounts the cycle of life, death and rebirth, and this was witnessed in the annual harvest. Therefore, the myth of Osiris and Seth was incorporated into the daily agricultural routines. In Ramesseum Dramatic Papyrus dated to the Middle Kingdom, it is recorded that the cattle employed to trample the barley during threshing were punished, presumably beaten, for being followers of Seth and contributing to the murder of Osiris. Osiris was represented by the barley and Seth was in the hooves of the cattle. Osiris's connection with the harvest is further emphasised on the twenty-sixth dynasty sarcophagus of Ankhnesneferibra:

> Hail you are the maker of grain, he who gives life to the gods with the water of his limbs, and bread to every land with the water than takes form under him ...

Barley has taken form out of the limbs of Osiris, when Thoth placed him in the Good Domain [embalming workshop].[40]

The local farmers, working on the fields, invoked the fertility of Osiris into their daily tasks through the singing of a song which was probably sung as a round between two groups or two men:

Q – O West! Where is the Shepherd? The shepherd of the West?
A – The shepherd is in the water with the fish. He speaks with the *phagos*-fish and converses with the *oxyrhynchus* fish.[41]

Other rituals associated with the harvest include the Driving of the Four Calves, which is depicted in numerous temples, and in Karnak, Ramses II is shown performing this ritual no less than six times. The calves were presented by the king to various gods in order to seek the grave or to tread the grave,[42] in reference to hiding the grave of Osiris from his brother Seth. The calves walked through the fields and pushed the seeds into the ground starting the process of rebirth and new life, which is a common, universal theme of Osiris and the harvest. Burying the seeds enabled them to be reborn as was the case with Osiris.

Osiris died, was reborn, and impregnated his wife after death. He was therefore seen as a fertility god, and this fertility was witnessed with the growth of the seeds. This seed growth was also used to represent the rebirth of the deceased by placing an Osiris bed into the tomb. These were also very similar to corn-mummies, a non-funerary ritual item for the cult of Osiris. The Osiris bed was a tray in the shape of Osiris lined with Nile mud and seeds, and the corn mummy was a three-dimensional figure of Osiris with an erect penis made of Nile mud impregnated with barley seeds. For both the corn mummy and the Osiris bed, once the seeds started to grow into the shape of Osiris, it represented the rebirth of Osiris and therefore by default the rebirth of the deceased.

The careful observation of the environment and the animals that inhabited it led to a rise of animal cults, some of which were said to have included fertility rites and sexualised rituals. However, the evidence we have of sexual acts associated with animal cults come from Greek chroniclers and may not be accurate. It is possible that this was information they were given which suited their desire for deviant behaviour but was not necessarily verified. Alternatively these practices were Graeco-Roman and therefore may not be applicable to the earlier periods of Egyptian history. For example, there are a number of Graeco-Roman figurines depicting women in sexual positions with baboons or baboons grasping oversized phalli. Baboons were sacred to the god Thoth,[43] the god of writing and intelligence, but there are no similar images from the Pharaonic Period, indicating this was not a common statue form at the time. Herodotus writing in the fifth century BCE tells us about a particularly graphic sexual ritual for the cult of Mendes:

> The Mendesians hold all goats in veneration, especially the male ones, whose keepers enjoy special honours. One of them is held in particular reverence and when he dies the whole province goes into mourning. Mendes is the Egyptian name both for Pan and for a goat. In this province not long ago a goat tupped a woman in full view of everybody – a most surprising incident.[44]

Mendes was the sacred animal of the fertility god Min, and therefore such a ritual may have passed the god's fertility onto the woman. Min was represented in ithyphallic form, wrapped in a cloak with one arm raised, and his phallus represented creation and fertility for humans, animals and crops.[45] Although there is no evidence of this ritualised sex-act from the Pharaonic Period, there are pictorial representations from the Graeco-Roman Period showing this ritual taking place.

Herodotus further records the festival of the cat goddess, Bastet:

> The procedure at Bubastis is this: they come in barges, men and women together, a great number in each boat; on the way, some of the women keep up a continual clatter with castanets and some of the men play flutes, while the rest both men and women, sing and clap their hands. Whenever they pass a town on the river-bank, they bring the barge close in-shore, some of the women continuing to act as I have said, while others shout abuse at the women of the place, or start dancing, or stand up and hitch up their skirts. When they reach Bubastis they celebrate the festival with elaborate sacrifices, and more wine is consumed than during all the rest of the year.[46]

Diodorus (60–57 BCE) describes a similar ritual at the installation of the sacred Apis Bull, a vessel for the ka of the creator god Ptah. For a period of forty days the bull was kept in a ritualistic quarantine before the main ceremony:

> Putting it on a state barge fitted out with a gilded cabin, they conduct it as a god to the sanctuary of Hephaestus at Memphis. During ... forty days only women may look at it; these stand facing it, and pulling up their garments show their genitals, but henceforth they are forever prevented from coming into the presence of this god.[47]

It was believed that the act of the women exposing themselves to the gods stimulated the fertility of the god. The forty-day period in which the new Apis Bull was kept in isolation makes reference to the forty days a new mother and her child were considered in danger and were kept isolated at this time. Therefore, the Apis Bull was believed to be in this neonate state of vulnerability and the women exposing themselves a means of protecting them.[48]

This act of women exposing themselves may very well have been practiced in Pharaonic cults as well as Graeco-Roman. Papyrus Chester Beatty I, dated to the reign of Ramses V (twentieth dynasty), tells a myth where the sun god, Ra, was depressed and needed cheering up:

> After a long time Hathor, lady of the southern sycamore, came and stood before her father, the master of the universe. She uncovered her vulva for his face, and the great god smiled at her.[49]

Whether this is considered as an erotic display is under question, as none of the descriptions of women exposing themselves seem particularly erotic or sexual; more matter of fact.

This myth is potentially further manifested into festival form, and in one Middle Kingdom tomb there is an image of *xnr* dancers performing at a funeral, naked with small exposed bare breasts.[50] It is possible this troupe of dancers also performed at temples in reference to Hathor's act, but it may have been considered inappropriate to depict this on temple walls. In Papyrus Westcar and the tale of the birth of the fifth dynasty kings, a dancing troupe shaking their sistra and menat necklaces, both sacred to Hathor, were asked to act as midwives to the woman, Rededjet, indicating there was clearly a connection between the cult of Hathor, childbirth and dancing.

The sistra and menat while being sacred to Hathor were in fact used by priestesses in all religious cults. The sistrum comprised a handle, often with a small face of Hathor with cow's ears, and an arch in bronze with bronze sticks threaded through, which moved when shaken. The menat was essentially a bead necklace with numerous strands. It was held by the counterpoise, which was a key-shaped piece of metal that counterbalanced the weight of the necklace when worn, and the beads made a rattling sound as they hit together when shaken. Some believe that the sistrum and menat necklaces could bestow life and therefore had a role to play in rebirth[51] or embodied the power of Hathor. The king is often depicted wearing an oversized menat necklace, and it is thought to represent Hathor herself and therefore ensured the king's rebirth:[52] 'For your virility the neck-ornaments of Hathor; may she lengthen your life to [the number of] years you desire'.[53]

Music calmed the gods and abated their anger, and none more so than the swooshing sound of these instruments,[54] which resembled the noise of Hathor's movement through the marshes. This noise was considered calming, and the name for the sistrum was the onomatopoeic *sesheshet*:[55] 'it banishes the irritation, it dispels the rage that is the heart of the goddess and makes her affable after her grimness'.[56]

Playing these instruments was an important ritual, and in the tomb of Queen Merysankh, the granddaughter and wife of Khafre, she is depicted 'shaking the papyrus for Hathor'.[57] This was an ancient festival mentioned in the Pyramid Texts, and some scholars suggest it derived from the practice of picking flowers for a lover, whereas other suggestions indicate it is the shaking of the papyrus rather than the plucking that was the most important aspect of the festival. King Wahankh-Intef (eleventh dynasty) describes in his tomb his desire to play music for the goddess:

I am indeed the one who causes the morning awakening of the sistrum player of Hathor every day, at whatever hour she wishes.

May your heart be content with the sistrum player. May you travel in peace.[58]

The ritualised music playing was probably choreographed where one musician shook the sistrum followed by another with the menat, rather than random shaking by all. Although music is associated with the goddess Hathor, it was actually devised by Thoth, the god of knowledge, learning and intelligence. This role of creating music and harmony being attributed to such an important deity emphasises the importance of the role of music in religion.

The Hathor cult was interspersed with festivals, which encouraged dancing, singing and alcohol consumption, which also no doubt led to sexual encounters. As the go-to goddess for conception, what better time to try to conceive a child than during a festival? At least two of her festivals were of a sexual nature; one was called the Opening of the Bosoms of the Women, and another where a large phallus was carried in procession.[59] Although the details of these festivals are not provided, there is clearly a sexual focus, which may have been an ideal place for men and women to mingle and instigate sexual relationships. Dancing and music were clearly important features, as Hathor:

> ... feeds on praise,
> Because the food of her desire is dancing,
> Who shines on the festival at the time of lighting [the lamps]
> Who is content with the dancing at night.[60]

This indicates that many of the festivals to Hathor took place at night, further emphasising the sexual and sensual aspect of her festivals. One of the most famous festivals was the Festival of Drunkenness, which may have been in commemoration of the myth of the Destruction of Mankind when Hathor in her form of

Sekhmet was sent to punish mankind for rebelling against the sun god. To stop her, the priests tricked her into drinking so much beer that she fell asleep. This festival was clearly an opportunity for the population to get drunk in the name of religion. For the Egyptians, drunkenness 'was not the same thing as ordinary befuddling of the senses'[61] but was rather believed to be a means of becoming closer to the goddess. Alcohol appeased the wrath of the goddess Sekhmet in the tale of the Destruction of Mankind, and it was believed to have the same effect on the followers of Hathor. However, the Egyptians were a practical people and believed:

> It is however good when people get drunk,
> When they drink ... with happy hearts.
> It is however good when mouths shout for joy,
> When nome-lords watch the shouting from their homes'.[62]

Hathor is normally depicted as a cow, a woman with cow's ears or a cow-horn headdress. She is a mother goddess as well as the goddess of love, music and sexuality. This aspect of her cult is represented quite clearly by her own name: *hwt Hr* or temple of Horus, and is depicted by a hieroglyph showing a temple with Horus inside. This represents her role as the mother of Horus (normally this is Isis but they soon became interchangeable) as well as the divine mother of all kings with the temple aspect of her name representing a womb. In other versions of the myths, Hathor is the wife of Horus of Edfu, showing that the relationship between the gods was fluid. Furthermore, she is often associated with the ithyphallic deity Min, and together they represent the masculine and feminine forms of sexuality.[63] Min was represented as mummiform with an enormous erect phallus, and one arm raised holding a flail. He is one of the few deities who can be traced to the earliest times, with two colossal statues dated prior to 3000 BCE being discovered at Koptos of a male deity clasping his erect penis in one hand. These are currently on display in the Ashmolean Museum, Oxford. During the reign of Ramses III, there was a four-day festival dedicated to the god Min, where the god and statues of ancestral kings were carried in procession, clearly associating the fertility of the god with the kings. However, Ramses III omitted Hatshepsut and the Amarna kings from this procession, as their reigns were believed to go against Maat. The king was expected to participate in the rituals of the festival in the form of shooting arrows to the four cardinal points, as well as making a show of harvesting crops.

Goods connected with the cult of Hathor were found buried in the foundation deposit at the cult temple of Min at Koptos. Min was an interesting deity, as he is one of the few deities who has his own sacred vegetable, the lettuce. This was believed to be an aphrodisiac due to the white liquid that seeps from the stem when cut, and he is rarely depicted without these lettuces behind him. In temple cults, flowers and vegetables are mostly offered to ithyphallic forms of Amun-Ra[64] or Min. Hathor also has a sacred tree, the Sycamore, which provided sustenance for the deceased in the form of figs and was therefore associated with rebirth.[65]

It needs to be considered that any over-sexualised rituals carried out may have been considered acceptable in the temples in relation to aspects of kingship and divinity, but this was a far cry from the religion of the populace of Egypt. As sex features in the state religion involving the gods and the royal family, sex and fertility was also a major feature of the everyday interaction of the ordinary people with the gods.

Elaborate temple rituals were not part of their religious practice, as most worship was carried out in the home within the front room of the house incorporating a shrine dedicated to ancestors and household deities. This is not to say that Egyptians did not participate in temple worship in the limited capacity that they were able. Temples on the whole were closed to the public and were only accessible to the king, priests and officials with special permission to enter. Therefore, for most people they were unable to appeal to the gods directly. At best, people left votive offerings at a chapel outside the main temple walls, addressed the god through ear chapels on the external part of a temple or, for the privileged few, slept in one of the temples, in order to receive divine messages from the gods that provided advice on their problems and needs. The Deir el Medina scribe, Qenhirkhopshef was a great believer in the power of sleep therapy and the importance of dreams, and among his personal archive was a book of dream interpretations. It is therefore not surprising that he tells us: 'I have slept in your forecourt. I have made stelae in the temple beside the lords of Djeseret [Deir el Bahri]'.[66]

Although he states he slept in the temple of Deir el Bahri, during the New Kingdom people could sleep at the temple at Deir el Medina, Denderah, Abydos, Sety I temple Serapeum at Memphis and the temple of Hathor at Deir el Bahri. It is thought that this practice continued until the Graeco-Roman Period. Hathor is described as a goddess who listens to: 'the requests of all maidens who weep'.[67]

She was titled the 'lady of happiness' and people also addressed her in order to maintain a happy relationship. It was customary to leave an offering to the deity if a request was made, and one statue base claims: 'if cakes are placed before her, she will not be angry'.[68] One couple to leave such offerings were the Deir el Medina scribe Ramose and his wife Mutemwia, who wanted to conceive a child. For them it was not successful, as they adopted their son, Qenhirkhopshef, who took over Ramose's role after his death.

In chapter 2 we met the young girl Taimhotep who was married to the High Priest of Ptah, Psherenptah. They paid a much higher price than cakes in their request to the god, Imhotep. He was the deified architect responsible for the construction of Djoser's step pyramid at Saqqara. During the Ptolemaic Period, he was a god of medicine and a draw for couples wishing to conceive. In their marriage, Taimhotep and Psherenptah were fortunate enough to have three daughters but desperately wanted a son:

> I was pregnant by him three times but did not bear a male child, only three daughters. I prayed together with the high priest to the majesty of the god ... Imhotep, son of Ptah.
>
> He heard our pleas, he hearkened to his prayers. The majesty of this god came to the head of the high priest in a revelation. He said 'Let a great work be done in the holy of holies of Ankhtawi, the place where my body is hidden. As a reward for it I shall give you a male child'.[69]

Although it is not clear whether the couple slept at his temple, the god revealed himself to Psherenptah in a dream, requesting a shrine should be built in Ankhtawi (just outside Memphis). Obviously, Psherenptah commissioned the sanctuary and Taimhotep was blessed with a son, whom she named Imhotep-Pedibast.[70] Herodotus also discussed this form of temple worship by stating:

> There is a woman who sleeps in the temple of the Theban Jupiter [the temple of Amun] and it is reported than these women have no intercourse with any man.[71]

Herodotus emphasised that this was not a form of temple prostitution or ritualised sex, but instead simply sleeping in the temple. In both the Story of Setne and the story of the Doomed Prince, childless couples slept in the temple in the hope of conceiving.[72]

One of the most popular deities worshipped in the home was Bes, the dwarf god of childbirth, music and dancing (*see* chapter 4). He was worshipped by women of childbearing age and was a protector of children. Furthermore, amulets in the form of Bes were worn by both women and children in life for protection of the latter and fertility of the former. Although a household deity, the dado in the palace bedroom of Amenhotep III at Malkata was decorated with images of Bes, no doubt to aid his fertility. The wives of Thutmosis III were also buried with a bracelet made of hollowed out golden Bes figures, which provided protection for the afterlife, showing that Bes was a god for rich and poor alike.

Throughout the Pharaonic Period there were no temples to Bes, as he was worshipped primarily in the home. However, there is evidence from the Ptolemaic Period at Saqqara of a small Bes shrine. The shrine, situated to the east of the temple of Teti, consisted of a few small rooms, located near an enclosure wall surrounding the now-lost Anubeum. The layout is similar to a typical New Kingdom house, and indicates there was a daily life association. The walls were constructed of mud-brick and limestone fragments and there were large statues of the god Bes standing 1–1.5 m tall, made from painted clay. Next to the statues were figures of nude ladies worshipping him and caressing his protruding stomach. There were also large platforms, which may have been used as sleeping platforms for dream therapy,[73] fertility treatment or even childbirth. It is even suggested that during the purification period after childbirth or even menstruation, some of the women in the community may have spent the time in the Bes chambers. Excavation at the site uncovered limestone votive statues of Bes, some ithyphallic, indicating fertility was unsurprisingly a major focus of his cult, as well as a number of erotic figures of couples making love. It has been suggested that these Bes chambers may have been used by cultic prostitutes dedicated to the goddess Astarte.[74] However, institutional prostitution is not an Egyptian practice, and the evidence for this is ambiguous. The cult developed further in the Roman Period, and the Roman historian Ammianus Marcellinus records an oracle of Bes in Upper Egypt.

It was not unusual to leave votive offerings at temples, especially those associated with fertility in one form or another. Each votive offering, while looking like interesting artefacts today, at the time were steeped with personal emotion, whether a man was asking the god to help with impotence or fertility, or a woman was asking to conceive or for a healthy birth, the effort to purchase or make a votive offering, visit the temple, wait in line, and recite the appropriate prayers was an emotional time and for many may have been a last resort. The most popular goddess as the recipient of sexualised votive offerings was Hathor. As she was a one-stop-shop for marital bliss, it is not surprising that there is one text where the woman is praying for 'a good child of this house, happiness and a good husband'.[75]

Phalli were popular votive offerings, although despite the life-size and realistic shape, there is no evidence they were used for anything else, although in the Turin Erotic Papyrus a woman is sitting on an upturned pot, showing external stimuli were not unheard of.[76] It has been suggested that, as many of the phalli offerings taper towards the end, this made them easier to hold, although whether this was part of a religious ritual or, whether they were inserted into something or used as a sexual aid is unknown.

Rarer than phalli are votive offerings in the form of vaginas or breasts. At the temple of Hathor at Deir el Bahri, a small blue frit, oval plaque was discovered bearing a relief of a pair of breasts. There was a hole at the top so the plaque could be suspended, although what the offering was hoping for is unspecified. The British Museum also has two plaques displaying the pubic triangle and a small slit, representative of a vulva, also found at the temple of Deir el Bahri.[77] Most of the offerings are hoping for something from the goddess. It is rare for votive offerings to be those of thanks for a prayer answered, and if there are thankful offerings, they are left in anticipation of a positive outcome to the prayer.

While the gods were able to help with problems of conception, approaching the temple on a daily basis may have been impractical as well as expensive for many people. Therefore, as an alternative many may have referred to a calendar of lucky and unlucky days for guidance on day-to-day activities, which included days to avoid having sex:

Day 7, 1st month of winter [22 November] very bad. Do not have intercourse with any woman in front of the eye of Horus [the sun]. Keep and make to burn brightly the fire which is in your house on this day.

Day 5, 2nd month of summer [22 August]. Very bad. Do not leave your house on his day. Do not embrace any woman. On this day the Ennead was created. The god Monthu rested on this day. He who is born on this day shall die during intercourse.[78]

By following the guidance of these calendars, perhaps the childless couple would safely conceive or at best avoid a calamity by not having intercourse on an unlucky day. This gives the impression that the Egyptians were a very superstitious and yet pious people, who turned to the gods in times of emotional need, in order to facilitate the conception of children and therefore give purpose to marriage and intercourse.

SEX IN THE AFTERLIFE

'He will be able to copulate on this earth at night and at day'[1]

The ancient Egyptians are often believed to be obsessed with death, as they spent a large amount of their lives preparing their tomb and commissioning and collecting goods to take into the afterlife. In fact, the complete opposite is true, as the concept of the Egyptian afterlife was a place just like Egypt where the deceased lived the same life they lived on earth for eternity, albeit in health, with an abundance of food, possessions and of course sexual activity. Unlike many cultures, access to religion and the afterlife in ancient Egypt was based on status and not gender;[2] the richer you were in life, the richer you were in the afterlife, as a successful afterlife maintained the level of lifestyle attained in life. It was rather unfortunate if one was a servant on earth, as it is likely that in the afterlife this position would be maintained and eternity was one of toil rather than pleasure.

Sex was fundamental to entering the afterlife, as like life on earth, the afterlife started with rebirth, for which male potency and fertility and the female ability to give birth were vital. Therefore, rather unsurprisingly, much of the decoration in the tomb and the funerary texts chosen had fertility characteristics all to aid the rebirth of the deceased. One Ramesside magic spell associates the very act of dying with sexual intercourse, especially for a woman dying in childbirth: 'you [*death*] shall not have intercourse [with this woman] ... you shall not associate with her, you shall not do to her anything bad or evil'.³

Furthermore, the Middle Kingdom Coffin Texts emphasise how much penetrative sex (*nk*) was an expected part of the afterlife. Spell 619 refers to *nk*ing 'with my wife', and Spell 576 tells the deceased to '*nk* in this land day and night' as well as assuring the man that 'the desire of the woman beneath him will come' each time he *nk*s.⁴ These texts guarantee regular sex with the deceased's wife, day and night in the afterlife. However, sex played an even greater role in the afterlife.

A number of female figurines with emphasised sexual organs, large hips and sometimes lying on a bed with a child have been found in various tombs, and many scholars have confidently stated that these were placed into the tombs to provide a sexual partner for the deceased. These assertions have led to debate, as these figurines were also found in female tombs, temples and houses, indicating there could be another broader reason. One scholar suggested these figures were able to revive male fertility in the way that Isis was able to bring Osiris back to life after death and impregnate herself with Horus. However, as these figures are wearing tripartite rather than bag wigs, which is more traditional for mourners, they are believed to be more likely associated with the *xnr* dancers and the cult of Hathor (*see* chapters 6 and 8).⁵ Their dancing at funerals may have been of a sexual nature and aided the deceased to be reborn in the afterlife. Furthermore, on the side of one such figure is the inscription; 'May a birth be given to your daughter Seh' (Berlin 14517), and on another; 'An offering that the king gives to the spirit of Khonsu; a birth for Tita' (Paris Louvre E8000), demonstrating that these figures had a fertility function. Unfortunately, the provenance of these two examples is unknown, meaning it is difficult to interpret their exact usage, although they are likely to be direct appeals to ancestors for help to conceive: a votive offering for the dead rather than for the gods, which provides some explanation for examples discovered in houses and temples.

It was not unheard of to appeal to the dead for such intervention in the lives of the living, and a letter to the dead was discovered at Denderah where a man asks his deceased father: 'Cause that there be born to me a healthy male child,'[6] indicating that fertility and children were a concern for both men and women. This act of beseeching the deceased indicates they were attributed with accelerated fertility with the ability to bestow it upon the living.

According to Egyptian beliefs, in order to be reborn in the afterlife, more than fertility was required. It was essential for the five elements of the human being to be reunited. Mummification enabled the physical body to be reborn, and the tomb inscriptions encouraged the repetition of the name of the individual. To repeat an individual's name ensured that they were not forgotten and could be reborn. In the Harem Conspiracy discussed in chapter 3, one of the conspirators had his name changed from Mersure (Re-Loves-Him) to Mesedsure (Re-Hates-Him), ensuring that his true name was forgotten and he would be denied an afterlife.

The final three elements of a human were a little more complex and included the shadow, which demonstrated the protection of the sun god both in life and the afterlife. The ka was particularly important and is often translated as spirit, whereas it was more like the life-force of the individual and was what gave representations of the deceased power and vitality. An ordinary human had one ka, the king had two (one each for Upper and Lower Egypt) and Hathor, the goddess of love and fertility, had seven kas.

The role of Hathor and her seven kas was an important one, as they predicted the destiny of a new-born baby and therefore also aided the deceased in their journey through the afterlife. Her connection with destiny was applied to all aspects of life, not simply birth and rebirth, and one of the New Kingdom love poems states: 'Lover I am destined for you by the Golden One [*Hathor*] of women'.[7]

If Hathor did not desire it, then lovers were destined to be apart.

O Golden One let it be in her heart,

Then I shall hasten to the brother,

And I shall kiss him in the presence of his comrades.[8]

The ka was an important element of the human body, as it was able to reside in any representation of the deceased, which goes some way to explain the numerous representations of both kings and the elite in temples and tombs. It was this element that was the focus of the funerary cults, which included the provision of food and drink for the deceased. 'Joining your ka' was a euphemism for dying, as it was the time when the human body was reunited with this element that had been present throughout life.

Another element of the human form that is often also translated as the soul is the ba, which was more like the personality of the deceased and was represented as a bird with a human face. Once the ba and ka were reunited in the afterlife, the deceased became an akh (spirit or blessed dead), which was considered a semi-divine being and was the focus of the family ancestor cults where the ancestors (akhw) were approached to help with issues concerning the living. Before the deceased was able to become an akhw, they were simply mwt, or dead, meaning they had not been transfigured into an immortal being. It has been suggested that the difference between akh and mwt is similar to the difference between the blessed dead and the damned in modern understanding.[9]

The ba is the element of the human being that truly interests us here, as it is this element that was free to copulate in the afterlife. The ba is always represented as a bird with a human face, normally thought to be that of the deceased. The bird demonstrates the freedom of the ba to travel after death as well as to act as a vehicle for the deceased to participate in various activities in the afterlife.[10] An image on the papyrus of Sutymes (Third Intermediate Period) shows the deceased holding his ba in his lap almost as if he were about to launch it into the air enabling it to fly off in search of food and sexual entertainment.[11]

The religious texts indicate that the ba left the body and the tomb every morning and returned in the evening. The Middle Kingdom Coffin Texts leave little doubt concerning its sexual nature:

> I have created my ba about me in order to make it know what I knew. For the sake of my corpse, my ba shall not burn, my ba shall not be held up by the bodyguard of Osiris. I copulate and my ba copulates; when my ba copulates with the men who dwell on the island of fire, I copulate with the goddesses.[12]

It is clear from this spell that the ba performs all the physical actions on behalf of the deceased, which in this case are clearly that of sexual intercourse. Even the name ba is a play on words, as it is remarkably similar to the word *b3h* or phallus. Furthermore, this is not the only connection between the ba and a phallus. In a wall scene in the Opet Temple at Karnak, there is an unusual figure of the ba of Amun-Ra hovering above a supine figure of Osiris. This ba is in the typical form of a bird with a human face, but with an enormous phallus emphasising its sexuality. Further reinforcement of the active sexuality of the ba can be found in Coffin Text spell 96:

> I (N) am this great ba of Osiris, by which means of which the gods have commanded him to copulate, which lives by striding by day, which Osiris has made of the efflux which in his flesh, of the seed which came forth from his phallus, in order that he may come forth on the day which he copulates. May thy seed go forth for thee into thy living Ba ... Osiris has made me his living ba, according as the gods have said, that I may come forth on the day which I copulate. I come forth, my ba in my form, on the day which I copulate.[13]

The exact meaning of this spell is obscure, but the ba, phallus and seed are all closely connected and emphasises the importance of the day when the deceased will copulate. It was not, however, only the bas of the ordinary population who were able to participate in sexual activity, as by the New Kingdom the bas of the gods also could: 'Who is he? He is Osiris ... He is the soul of Re, with whom, he himself copulated'.[14]

This ability to have sexual intercourse in the afterlife was essential for rebirth, and therefore the loss of sexual ability insinuated a loss of power. Chapter 39 of the Book of the Dead addresses Apophis, the enemy of the sun god Ra:

> You shall not become erect, you shall not copulate. O Apophis, you enemy of Ra. Opposition is made against you, O you whom Ra hates when he looks on you.[15]

This desire for an enemy to become impotent means a loss of power, and therefore an inability to be reborn. This adds a ritualistic element to the removal of the enemies' penis following a battle. The more practical reason was as a means of counting the enemy dead, but it also ensured that the enemies were unable to bring themselves back into existence through the masculine power of rebirth.[16]

Such impotence was also connected with old age, making the excessive sexual activity in the afterlife a clear representation of renewed youth following rebirth. The Middle Kingdom tale of Sinuhe describes the impotence of the aging fugitive:

> Return to Egypt! And you will see the residence where you grew up, kiss the earth and the Great Portal, and join the friends. For today you have already begun to be old, have lost the ability to beget (*b33wt*), and have in mind the day of burial, the passing to blessedness.[17]

The translation of the word *b33wt* is obscure, but as it has a penis determinative it is likely to mean to beget, to be potent, or to be erect, none of which Sinuhe was able to do as an old man. But it was something he could look forward to doing again in the afterlife.

This masculine fertility, and by association, the ability to be reborn, was considered very powerful, and in the creation stories the male creator deities were able to self-create, showing they contained both male and female potency (*see* chapter 8). They were able to create themselves, often via a sexual act such as masturbation or ejaculation. The creator god Atum was one such god who copulated with his hand. His hand was called Djeret and acted as the feminine vessel essential for rebirth.[18]

As discussed in chapter 8, Osiris, the god of the underworld, was also a god of great fertility. In the scenes of his resurrection, he is depicted with his hand around his erect phallus as Isis, in the form of a kite, hovers above him. This indicates he was able to re-create himself through the act of masturbation. Isis, his sister and wife, had a supporting role in this act, initially exciting Osiris so he was able to complete the required act, and then acting as a vessel to carry their son, Horus.[19] Moreover, this ability to beget a son after his death was a sign of great sexual prowess and power.[20] Osiris was therefore the deity who ensured rebirth. Every deceased individual (male or female) was referred to as the Osiris, making them male for the rebirth, albeit a male who possesses both male and female reproductive characteristics.[21]

The masculinisation of women did not stop at calling her the Osiris, as sometimes the funerary goods belonging to women were masculine in style, with, for example, male striped headdresses and androgynous, Osiriform bodies and golden skin like the sun god.[22] Some coffins belonging to women also have Book of the Dead spells written in the masculine rather than the feminine form, which some Egyptologists simply put down to scribal mistakes, quick copying, poor adaptation of male objects, or that the deceased bought an off-the-shelf item.[23] However, considering some good quality, expensive coffins, such as that of Henutmehyt in the British Museum, have a combination of masculine and feminine terminology indicates it was deliberate, as on such high-end goods, scribal errors of this type would have been considered unacceptable.[24] Moreover, such masculinisation of women's funerary equipment generally appears *only* on expensive coffins, and it could be suggested that only the wealthy, educated, priestly classes were totally aware of the importance of masculine terminology for a successful rebirth.[25]

It is only in the Graeco-Roman Period that women started combining their names with the goddess Isis or Hathor for rebirth rather than Osiris.[26] There is only one goddess, Neith, prior to this period that also possessed male and female characteristics enabling her to re-create alone. Neith is the goddess of war, but appears in the New Kingdom book of 'That Which is in the Beyond' in the fourth, tenth and eleventh hours of the nocturnal journey of the sun god, as a child, as the Queen of Upper and Lower Egypt and as a pregnant goddess to whom the sun god will be born. She possesses both male and female characteristics and is able to give birth to the ultimate creator, the sun god, without the need for copulation with a male. At the temple of Khnum at Esna, this theme is continued as Neith is shown emerging from the primeval waters as a cow goddess representing her role as both the mother and father of all gods.[27] All cow goddesses are nurturers, and from the New Kingdom Book of the Dead Hathor is also shown in this form emerging from the western mountain in her role as protector of the realm of the dead.

Men, who could not connect their name with Neith, were unable to guarantee her presence and therefore her role in their rebirth. However, as long as a female image was present, they were provided with a vessel or womb within which they could be reborn. This could simply be in the form of female offering-bearer statues, depicted carrying trays of food providing sustenance for eternity,[28] but the most common feminine vessel in a tomb was the mummy (*khat*) or the coffin (*wt*), although this is purely based on the feminine words used for each.[29]

The sky goddess Nut is often depicted on the inside of the lids of coffins stretched over the deceased, meaning she is able to aid him with rebirth in the same manner she swallows the sun at dusk and gives birth to him afresh in the morning (*see* chapter 8). Therefore, the sarcophagus was sometimes referred to as the 'womb of Nut', within which the rebirth took place.[30] Coffins were made of wood, a valuable resource in Egypt, and the most expensive were made of imported cedar planks. Although imported cedar was valuable and therefore desirable, being buried in a coffin of native sycamore wood had religious significance, as the sycamore tree was associated with Hathor, the divine mother goddess.

Hathor in her role as Lady of the Sycamore was also essential for the sustenance of the deceased and therefore their prolonged existence in the afterlife. The sycamore tree was often depicted in the tomb, sometimes with Hathor emerging from the branches to pass liquid to the deceased, providing them with nourishment. Hathor, however, was not the only goddess presented as the Lady of the Sycamore. The role was also held by Nut and Isis. It was not only the sustenance provided by the tree goddess that was important for the deceased but also the shade provided by the branches, and in spell 52 of the Book of the Dead the deceased is proud the be able to sit in the shade of the tree. In the Admonitions, the author emphasises the pleasure of sleeping in the shade:

It is however good when beds are readied,
The masters' headrests safely secured;
When every man's need is filled by a mat in the shade,
And a door shut on one who slept in the bushes.[31]

In order to increase the chances of a successful rebirth, mummies were sometimes sexualised. For example, Tutankhamun was embalmed with his penis in the erect position, enabling him to re-create himself in the afterlife, like Osiris. This was not in fact unusual, as many male mummies have been found with enhanced penises which were moulded from linen. In order to protect the penis in the afterlife, it was also not unusual in the Late Period for mummies to have a phallus-shaped amulet on either side of their penis made from serpentine, gold or a dark stone.[32] Women were generally given artificial nipples, which helped them to lactate in the afterlife, reinforcing their role as fertile mother.

Mummy 1770 from Manchester Museum was given both breasts and a penis fashioned out of linen. This has been attributed to the priests not knowing the sex of the body when they rewrapped her and therefore, in order to ensure she was reborn, they gave her both masculine and feminine sexual organs. Cooney suggests that she was in fact given both, not to cover an error, but to preserve the masculine and feminine characteristics needed to ensure rebirth. She suggests that this practice may have been more common than the evidence suggests due to years of unscientific unwrapping destroying such evidence.[33]

It seems therefore that gods and deceased men could spend their afterlives copulating, and it was almost essential to ensure their safe rebirth in the afterlife, and this is emphasised in the Coffin Texts:

Concerning every man who know (the formula), he will be able to copulate on this earth at night and at day, and the hearts of women will come to him at any time he desires.[34]

For women, sex and the afterlife was a very different experience. And Herodotus claims that for some women sex in the afterlife may have started while in the necrophiliac hands of the embalmers:

Wives of notable men, and women of great beauty and reputation, are not at once given over to the embalmers, but only after they have been dead three or four day; this is done that the embalmers may not have carnal intercourse with them. For it is said that one was found having intercourse with a woman newly dead, and was denounced by his fellow workmen.[35]

The mummy of Meresankh III, the daughter of Khufu's son Kawab, was not buried for 272 days, which was over and above the recommended 70,[36] and it has been suggested this was to prevent the embalmers abusing the body. Such deviant practices aside, for which there is no archaeological proof anyway, the fact of the matter was that the afterlife for women was far less free than it was for men. In the afterlife, the role of the woman was as a fertile mother and therefore sexual intercourse was not for enjoyment.

It was extremely rare for a woman to have her own tomb, as she was buried in the tomb of her husband if she was married or in the tomb of her father if she was not. However, it was not unknown for a woman to be absent from her husband's tomb. While it may be tempting to look for a social reason behind such an absence, such as divorce, death, unmarried status or even homosexuality, the reality is likely to be based in religion and fertility.

Generally, a wife represented in her husband's tomb had a role to play in his rebirth in the form of female fertility and reproduction. However, the significance of this female role in her husband's rebirth changed over time. In the Old Kingdom, wives were not always depicted in the tombs, as their role was less important than in the New Kingdom (*see* chapter 5).[37] In a study of 456 New Kingdom tombs, only 97 (21 per cent) name the husband but not the wife, and only in 31 (7 per cent) tombs is the wife completely excluded. However, some tombs depict children, which indicates the man is married,[38] and emphasises his fertility. It was therefore clearly unusual in the New Kingdom for a man not to depict his wife in his tomb. In the Middle Kingdom Coffin Texts there are also numerous spells concerning the deceased man's wife and family showing they were essential for a successful rebirth.[39]

In the tombs where the wife is present, she accompanied the deceased in scenes of great importance for rebirth in the afterlife. The most important scene that always includes the deceased's wife and often his children is the Fishing and Fowling scene, which appears in noble tombs from the Old Kingdom onwards. The whole scene is one of fertility, from the masculine stance of the tomb owner in the active role of spearing fish or catching birds, to the images of his family surrounding him. All participants were represented in their best party clothes, which may include an unguent-soaked dress for the wife, unguent cones on their heads, and the deceased and his wife draped in lotus flowers. Even the children represented are shown holding or pulling lotus flowers from the water or holding baby ducks in their hands. The women and children are only presented in complimentary roles and are often saying things like: 'Oh Meri, do give me those [beautiful birds as you love me]', 'Milord, bring me this oriole'.

Women in scenes like this one are generally submissive and inactive as a clear contrast to the activity of the men in the scene.[40] It has been suggested that to a certain extent this reflects the social order of things in ancient Egypt, as women were generally the supporting characters as the men were educated, employed and active, and ideologically women were not in a position to do the things they requested the men do for them.[41]

The role of the wife, however, is not only to allow the tomb owner to display his masculinity but also as a metaphor for sexual activity in the afterlife providing him with a partner in order to revivify his sexuality[42] and to demonstrate his potency.[43] However, due to the potential power of sexual activity, while sexual activity is hinted at in the tomb, there are no images of couples having sex, other than a single hieroglyph at Beni Hasan. This absence could be an indication that such images were in fact too powerful to depict in the tomb for eternity.[44]

The fish that are normally impaled on the end of the spear in these Fishing and Fowling scenes also have fertility significance. One is the *tilapia nilotica* fish, which when threatened by a predator takes its young into its mouth and then spits them out again, unharmed. To the observant ancient Egyptian, the fish apparently killed its young and then they were reborn. The connection with the deceased and his desire to be reborn into the afterlife is clear.[45] There is also a connection between the fish depicted on the end of the spears in these scenes and the myth of Osiris and Seth. According to Plutarch, the *lepidotus*, the *phagrus* and the *oxyrrhyncus* fish were responsible for eating the phallus of Osiris, and therefore to catch one in the afterlife bestowed great fertility on the deceased.

Another popular tomb scene from the Old Kingdom onwards was the so-called pilgrimage to Abydos that every Egyptian was expected to make, either in life or after death. The wife of the tomb owner always accompanied him in this scene, where she is presented seated on the boat for both the outward and return journey. However, it seems unlikely that many actually made this pilgrimage in real life and, instead, this represented a spiritual visit rather than a mortal visit.

For those who could afford to go, it was considered a particularly important site to visit, as it was believed to be the burial site of the god Osiris and therefore visiting the site associated the deceased with Osiris and improved their chances of rebirth. A number of kings took this journey one step further and constructed cenotaphs or fake tombs at Abydos, enabling their ka to be buried in their traditional tomb in the Valley of the Kings as well as in the symbolic burial place of the Osiris. One of the most impressive is the cenotaph of Sety I, which is commonly known as the Osireion. The construction is subterranean and resembles the Theban tomb of Sety with square pillars and a sarcophagus chamber constructed of red granite. It was started by Sety I but not completed until the reign of his grandson Merenptah. The coffin was placed on a mound in the centre surrounded by a channel of water reminiscent of the mound of creation. The ceiling of this chamber bears an image of the goddess Nut with the sun god travelling through her body on his nocturnal journey. At the time of construction, there was a small canal that filled from the Nile and therefore rose and fell with the inundation and simultaneously represented the primeval waters of Nun and the watery death of Osiris himself. The entrance corridor to the tomb was decorated with scenes from the Book of Gates, enabling Osiris to enter the afterlife safely. This structure is truly unique in Egypt as the only one surrounded by water.

Between the mortuary temple and the cenotaph of Sety I, there were a row of trees that were nurtured by the canal and therefore represented the cycle of life. Since the Aswan dam was built, the Nile no longer rises, and the Osireion is continually under water deep enough to accommodate fish.

From the Middle Kingdom onwards, rich noblemen also constructed cenotaphs known as mehat chapels at the site of Abydos. These were not as elaborate as the Osireion and often comprised a small mud-brick enclosure with a structure large enough to accommodate one or a number of stela which were dedicated to Osiris but also named the owner as a means of connecting them to the god. These cenotaphs lined the processional way for the Mysteries of Osiris which were carried out here, and presented a place where family members could make offerings to their ancestors. Some of the inscriptions on the stela state:

> I made a mehat at the terrace of the great god ... so that I might receive offerings in the presence of the great god and that I might inhale his incense.[46]

Although these were not tombs, the inscriptions found within were similar to those found in tombs, and their position at Abydos may have been a way for the deceased to share a tomb with the god,[47] further guaranteeing their rebirth into the afterlife.

The most common funerary scene in non-royal tombs is the banqueting scenes, which are a representation of the funerary feast where the living and the dead were able to get together one last time. These scenes are comprised of a number of erotic elements, which include women in large wigs, floral collars, and fine linen, holding menat necklaces associated with the Hathor cult or feeding each other mandrake fruits which were a symbol of love and was often used in aphrodisiacs. However, as discussed in chapter 5, such acts of affection between the women at the banquets are never interpreted as same-sex relationships, despite this erotically charged symbolism. Other aspects of sexuality at these banquets can be identified in the naked servants pouring drinks. This act was a play on words, as pouring, shooting and ejaculating were the same word (*sti*) in Egyptian showing they were all considered erotic. This linguistic aspect also connects sexual acts with the hunting scenes discussed above (to shoot and to ejaculate).[48] The banquet scenes are often accompanied by musicians and dancers performing erotic dances in order to rejuvenate the deceased tomb owner enabling him to be fertile in the afterlife.[49] These banquets may represent the Beautiful Festival of the Valley, which was celebrated with processions to the west bank, and families attended the tombs of their ancestors to enjoy a meal with them. They also placated the deceased with music played with the sistrum and the menat in honour of Hathor.[50]

Such scenes as the banquet scenes depict both men and women wearing scented unguent cones on their heads, and, as discussed in chapter 1, these are often believed to represent perfume and eroticism through scent. Not all of the wearers of an unguent cone are deceased, especially in the banquet scenes where the living and dead get together in the tomb chapel. However, it is suggested that as these cones were presented in tombs for over 1500 years, there is likely to be a deeper meaning. Padgham believes that, based on a study of the different scenes where the cone was most frequently worn, the cone could in fact represent the ba, the element of the human psyche that could travel and perform sexually after death. The cones appear to be worn by the deceased in scenes where the ba is present for the ceremony or ritual event, which may be the Opening of the Mouth ritual, the Beautiful Festival of the Valley, the funerary banquet or even the distribution of shebyu collars by the king to a favoured courtier.[51] As the king is a divinity associated with the sun god, being awarded a collar by the king/god was a special, life-changing event. According to the study, only once the tomb owner who has received the collars appears with the cone on his head, and once his ba appears he is able to communicate with the sun god and to a degree demonstrate his own divine being.[52]

In these scenes, the living are also presented with unguent cones on their heads, and it is suggested that this is in reference to their own bas which remain with them throughout life although not normally acknowledged until death. As the deceased tomb owner was able to attend the banquet of the living, the presence of the bas (cones) of the living enabled them to interact with the dead.[53]

This was essentially the role of tomb chapels, to bring the living and the dead together. On special occasions and festivals, the family attended the tomb and had a meal in the chapel enabling the deceased and the living to feast together. This sums up the funerary beliefs of the ancient Egyptians. There was a fine line between the world of the living and the world of the dead, which could cross over at times like this as well as with the deceased, aiding (or hindering) the lives of the living. It is therefore not surprising that fertility in life was equally important in the afterlife, and maintaining a healthy sex life was the only means of remaining fertile and being reborn in the afterlife.

NOTES

Introduction: The Ancient Egyptian Attitude to Sex

1. Manniche, L., 1997: *Sexual Life in Ancient Egypt*. London. Kegan Paul International. p. 74.

2. *Ibid.*, 33.

3. Toivari-Viitala, J., 2001: *Women at Deir el Medina: A Study of the Status and Roles of the Female Inhabitants in the Workmen's Community During the Ramesside Period*. Leiden. Nederlands Instituut voor het Nabije Oosten. p. 154.

4. Manniche 1997, 33.

5. *Ibid.*, 31.

6. *Ibid.*, 28.

7. Frankfurter, D., 2001: 'The Perils of Love: Magic and Countermagic in Coptic Egypt' in *The Journal of the History of Sexuality*, Vol 10, Number 3/4, pp. 480–500. p. 493.

8. P. Lansing 14.8 dated to the Ramesside Period.

9. Toivari-Viitala 2001, 142.

10. Manniche 1997, 33.

11. *Ibid.*, 80.

12. *Ibid.*, 34.

13. Toivari-Viitala 2001, 146.

14. Meskell, L., 2000: 'Re-em(bed)ding Sex: Domesticity, Sexuality, and Ritual in New Kingdom Egypt' in Schmidt R. & Voss, B (Eds.). *Archaeologies of Sexuality*. London. Routledge. p. 258.

15. *Ibid.*, 257.

16. Toivari-Viitala 2001, 141.

17. Meskell 2000, 260.

18. Toivari-Viitala 2001, 158.

19. *Ibid.*, 153.

20. Manniche 1997, 7.

21. Toivari-Viitala 2001, 143–4.

22. Mertz, B., 1966: *Red Land, Black Land*. London. Harper Press. p. 53.

23. Szpakowska, K., 2012: 'Hidden Voices: Unveiling Women in Ancient Egypt' in James, S. L. and Dillon, S. (Eds.), *A Companion to Women in the Ancient World* (pp. 25–38). Oxford: Wiley-Blackwell. p. 26.

24. Sélincourt, A., (Translator) 1972: *Herodotus*. London. Penguin. p. 154.

25. *Ibid.*, 143.

26. Manniche 1997, 100.

27. *Ibid.*, 104.

28. Green, L., 2001: 'The Hand of God' Sacred and Profane Sex in Ancient Egypt' in *KMT Volume 12 Number 4*. p. 57.

1: Idealised Beauty

1. Manniche, L., 1999: *Sacred Luxuries: Fragrance, Aromatherapy and Cosmetics in Ancient Egypt*. London. Opus Publishers Ltd. p. 101.

2. Davis, W., 1989: *The Canonical Tradition in Ancient Egyptian Art*, Cambridge. Cambridge University Press. p. 168.

3. Robins, G., 1997: *The Art of Ancient Egypt*. London. British Museum Press. p. 107.

4. Meskell 2000, 254.

5. Toivari-Viitala 2001, 144–5.

6. Manniche 1997, 94.

7. *Ibid.*, 75.

8. Meader, J., & Demeter, B., 2004: 'The Egyptian Blue Water Lily' in *KMT* Vol 16 No 2. p. 63.

9. *Ibid.*, 61.

10. Lichtheim, M., 1997: *Moral Values in Ancient Egypt*, Vandenhoeck & Ruprecht. p. 55.

11. Manniche 1999, 99.

12. *Ibid.*, 102.

13. *Ibid.*, 101.

14. Lichtheim, M., 1976: *Ancient Egyptian Literature; Volume II.* Berkeley. University of California Press. p. 183.

15. Hare, T., 1999: *Remembering Osiris; Number, Gender and the Word in Ancient Egyptian Representational Systems.* Stanford. Stanford University Press. p. 142.

16. Robins, G., 1999: 'Hair and the Construction of Identity in Ancient Egypt, c. 1480–1350 B.C.' in *Journal of the American Research Center in Egypt*, Vol. 36 (1999), p. 58.

17. Szpakowska 2012, 29.

18. Hare 1999, 140.

19. Janssen, R., 1995/1996: 'An Ancient Egyptian Erotic Fashion: Fishnet Dresses' in *Kmt 6 (4)* Winter 1995/6. p. 42.

20. Manniche 1997, 88.

21. Lichtheim 1976, 183.

22. Manniche 1999, 137.

23. Humber, C., 2008: 'Ancient Egyptian Eye Paint' in *Ancient Egypt Magazine* Vol. 8 No. 6 issue 48. p. 41.

24. Dayagi-Mendels, M., 1989: *Perfumes and Cosmetics in the Ancient World.* Jerusalem, Israel Museum. p. 44.

25. Humber 2008, 43.

26. *Ibid.*, 41.

27. Dayagi-Mendels 1989, 29.

28. McCreesh, N.C., et al. 2011: 'Ancient Egyptian Hair Gel: New Insight into Ancient Egyptian Mummification Procedures through Chemical Analysis' in *Journal of Archaeological Science* Vol 38, No. 12. pp. 3432–3434.

29. Taylor, J., and Antoine, D., 2014: *Ancient Lives, Ancient Discoveries; Eight Mummies, Eight Stories*. London. British Museum Press. p. 130.

30. Robins 1999, 59.

31. *Ibid.*, 67.

32. Manniche 1997, 69.

33. Manniche 1999, 131.

34. *Ibid.*, 91.

35. Fletcher, J., 2000: *Chronicle of a Pharaoh; the Intimate Life of Amenhotep III*. Oxford. Oxford University Press. p. 83.

36. Lichtheim 1976, 205.

37. Tyldesley, J., 1994: *The Daughters of Isis*. London. Viking. p. 155.

38. Fletcher 2000, 82.

39. Stevens Cox, J., 1977: 'The Construction of an Ancient Egyptian Wig (c. 1400BC in the British Museum)' in *Journal of Egyptian Archaeology* Vol. 63. pp. 67–70.

40. Manniche 1999, 129–31.

41. Watterson, B., 1997: *Women in Ancient Egypt*. Gloucestershire. Sutton Publishing. p. 115.

42. Lucas, A., 1930: 'Cosmetics Perfumes and Incense in Ancient Egypt' in *Journal of Egyptian Archaeology* Vol. 16 No. 1/2. 41–53. p. 46.

43. Robins, G., 1993: *Women in Ancient Egypt*. London. British Museum Press. p. 77.

44. Tassie, G.J., 2003. 'Identifying the Practice of Tattooing in Ancient Egypt and Nubia' in *Papers from the Institute of Archaeology* 14, pp. 87–88.

45. Booth C. 2001: 'Possible Tattooing Instruments in the Petrie Museum' in *Journal of Egyptian Archaeology* Vol 87, pp. 172–5.

46. Tassie 2003, 99.

47. *Ibid.*, 91.

48. Strouhal, E., 1992: *Life in Ancient Egypt*. Cambridge. Cambridge University Press. p. 89.

49. Tassie 2003, 89.

50. Pinch, G., 1993: *Votive Offerings to Hathor*. Oxford. Griffith Institute. p. 213.

51. Keimer, L., 1948: 'Remarques sur les Tatouage dans l'Égypte Ancienne' in *Mémoires del.Institute d.Egypte,* Vol. 53, p. 1.

52. Tassie 2003, 91.

53. Bianchi, R. S., 1988. 'Tattoo in Ancient Egypt', in A Rubin (Ed.), *Marks of Civilisation*, pp. 21–28. Los Angeles: Museum of Cultural History, Regents of the University of California. pp. 26–7.

54. Manniche 1997, 44.

55. Padgham, J., 2012: *A New Interpretation of the Cone on the Head in the New Kingdom Egyptian Tomb Scenes*. Oxford. BAR International Series 2431.

56. Manniche 1999, 95.

57. Manniche 1997, 30.

58. Pinch 1993, 213.

59. *Ibid.*, 241.

2: *Love and Marriage*

1. Manniche 1997, 89–91.

2. Graves-Brown, C., 2010: *Dancing for Hathor; Women in Ancient Egypt*. London. Continuum. p. 35.

3. Lichtheim, M., 1980: *Ancient Egyptian Literature Vol III; The Late period*. Los Angeles. University of California Press. p. 62.

4. Reymond, E.A.E., 1981: 'From the Records of a Priestly Family of Memphis Vol I' in *Agyptologische Abhandlungen* Band 38. Otto Harrassowitz. Weisbaden. p. 166.

5. Lichtheim 1997, 63.

6. Graves-Brown 2010, 132.

7. Chester Beatty I in Manniche 1997, 79.

8. Whale, S., 1989: *The Family in the Eighteenth Dynasty of Egypt*. Sydney. The Australian Centre for Egyptology. p. 251.

9. Manniche 1997, 28.

10. Toivari-Viitala 2001, 57.

11. Whale 1989, 253.

12. Papyrus Harris 500 in Simpson, W.K., 2003: *The Literature of Ancient Egypt: An Anthology of Stories, Instructions, Stelae, Autobiographies, and Poetry: An Anthology of Stories, Instructions and Poetry.* London. Yale University Press. p. 314.

13. Manniche 1997, 89–91.

14. *Ibid.*, 80.

15. Fox, M.V., 1981: '"Love" in the Love Songs' in *The Journal of Egyptian Archaeology*, Vol. 67 p. 82.

16. Manniche 1997, 80.

17. Cairo 25218 in Manniche 1997, 87.

18. Papyrus Oxyrhynchus XXXIX 2891 in Montserrat, D., 1996: *Sex and Society in Graeco-Roman Egypt.* London. Kegan Paul. p. 113.

19. Monserrat 1996, 113–14.

20. Lesko, B., 1996: *Remarkable Women of Ancient Egypt.* Providence. BC Scribe Publication. p. 113.

21. Manniche 1999, 92.

22. Lichtheim 1976, 183.

23. Manniche 1997, 78.

24. Tyldesley 1994, 50.

25. Manniche 1997, 75.

26. Tyldesley 1994, 46.

27. Pestman, P., 1961: *Marriage and Matrimonial Property in Ancient Egypt.* Leiden. E.J. Brill. p. 9.

28. Toivari-Viitala 2001, 155.

29. *Ibid.*, 157.

30. Robins 1993, 65–6.

31. Tyldesley 1994, 46.

32. Toivari-Viitala 2001, 53.

33. Lichtheim, 1976, 137.

34. Manniche 1997, 93.

35. Reeves, C., 1992: *Egyptian Medicine*. Buckinghamshire. Shire Egyptology. p. 19.

36. Toivari-Viitala 2001, 205.

37. Tyldesley 1994, 51.

38. Szpakowska, K., 2008: *Daily Life in Ancient Egypt*. Oxford. Blackwell Publishing. Note 94, p. 43.

39. Szpakowksa 2012, 32.

40. Toivari-Viitala 2001, 162.

41. Wilfong, T., 1999: 'Menstrual Synchrony and the "Place of Women" in Ancient Egypt' in Teeter E. & Larson J. (Eds.) *Gold of Praise; Studies on Ancient Egypt in Honor of Edward F. Wente*. Chicago. Oriental Institute. p. 420.

42. Wilfong 1999, 426.

43. Macy Roth, A., 1991: *Egyptian Phyles in the Old Kingdom: The Evolution of a System of Social Organisation*. Chicago. Oriental Institute. p. 71.

44. Nunn, J., 1996: *Ancient Egyptian Medicine*. London. British Museum Press. pp. 170–71.

45. Manniche 1997, 97.

46. Robins 1993, 58.

47. Tyldesley 1994, 54.

48. Meskell, L., 2002: *Private Life in New Kingdom Egypt*. Oxford. Princeton University Press. p. 101.

49. Toivari-Viitala 2001, 61.

50. Tyldesley 1994, 54.

51. Toivari-Viitala 2001, 72.

52. Pestman 1961, 17.

53. *Ibid.*, 20.

54. *Ibid.*, 19.

55. Černý, J., & Peet, T.E., 1927: 'A Marriage Settlement of the Twentieth Dynasty: An Unpublished Document from Turin' in *The Journal of Egyptian Archaeology* Vol. 13, No. 1/2. pp. 30–39.

56. Whale 1989, 240.

57. Manniche 1997, 97.

58. Tyldesley 1994, 67-8.

59. O.Berlin 10627, twentieth dynasty in Meskell 2002, 65.

60. Robins 1993, 98.

61. Parkinson, R., 1995: 'Homosexual Desire and Middle Kingdom Literature' in *Journal of Egyptian Archaeology* Vol. 81. p. 61.

62. Whale 1989, 245.

63. Robins, G., 1994–1995: 'Women and Children in Peril' in *KMT 5 (4)*. p. 27.

64. Donker Van Heel, K., 2014: *Mrs. Tsenhor a Female Entrepreneur in Ancient Egypt*. Cairo. American University in Cairo Press. p. 81.

65. Lichtheim 1976, 212.

66. Whale 1989, 245.

67. *Ibid.*, 248.

68. *Ibid.*, 249.

69. Robins 1993, 63.

70. Meskell 2002, 95.

71. Toivari-Viitala 2001, 19.

72. Pestman, 1961, 9.

73. Toivari-Viitala 2001, 56.

74. Lichtheim 1980, 128.

75. Toivari-Viitala 2001, 65.

76. McDowell, A.G., 1999: *Village Life in Ancient Egypt: Laundry Lists and Love Songs*. Oxford. Oxford University Press. p. 46.

77. Meskell 2002, 97.

78. Tyldesley 1994, 54.

79. Donker Van Heel, K., 2014: *Mrs. Tsenhor a Female Entrepreneur in Ancient Egypt*. Cairo. American University in Cairo Press. p. 65. & Lichtheim 1980, 39.

80. Toivari-Viitala 2001, 33.

81. *Ibid.*, 34.

82. *Ibid.*, 33.

83. Goedicke, H., 1984: *Studies in the Hekanakhte Papers*. Baltimore. Halgo Inc. pp. 17–19.

84. Toivari-Viitala 2001, 36.

85. Tyldesley 1994, 49.

86. Toivari-Viitala 2001, 36.

87. Manniche 1997, 21.

88. Toivari-Viitala 2001, 37.

89. *Ibid.*, 36.

90. *Ibid.*, 28–9.

91. Pestman 1961, 79.

92. Robins 1993, 64.

93. Donker van Heel, K., 2013: *Djekhy and Son: Doing Business in Ancient Egypt*. Cairo. American University in Cairo Press. p. 47.

94. Robins 1993, 67.

95. Watterson 1997, 69.

96. Lichtheim 1976, 143.

97. Manniche 1997, 10.

98. Eyre, C., 1984: 'Crime and Adultery in Ancient Egypt' in *The Journal of Egyptian Archaeology* Vol. 70. p. 93.

99. *Ibid.*, 104.

100. *Ibid.*, 94.

101. Mertz 1966, 65.

102. Tyldesley 1994, 61.

103. Manniche 1997, 60.

104. Lichtheim 1976, 203–11.

105. Ryholt, K., 1999: *The Story of Petese son of Peletum*. Carsten Niebuhr Institute of Near Eastern Studies. p. 83.

106. McDowell 1999, 49.

107. *Ibid.*, 48–49.

108. Ryholt 1999, 70.

109. Donker van Heel 2013, 47.

110. McDowell 1999, 43.

111. Janssen, J., 1982: 'Two Personalities', in Demarée, R.J., and Janssen, J.J., (Eds.) *Gleanings from Deir el-Medîna*. Leiden. Nederlands Instituut voor het Nabije Oosten. p. 114.

112. Romer, J., 1984: *Ancient Lives: Daily Life in Egypt of the Pharaohs*. New York Henry Holt and Company. p. 84.

113. Robins 1993, 70.

114. Toivari-Viitala 2001, 219.

115. Lichtheim 1980, 169–70.

116. Lichtheim 1976, 143.

117. Manniche 1997, 21.

118. Watterson 1997, 71.

119. Meskell 2002, 99.

120. Watterson 1997, 72.

121. Lesko 1996, 38–9.

122. McDowell 1999, 42.

123. Pestman 1961, 67–8.

124. Watterson 1997, 66.

125. Toivari-Viitala 2001, 90.

126. Pestman 1961, 72.

127. Montserrat 1996, 100.

128. Morton, R., 1995: 'Sexual Attitudes, Preferences and Infections in Ancient Egypt' in *Genitourin Med*. 71. p. 182.

129. Toivari-Viitala 2001, 238.

130. *Ibid.*, 87.

131. Janssen 1982, 115.

3: Sex and the Pharaohs

1. Kitchen, K., 1982: *Pharaoh Triumphant; The Life and Times of Ramses II*. Cairo. American University in Cairo Press. p. 88.

Notes

2. Manniche 1997, 36.

3. URK IV 219 in Manniche 1997, 59–60.

4. Ayad, M., 2009: *God's Wife, God's Servant*. London. Routledge. p. 7.

5. Tyldesley, J., 2000: *Ramesses; Egypt's Greatest Pharaoh*. London. Penguin. p. 124.

6. Fletcher 2000, 115.

7. *Ibid.*, 80.

8. *Ibid.*, 147.

9. Tyldesley, J. 2006: *Chronicle of the Queens of Egypt*. London Thames and Hudson. p. 114.

10. *Ibid.*, 18.

11. Reynolds, J., 1914: 'Sex Morals and the Law in Ancient Egypt and Babylon' in *Journal of the American Institute of Criminal Law and Criminology* Vol. 5, No. 1. p. 21.

12. Bleeker, C.J., 1973: *Hathor and Thoth; Two Key Figures of the Ancient Egyptian Religion*. Leiden. E.J. Brill. p. 55.

13. Tyldesley 1994, 197.

14. Tyldesley, J., 2014a: 'Egypt's Earliest Queens' in *Ancient Egypt Magazine* Vol. 15, No. 1 Iss. 85. p. 19.

15. Wegner, J., 2002: 'A Decorated Birth-Brick from South Abydos' in *Egyptian Archaeology* No. 21. p. 8.

16. Manniche 1997, 29.

17. Quirke, S., 1992: *Ancient Egyptian Religion*. London. British Museum Press. pp. 66–7.

18. Hart, G., 1990: *Egyptian Myths*. London. British Museum Press. p. 34.

19. Hart 1990, 40.

20. Tyldesley 2000, 119.

21. Fletcher 2000, 148.

22. For a full discussion of this letter go to Booth, C., 2009: *Horemheb: The Forgotten Pharaoh*. Stroud. Amberley and Booth, C., 2007: *The Boy Behind the Mask*. Oxford. Oneworld.

23. EA22 in Schniedewind, W., & Cochavi-Rainey, Z., (Eds.), 2015: *The El-Amarna Correspondence: A New Edition of the Cuneiform Letters from the Site of El-Amarna Based on Collations of all Extant Tablets*. Leiden. Brill. p. 183.

24. Arnold, D., 1996: *The Royal Women of Amarna: Images of Beauty from Ancient Egypt*. New York. Metropolitan Museum of Art Press. p. 14.

25. Fletcher 2000, 146.

26. Kitchen, K., 1982: *Pharaoh Triumphant; The Life and Times of Ramses II*. Cairo. American University in Cairo Press. p. 83.

27. *Ibid.*, 84.

28. *Ibid.*, 88.

29. *Ibid.*, 86.

30. Hart 1990, 67.

31. Tyldesley 2006, 145.

32. Redford, S., 2002: *The Harem Conspiracy: The Murder of Ramesses III*. Illinois. Northern Illinois University Press. p. 54.

33. Tyldesley 1994, 181.

34. Redford 2002, 50.

35. Tyldesley 1994, 190.

36. Redford 2002, 18.

37. Quirke 1992, 126.

38. Hawass, Z., et al., 2012: 'Revisiting the Harem Conspiracy and Death of Ramesses III: Anthropological, Forensic, Radiological and Genetic Study' in *British Medical Journal* 345. p. 3.

39. *Ibid.*, 2.

40. Tyldesley 2006, 58.

41. Lichtheim, M., 1975: *Ancient Egyptian Literature Vol. I*. Berkeley. University of California Press. p. 225.

42. EA1 in Schniedewind & Cochavi-Rainey 2015, 59.

43. Redford 2002, 57.

44. Tyldesley 1994, 185.

45. Redford 2002, 57.

46. Fletcher 2000, 148.

47. Redford 2002, 52.

48. Tyldesley 2006, 124.

49. Redford 2002, 51.

50. Fletcher 2000, 132.

51. Redford 2002, 51.

52. Quirke 1992, 92.

53. Tyldesley, J., 1996: *Hatchepsut; the Female Pharaoh*. London. Penguin. p. 191.

54. *Ibid.*, 181.

55. Tyldesley 1996, 185.

56. Quoted in Lovric, M., 2001: *Cleopatra's Face; Fatal Beauty*. London. British Museum Press. p. 73.

57. Propertius 50–15 BC in Lovric 2001, 47 & Walker, S., & Ashton, S-A., 2006: *Cleopatra*. Bristol. Bristol University Press. p. 64.

58. Aurelius Victor quoted in Lovric 2001, 52.

59. Parkinson, R., 1991: *Voices From Ancient Egypt*. London. British Museum Press. pp. 54–6.

60. Redford 2002, 60.

61. Janssen 1995–1996, 42.

62. *Ibid.*, 43.

63. *Ibid.*, 47.

4: *Childbirth*

1. Stetter C. 1993: *The Secret Medicine of the Pharaohs; Ancient Egyptian Healing*. Chicago. Edition Q. p. 87.

2. Selene-Sayell, L., 2012-2013: 'Servants of Heket; Midwifery and Birth in Ancient Egypt' in *Ancient Egypt* Vol. 13, No. 3. p. 13.

3. Lichtheim 1976, 138.

4. Harer, W.B. 2013: 'Obstetrics in Ancient Egypt' in *KMT* Vol. 24, No. 2. p. 49.

5. Tyldesley 1994, 77.

6. Lichtheim 1976, 141.

7. Harer 2013, 46.

8. Quirke 1992, 107.

9. Janssen, R., & Janssen, J., 1990: *Growing Up in Ancient Egypt*. London. Rubicon Press. p. 6.

10. Harer 2013, 46–7.

11. Ayad 2009, 49.

12. Macy-Roth, A. & Roehrig, C., 2002: 'Magical Bricks and the Bricks of Birth' in *Journal of Egyptian Archaeology* Vol. 88. p. 136.

13. *Ibid.*, 137.

14. Quirke 1992, 126.

15. Robins 1994, 33.

16. Bleeker 1973, 83.

17. Stetter 1993, 87.

18. Lichtheim 1980, 128.

19. Töpfer, S., 2014: 'The Physical Activity of Parturition in Ancient Egypt: Textual and Epigraphical Sources' in *Dynamis* 34(2). p. 326.

20. *Ibid.*, 327.

21. *Ibid.*, 322.

22. *Ibid.*, 324.

23. Quirke 1992, 69.

24. Toivari-Viitala 2001, 161.

25. Robins 1993, 82.

26. Ghalioungui, P., 1963: *Magic and Medical Science in Ancient Egypt*. London. Hodder and Stoughton. p. 123.

27. Lichtheim, 1976, 188.

28. Hart 1990, 46.

29. Stetter 1993, 88.

30. *Ibid.*, 89.

31. Selene-Sayell 2012/2013, 15.

32. Chamberlein, G., 2004: 'Historical Perspectives on Health Childbirth in Ancient Egypt' in *JRSH* 124(6). p. 284.

33. Some translate this as placed on four bricks.

34. Lichtheim 1975, 220.

35. Toivari-Viitala 2001, 173.

36. Meskell 2002, 70.

37. *Ibid.*, 172.

38. Toivari-Viitala 2001, 178.

39. Töpfer 2014, 322.

40. Robins 1993, 83.

41. Töpfer 2014, 328.

42. Selene–Sayell 2012/2013, 10.

43. Dupras, T., et al, 2015: 'Birth in Ancient Egypt: Timing, Trauma and Triumph? Evidence from the Dakleh Oasis' in Ikram, S., et al. (Eds.) *Egyptian Bioarchaeology; Humans, Animals, and the Environment.* Sidestone Press. p. 56.

44. Macy-Roth & Roehrig 2002, 129.

45. Töpfer 2014, 331.

46. *Ibid.*, 331.

47. Harer 2013, 47.

48. *Ibid.*, 47–48.

49. Chamberlein 2004, 285.

50. Macy-Roth & Roehrig 2002, 121.

51. *Ibid.*, 122.

52. *Ibid.*, 133.

53. Töpfer 2014, 330.

54. *Ibid.*, 325.

55. Macy-Roth & Roehrig 2002, 130.

56. Wegner 2002, 3.

57. Macy-Roth & Roehrig 2002, 139.

58. Toivari-Viitala 2001, 174.

59. Meskell L. 1999: *Archaeologies of Social Life.* London. Blackwell Publishers. p. 100.

60. Toivari-Viitala 2001, 175.

61. *Ibid.*, 177.

62. 2013, 48.

63. Toivari-Viitala 2001, 176.

64. Graves-Brown 2010, 62.

65. Robins 1993, 87.

66. Tyldesley 1994, 75.

67. Watterson 1997, 91.

68. Montserrat 1996, 30–31.

69. Robins 1993, 83.

70. Toivari-Viitala 2001, 181.

71. *Ibid.*, 180.

72. Lichtheim 1976, 169.

73. Chamberlein 2004, 286.

74. Stetter 1993, 88.

75. Tyldesley 1994, 78.

76. Meskell 1999, 102.

77. Selene-Sayell 2012/2013, 14.

78. Dupras et al 2015, 62.

79. *Ibid.*, 64.

5: Homosexuality

1. Montserrat 1996, 141.

2. Meskell 1999, 91.

3. *Ibid.*, 97.

4. *Ibid.*, 92.

5. Graves-Brown 2010, 103.

6. Johnston, J.J., 2010: *Beyond Isis and Osiris: Alternative Sexualities in Ancient Egypt*. London. University College London. p. 2.

7. Parkinson 1995, 68.

8. Goedicke, H., 1967: 'Unrecognized Sportings' in *Journal of the American Research Center in Egypt* Vol. 6. p. 100.

9. Devaud, E., 1916: *Les Maximes de Ptahhotep : d'Apres le Papyrus Prisse, les Papyrus 10371/10435 et 10509 du British Museum, et la Tablette Carnarvon*. Fribourg, Suisse. Col 9, line 13 – Col 10, line 5.

10. *Ibid.*, Col 9, line 13 – Col 10, line 5.

11. Parkinson 1995, 69.

12. Meskell 1999, 94.

13. *Ibid.*, 93.

14. A nome is a regional division of Egypt, rather like modern counties or boroughs.

15. Parkinson, R., 2008: 'Boasting About Hardness Constructions of Middle Kingdom Masculinity' in Graves-Brown, C. (Ed.) *Sex and Gender in Ancient Egypt*. Swansea. University of Wales Press. p. 122.

16. Parkinson 1995, 74.

17. Macy-Roth, A., 1999: 'The Absent Spouse: Patterns and Taboos in Egyptian Tomb Decoration' in *The Journal of the American Research Center in Egypt*. Vol 36. p. 37.

18. Whale 1989, 244–5.

19. Montserrat 1996, 140.

20. Robins 1993, 72.

21. Parkinson 1995, 61.

22. Manniche 1997, 98.

23. Quoted in Montserrat 1996, 140.

24. Parkinson 1995, 62.

25. *Ibid.*, 61.

26. *Ibid.*, 64.

27. *Ibid.*, 66.

28. Ryholt, K., 2005: *The Petese Stories II*. Carsten Niebuhr Institute of Near Eastern Studies p. 101.

29. Morton 1995, 183.

30. Reynolds 1914, 22.

31. Breasted, J.H., 1906: *Ancient Records of Egypt Vol. I*. University of Illinois Press. p. 253.

32. Parkinson 1995, 62.

33. *Ibid.*, 62.

34. Goedicke 1967, 102.

35. Parkinson 1995, 64. Translation from German by Elisabeth Kerner.

36. *Ibid.*, 68.

37. Goedicke 1967, 101.

38. Lichtheim 1975, 166.

39. Goedicke 1967, 101.

40. Parkinson 1995, 59.

41. Lichtheim 1976, 183.

42. Parkinson 1995, 68.

43. Parkinson 2008, 119.

44. Parkinson 2009, 120 & Hare 1999, 148.

45. Hare 1999, 145.

46. *Ibid.*, 107.

47. Montserrat 1996, 141.

48. Parkinson 1995, 65.

49. *Ibid.*, 71.

50. Meskell 1999, 95.

51. Montserrat 1996, 142.

52. Kelly Simpson, W., 1972: *The Literature of Ancient Egypt*. London. Yale University Press. p. 100.

53. Hart 1990, 37.

54. Parkinson 1995, 203.

55. Parkinson 2008, 115.

56. Meskell 1999, 94.

57. Parkinson 1995, n. 61.

58. Riefstahl, E., 1972: 'An Enigmatic Faience Figure' in *Miscelllanea Wilbouriana 1*. Brooklyn. The Brooklyn Museum. p. 143.

59. Riefstahl, 1972, 143.

60. Parkinson 1995, 63.

61. Parkinson 2008, 132.

62. DuQuesne, T., 2008: 'Power on Their Own: Gender and Social Roles in Provincial New Kingdom Egypt' in Graves-Brown. C. (Ed.) *Sex and Gender in Ancient Egypt.* Swansea. University of Wales Press. pp. 57–8.

63. Lichtheim 1976, 88.

64. Quirke, S., & Spencer, J., 1995: *The British Museum Book of Ancient Egypt.* London. British Museum Press. p. 79.

65. Reeder, G., 2008: 'Queer Egyptologies of Niankhkhnumn and Khnumhotep' in Graves-Brown, C. (Ed.) *Sex and Gender in Ancient Egypt,* Swansea. Classical Press of Wales Publications. pp. 143–44.

66. Parkinson 2008, 119.

67. Baines, J., 1985: 'Egyptian Twins' in *Orientalia* 54, p. 469.

68. Vasiljević, V., 2008: 'Embracing His Double: Niankhkhnum and Khnumhotep' in *Studien Zur Altägyptischen Kultur* 37. Hamburg: Helmut Buske Verlag. p. 366.

69. Reeder 2008, 146.

70. Reeder, G., 2000: 'Same-Sex Desires, Conjugal Constructs, and the Tomb of Niankhkhnum and Khnumhotep,' in *World Archaeology* Vol. 32, No. 2. p. 200.

71. Reeder 2008, 147.

72. *Ibid.,* 147.

73. *Ibid.,* 146.

74. Reeder 2008, 151.

75. Cherpion quoted in Reeder 2008, 145.

76. Reeder 2000, 202.

77. *Ibid.,* 196.

78. Reeder 2008, 148.

79. *Ibid.,* 149.

80. Parkinson 2008, 118.

81. Macy-Roth 1999, 38.

82. *Ibid.*, 39.

83. Parkinson 1995, 62.

84. Baines 1985, 464.

85. O'Connor, D., 2005: 'The Enigmatic Tomb Chapel of Niankh-Khnum and Khnumhotep: A New Interpretation', abstract of the paper delivered at the conference Sex and Gender in Ancient Egypt, University of Wales, Swansea.

86. Parkinson 2008, 119.

87. Vasiljević 2008, 364.

88. Reeder 2000, 197–8.

89. *Ibid.*, 196.

90. Vasiljević 2008, 369 & Baines 1985, 468.

91. Reeder 2008, 145.

92. *Ibid.*, 148.

93. Baines 1985, 480.

94. Newberry, P., 1928: 'Akhenaten's Eldest Son-in-Law Ankhkheperure' in *The Journal of Egyptian Archaeology* Vol. 14, No. 1/2. p. 7.

95. Reeves, N., 2001: *Akhenaten: Egypt's False Prophet*. London. Thames and Hudson. p. 168.

96. Parkinson, R., 1991: *Voices from Ancient Egypt*. London. British Museum Press. p. 54.

97. *Ibid.*, 54–6.

98. *Ibid.*, 54.

99. *Ibid.*, 73.

100. Montserrat 1996, 143.

101. Meskell 1999, 95.

102. Parkinson 1995, 75.

103. Manniche 1997, 24.

104. Parkinson 1995, 61.

105. Manniche 1997, 22.

106. *Ibid.*, 102.

107. *Ibid.*, 102.

108. *Ibid.*, 22.

109. Parkinson, R., 1993: 'Niankhkhnum and Khnumhotep; Lovers or Twins' (letter) in *KMT 4.3*. p. 3.

110. Farrer, S., 2005: 'Is This the Earliest Image of a Gay Couple?' in *The Times Higher Education Supplement 1715*. p. 18.

6: *Prostitution*

1. Halioua, B. & Ziskind, B., 2005: *Medicine in the Days of the Pharaohs*. London. Harvard University Press. p. 175.

2. Montserrat 1996, 107.

3. *Ibid.*, 129.

4. Morton 1995, 183.

5. Manniche 1997, 100.

6. Eyre 1984, 96.

7. Pestman 1961, 54 & 56.

8. Manniche 1997, 95.

9. Halioua & Ziskind, 2005, 175.

10. Lichtheim 1976, 171.

11. Montserrat 1996, 121.

12. Tyldesley 1994, 51.

13. Montserrat 1996, 110.

14. Manniche 1997, 31.

15. *Ibid.*, 98.

16. Sélincourt 1973, 179.

17. *Ibid.*, 177.

18. Ankhsheshonq in Manniche 1997, 98–9.

19. Montserrat 1996, 109.

20. Sélincourt 1973, 182–3.

21. *Ibid.*, 182.

22. Montserrat 1996, 110.

23. Sélincourt 1973, 182–3.

24. Manniche 1997, 18.

25. Houlihan, P., 2001: *Wit and Humour in Ancient Egypt*. London. Rubicon Press. p. 130.

26. Romer 1984, 98.

27. Manniche 1997, 107.

28. Romer 1984, 98.

29. Manniche 1997, 109.

30. Janak, J., & Navratilova, H., 2008: 'People vs. P. Turin 55001' in Graves-Brown, C. (Ed.) *Sex and Gender in Ancient Egypt*. Swansea. University of Wales Press. p. 65.

31. Manniche 1997, 63.

32. DuQuesne 2008, 66.

33. *Ibid.*, 65.

34. *Ibid.*, 67.

35. Houlihan 2001, 134.

36. *Ibid.*, 135.

37. Toivari-Viitala 2001, 148.

38. *Ibid.*, 151.

39. Manniche 1997, 15.

40. Graves-Brown 2010, 44.

41. Meskell 2002, 102.

42. Toivari-Viitala 2001, 146.

43. Hare 1999, 140.

44. Toivari-Viitala 2001, 148.

45. Bleeker 1973, 54.

46. Houlihan 2001, 137.

47. *Ibid.*, 126.

48. Winlock, H., 1932: 'The Museum's Excavations at Thebes,' in *BMMA* 27, p. 36.

49. Pinch 1993, 213.

50. Toivari-Viitala 2001, 150–1.

51. Manniche 1997, 18.

52. Toivari-Viitala 2001, 150.

53. *Ibid.*, 151.

54. *Ibid.*, 152.

7: *Sex and Medicine*

1. Nunn 1996, 194.

2. Sélincourt 1973, 203.

3. Save-Soderbergh, T., 1958: *Pharaohs and Mortals*. London. Robert Hale Limited. p. 147.

4. Szpakowska 2008, 220.

5. Taylor & Antoine 2014, 168.

6. Manniche 1999, 125.

7. Ghalioungui1963, 119.

8. Reeves 1992, 53.

9. Szpakowska 2008, 221.

10. Watterson 1997, 77.

11. Ghalioungui 1963, 126.

12. Watterson 1991, 85.

13. Nunn 1997, 192.

14. Tyldesley 1994, 70.

15. Manniche 1997, 103.

16. Shokeir, A., & Hussain, M., 2004: 'Sexual Life in Pharaonic Egypt: Towards a Urological View' in *International Journal of Impotence Research* 16. p. 386.

17. Manniche 1997, 104.

18. *Ibid.*, 104.

19. Mertz 1966, 51.

20. Frankfurter 2001, 496.

21. McDowell, 1999, 33.

22. Manniche 1997, 105.

23. Manniche 1999, 121.

24. Watterson 1991, 111.

25. *Ibid.*, 112.

26. Manniche, L., 1989: *An Ancient Egyptian Herbal.* London. British Museum Press. p. 46.

27. Manniche 1999, 118.

28. Tyldesley 1994, 152.

29. Nunn 1996, 197.

30. Robins 1993, 78.

31. Wilfong 1999, 423.

32. Nunn 1996, 196.

33. Robins 1994, 27.

34. Meskell 2002, 68.

35. Ghalioungui, P., Khalil, S.H. & Ammar, A.R., 1963: 'On an Ancient Egyptian Method of Diagnosing Pregnancy and Determining Foetal Sex' in *Medical History* 7(3). p. 245.

36. Robins 1993, 80.

37. Robins, G., 1994/1995: 'Women and Children in Peril? Pregnancy, Birth and Infant Mortality in Ancient Egypt' in *KMT* 5 no.4. p. 27.

38. Chamberlein 2004, 285.

39. Nunn 1996, 194.

40. Robins 1993, 83.

41. Toivari-Viitala 2001, 169.

42. Selene-Sayell 2012/2013, 11.

43. Nunn 1996, 195.

44. Toivari-Viitala 2001, 164 n 216.

45. Manniche 1999, 121.

46. Stetter 1993, 89.

47. Wilfong 1999, 423.

48. Nunn 1996, 194.

49. Reeves 1992, 19.

50. Nunn 1996, 199.

51. *Ibid.*, 196.

52. Szpakowska 2008, 213.

53. Montserrat 1996, 86.

54. Nunn 1996, 196.

55. Toivari-Viitala 2001, 169.

56. Donker van Heel 2014, 162.

57. Watterson 1997, 89.

58. Toivari-Viitala 2001, 168.

59. Kozieradska-Ogunmakin, I., 2015: 'A Case of Metastatic Carcinoma in an Old Kingdom Skeleton from Saqqara' in Ikram, S. et al. (Eds.) *Egyptian Bioarchaeology; Humans, Animals and the Environment*. Leiden. Sidestone Press. pp. 84–5.

60. Manniche 1997, 18.

61. Ghailounghi 1963, 120.

62. Morton 1995, 184.

63. *Ibid.*, 184.

8: *Sex and Religion*

1. Lichtheim 1980, 62.

2. Coffin Text 80, lines 48–51 in Allen, J.P., 1988: *Genesis in Egypt; the Philosophy of Ancient Egyptian Creation Accounts*. New Haven. Yale. p. 25.

3. Ayad 2009, 93.

4. *Ibid.*, 94.

5. Lichtheim 1997, 43.

6. Ayad 2009, 94.

7. Allen J.P 2014: *Middle Egyptian: An Introduction to the Language and Culture of Hieroglyphs*. Cambridge. Cambridge University Press. p. 194.

8. Faulkner, R., 1969 (1998 ed): *The Ancient Egyptian Pyramid Texts*. Oxford. Oxford University Press. p. 246.

9. Allen 1988, 28.

10. Frankfort, H., de Buck, A., & Gunn, B.G. 1933: *The Cenotaph of Seti I at Abydos*, Volume 39, Part 1. p. 73.

11. Hart 1990, 30.

12. *Ibid.*, 21.

13. Ayad 2009, 82.

14. Hart 1990, 25.

15. Quirke S. 2014. *Exploring Religion in Ancient Egypt*. London. Wiley-Blackwell. p. 143.

16. Manniche 1999, 55.

17. *Ibid.*, 52–3.

18. Lucas 1930, 48.

19. Dodson, A., 2004: 'The God's Wives of Amun' in *Ancient Egypt* Vol. 4, Iss. 6. p. 23.

20. *Ibid.*, 25.

21. *Ibid.*

22. Lesko 1996, 42.

23. Dodson 2004, 24.

24. Dodson, A., 2002: 'The Problem of Amenirdis II and the Heirs to the Office of God's Wife of Amun During theTwenty-Sixth Dynasty' in *The Journal of Egyptian Archaeology* Vol. 88. p. 181.

25. Manniche 1997, 12.

26. Ayad 2009, 103.

27. *Ibid.*, 7.

28. *Ibid.*, 99.

29. Lesko, B., 1999: *The Great Goddesses of Egypt*. Norman. University of Oklahoma Press. p. 246.

30. Bleeker 1973, 95.

31. Lesko 1999, 127.

32. Hare 1999, 134.

33. *Ibid.*, 152.

34. Nunn 1996, 84.
35. Mojsov, B., 2005: *Osiris: Death and Afterlife of a God*. Oxford. Blackwell. p. 37.
36. Manniche 1997, 12.
37. Hart 1990, 42.
38. Pinch 1993, 239.
39. Sélincourt 1973, 149.
40. Quirke 1992, 57–8.
41. Manniche, L., 1991: *Music and Musicians in Ancient Egypt*. London. British Museum Press. p. 17.
42. Ayad 2009, 106.
43. Frankfurter 2001, 489.
44. Sélincourt 1973, 148.
45. Pinch 1993, 239.
46. Sélincourt 1973, 153.
47. Manniche 1997, 10.
48. Montserrat 1996, 169.
49. Manniche 1997, 53.
50. Pinch 1993, 213.
51. Lesko 1999, 114.
52. *Ibid.*, 118.
53. Bleeker 1973, 44.
54. Ayad 2009, 35.
55. *Ibid.*, 37.
56. Bleeker 1973, 60.
57. Lesko 1999, 85.
58. Ayad 2009, 50.
59. Lesko 1999, 115.
60. *Ibid.*, 126.
61. Bleeker 1973, 91.
62. Lichtheim 1997, 50.

63. Pinch 1993, 239.

64. Ayad 2009, 45.

65. Bleeker 1973, 29.

66. Quirke 1992, 136.

67. Lesko 1999, 114.

68. *Ibid.*, 114.

69. Lichtheim 1980, 62.

70. Booth, C., 2006: *The People of Ancient Egypt*. Stroud. Tempus. p. 270.

71. Manniche 1997, 14.

72. Pinch 1993, 223.

73. Kemp, B., 2005: *Ancient Egypt; Anatomy of a Civilisation*. London. Routledge. p. 382.

74. Montserrat 1996, 125.

75. Pinch 1993, 222.

76. Manniche 1997, 48.

77. Pinch 1993, 210–11.

78. Manniche 1997, 100.

9: *Sex in the Afterlife*

1. Manniche 1997, 105.

2. Wilfong 1997, 20.

3. Robins 1993, 85.

4. Parkinson 1995, 64.

5. Pinch 1993, 215.

6. *Ibid.*, 218.

7. Lesko 1999, 116.

8. Bleeker 1973, 41.

9. Quirke 1992, 158.

10. Reeder G., 1998: 'Musings on the Sexual Nature of the Human-Headed Ba Bird' in *KMT* Vol. 9 3. p. 74.

11. *Ibid.*, 75.

12. Coffin Texts I 360c–366b, spell 75 in Reeder 1998, 73.

13. Reeder 1998, 75.

14. Spell 17 Book of the Dead in Faulkner, R., 1972: *The Ancient Egyptian Book of the Dead*. London. British Museum Press. p. 44.

15. Cooney, K., 2008: 'The Problem of Female Rebirth in New Kingdom Egypt: The Fragmentation of the Female Individual in Her Funerary Equipment' in Graves-Brown, C. (Ed.): *Sex and Gender in Ancient Egypt*. Swansea. University of Wales Press. p. 2.

16. *Ibid.*

17. Parkinson 2008, 128.

18. Cooney 2008, 1.

19. *Ibid.*, 2.

20. Manniche 1997, 29.

21. Cooney 2008, 4.

22. *Ibid.*, 6.

23. *Ibid.*, 10.

24. *Ibid.*, 12.

25. *Ibid.*, 15.

26. *Ibid.*, 5.

27. Tyldesley, J., 2014: 'Neith: the Warrior Goddess' in *Ancient Egypt Magazine* Vol. 14, Iss. 6. p. 59.

28. Cooney 2008, 3.

29. *Ibid.*, 17.

30. Allen, P., 2015: *The Ancient Egyptian Pyramid Texts*. Atlanta. SBL Press. p. 11.

31. Lichtheim 1997, 50.

32. Andrews, C., 1994: *Amulets of Ancient Egypt*. London. British Museum Press. p. 71.

33. Cooney 2008, 16.

34. Manniche 1997, 105.

35. *Ibid.*, 28.

36. Tyldesley, J., 2014b: 'Queens of the Old Kingdom (1) The Pyramid Queens' in *Ancient Egypt* Oct/Nov Vol. 15, No. 2, Iss. 86. p. 18.

37. Macy-Roth, 1999, 41.

38. *Ibid.*, 41.

39. Parkinson 1995, 60 n. 27.

40. Routledge, C., 2008: 'Did Women "Do Things" in Ancient Egypt? (c.2600–1050 BCE)' in Graves-Brown, C. (Ed.): *Sex and Gender in Ancient Egypt*. Swansea. University of Wales Press. p. 159.

41. *Ibid.*, 168.

42. Meskell 1999, 99.

43. Routledge, 2008, 160.

44. Manniche 1997, 43.

45. *Ibid.*, 40.

46. Snape, S., 2011: *Ancient Tombs; The Culture of Life and Death*. London. Wiley-Blackwell. p. 124.

47. O' Connor, D., 2009: *Abydos: Egypt's First Pharaoh's and the Cult of Osiris*. London. Thames and Hudson. p. 96.

48. Manniche 1997, 42.

49. Meskell 2000, 256.

50. Ayad 2009, 50.

51. Padgham 2012, 103.

52. *Ibid.*, 104.

53. *Ibid.*, 105.

INDEX